Praise for *Parenting Solutions*

"Joan Rice has a wealth of knowledge to help parents strive to grow and benefit their children. Her teachings will guide parents and offer tools that really work."

—*Linda Matsumoto, Director of Parent Education, Burbank Adult School*

"The author's approach is kind, gentle, simple, encouraging, and practical. It is also easy to read, which is of tremendous importance for busy parents. I recommend this book."

—*Sally M. Ames, M.A., Parent Education Coordinator, San Luis Coastal Adult School, San Luis Obispo, CA*

"In searching for a textbook for my Parent Education Class, I wanted something that would be a personal and practical approach to parenting and early childhood and that would be easily understood by its readers. Joan Rice has presented such a book."

—*Judith Dal Porto, M.A., Director, Allan Hancock College Parent Participation Program*

"*Parenting Solutions* allows parents to think through everyday living experience with practical solutions. It is a well-researched step by step approach that I recommend to all parents in our parenting programs."

—*Margaret Kornberg, B.S. Early Childhood Education, M.A. Guidance and Counseling, Educator, Community Educational Centers, Doylestown, PA*

"*Parenting Solutions* is a valuable resource for families. It is concise and specific to topic areas. This makes it easily accessible for busy parents. She has summarized the leading research on child development and given practical solutions that she has tested throughout her career. I hope to use this with families as well as in my teacher-training classes."

—*Jeffra Nandan, MSW, Assessor for the National Association for the Education of Young Children, College Faculty, Child Development, Family Resource Centers, Inc., Princeton, NJ*

"Unique and caring parenting book…. I highly recommend *Parenting Solutions* as a therapist and as a chaplain."

—*Timothy S. Heater, MSW, M.Div.*

Additional Praise from Parents

"Thank you for all of your time, experience, and knowledge in helping me in my journey through motherhood. You have been a wonderful resource for me, a person to turn to when I question myself." —Pamela B.

"Thank you for giving me the skills and tools that I need to be a better mother." —Angela S.

"You have enriched our lives and made child rearing easier for us. Your advice has made my life better." —Dana S.

"I admire you for spending your life helping children and parents. Over the years you have touched more lives than can even be counted." —Stacy H.

"Thank you for helping my daughter and me have a better relationship and lifestyle." —Regina S.

"Thank you for all you've done to teach and serve our family. You have inspired me and so many other moms to be more caring and capable with our little ones. Thank you for being a big part of our growth!" —Linda Z.

"Thank you for the kindness, wisdom and energy you have put towards my children." —Heather P.

"I have learned so much from you. While you instructed me to tell my kids, 'I know you can do this. I believe in you,' it felt like you were telling me the same thing. Your gentle nature gave me the confidence to do the right thing, not necessarily the easiest thing, for my children. You've made the world a better place. I know I am a better mom because of you—and my children are better off because of you." —Melissa J.

"What I feel most encouraged by is how you taught us to build a child's self-esteem and confidence. We are looking for those moments in each day that we can pass love, belief, and acceptance onto them. Regardless of the pace or attitudes of the day—that is something I can do and go to bed feeling good about." —Jill M.

"Because of you, I am a better parent." —Dionne B.

PARENTING SOLUTIONS

PARENTING SOLUTIONS

Encouragement for Everyday Parenting Concerns

JOAN RICE

B.S.N., R.N., Parent Educator, Pediatric Nurse

PARAGON HOUSE
St. Paul, Minnesota

For Julia, Benjamin, and Marc—my three children—their spouses, my grandchildren, and to the thousands of families that have given me the privilege of sharing their lives over the past 30 years.

Published in the United States by
Paragon House
1925 Oakcrest Avenue
St. Paul, MN 55113

Julia Colon, Elizabeth Hawkins, Dionne Bolton, Karina Chavez, and Jenn Lins each donated photos.
All other photos are courtesy of James Colon, Photographer, California Image and Design, www.CAimage.us.

Solutions and strategies presented in this book are not all inclusive, nor do they take the place of advice from your health care provider. Consult with your peditrician or other health care provider about your concerns.

The term "parent" is used in this book to refer to the persons who are the primary caregivers for a child, such as mother, father, grandmother, grandfather, aunt, uncle, older sibling, or foster parent. Most of the solutions can be used by teachers as well.

Library of Congress Cataloging-in-Publication Data

Rice, Joan, 1948-
 Parenting solutions : encouragement for everyday parenting concerns / Joan
Rice.
 p. cm.
 Includes bibliographical references and index.
 Summary: "Guidebook for parents provides answers for the day to day issues
parents with young children face, by a parenting expert"--Provided by
publisher.
 ISBN 978-1-55778-879-5 (pbk. : alk. paper)
 1. Parenting. 2. Child rearing. I. Title.
 HQ769.R4665 2009
 649'.122--dc22
 2008041028

Manufactured in the United States of America

The paper used in this publication meets the minimum requirements of American National Standard for Information Sciences—Permanence of Paper for Printed Library Materials, ANSI Z39.48-1992.

10 9 8 7 6 5 4 3 2 1

For current information about all releases from Paragon House,
visit the web site at www.paragonhouse.com

Contents

• Misunderstandings about "Ferberizing" • Ways to Soften the Ferber Method • Alternatives to All Night Nursings • The Family Bed • Sleeping in My Own Bed • A Word about Colic and Acid Reflux • Sleep Disruptions from New Developmental Steps • Nightmares • Night Terrors

Copyright Permissions

♦ *in text indicates reference to copyright permissions on this page.*

Brazelton, T. Berry, M.D. and Joshua D. Sparrow, M.D. *Discipline the Brazelton Way.* New York: Perseus Books, 2003. Permission to use an excerpt from page 51 on their view of spanking is granted by Perseus Books Group Permissions Department.

Brazelton, T. Berry, M.D. *Doctor and Child.* New York: Delacorte Press, 1976. Permission to use excerpts from pages 134–140 on the signs of readiness for toilet learning, his Step-by-Step Method, and the results of his study of using this method is granted by Dell Publishing, a division of Random House Inc.

Brazelton, T. Berry, M.D. and Stanley I. Greenspan. *The Irreducible Needs of Children.* New York: Perseus Publishing, 2001. Permission to use a section of "Introduction to Recommendations, A Child's Day" is granted by Perseus Books Group Permissions Department.

Brazelton, T. Berry, M.D. *To Listen to a Child: Understanding the Normal Problems of Growing Up.* Reading, Massachusetts: Addison-Wesley Publishing Company, 1984. Permission to use an excerpt from page 121 discussing his recommendations for daytime sleep is granted by Perseus Books Group Permissions Department.

Brazelton, T. Berry, M.D. *Touchpoints: Your Child's Emotional and Behavioral Development.* New York: Perseus Books, 1992. Permission to use an excerpt from pages 252–53 about his definition of limits is granted by Perseus Books Group Permissions Department.

Department of Health Education, Boston Children's Hospital Medical Center. *Accident Handbook: A New Approach to Children's Safety.* New York: Dell Publishing, 1966. Permission to list the precursors to accidents on page 5 is granted by the Archives of Children's Hospital, Boston, MA.

Ferber, Richard, M.D. *Solve Your Child's Sleep Problems.* New York: Simon and Schuster, Inc., 1985. Permission to use excerpts from pages 66 and 78 is granted by the Permissions Department of Simon and Schuster, Inc.

Karp, Harvey, M.D. *The Happiest Baby on the Block.* New York: Bantam Dell, 2002. Permission to summarize the Five S's to calm a baby is granted by the Permissions Department of Random House Inc.

Pantley, Elizabeth. *The No-Cry Sleep Solution: Gentle Ways to Help Your Baby Sleep Through the Night.* New York: McGraw Hill, 2002. Permission to use the excerpt "The Pantley Gentle Removal Plan" from pages 126–27 is granted by the Contracts, Copyrights, and Permissions Department of McGraw Hill Education Department.

Sears, William, M.D. and Martha Sears, R.N. *The Attachment Parenting Book: A Commonsense Guide to Understanding and Nurturing Your Baby.* New York: Little, Brown and Company, 2001. Permission is granted to use excerpts from pages 96, 99–101 by Little, Brown, and Company.

Introduction

My journey in writing this parenting book began when my youngest son, in his early twenties, was helping me move my parenting materials from one closet to another. Each workshop had a labeled canvas bag with notes, handouts, books, and so on. He looked at me and said, "Mom, each of these bags is a chapter! You need to write a parenting book! I want to know what you have been teaching all these years!"

I responded by saying that I hoped I would be around when he had children, and he could call me. He said he wanted to know my *philosophy of parenting*; he didn't want to call me for every little thing. This was the greatest gift! He valued what I have devoted my life to and wanted me to share it with him and with all my students—past, present and future.

Over the next 5 years, he never stopped encouraging me. My daughter's first child was expected as I began. As I finished each chapter, I would give her a copy. She critiqued it and gave me suggestions (her undergraduate degree is in Early Childhood Studies). When my new grandson arrived, my daughter was able to benefit from my chapters as I wrote them. The book evolved as a gift of love and is the essence of what one needs to know as a parent.

Parenting Solutions offers much-needed support and encouragement.

Instead of having to sift through the hundreds of parenting books, I have done the work for you, providing the most helpful information possible and synthesizing a philosophy that will work for you. Each chapter of *Parenting Solutions* will be like attending a thought-provoking, behavior-changing parenting workshop.

As an experienced parent educator, pediatric nurse, credentialed teacher, and mother of three, I have much to share. Because I have taught parenting classes for more than 30 years, I have developed a deep understanding of what concerns parents. I am on the front lines every day in my current parenting classes, where parents express their frustrations and concerns. Many are floundering and unsure of ways to handle troublesome behaviors.

I am able to give you specific strategies to change behaviors on multiple topics. I have captured *the essence of parenting* with clear and concise guidance on specific topics that can solve problems and issues that arise daily. Each chapter is a workshop that I have presented numerous times, in many venues, that zeroes in on a specific topic and gives specific, behavior-changing solutions that can be applied immediately.

My book is a written reflection of how each of my parenting workshops offers immediate, effective strategies for handling difficult and challenging parenting issues. I have received repeated positive feedback from parents telling me that they had great success with the strategies we came up with together. Many have told me that the atmosphere in their homes has positively changed. Many have excitedly admitted that their relationships with their children have improved immeasurably. My goal is to empower you with usable strategies and give you the self-confidence to implement them.

Parents have repeatedly asked me to put my workshops in written form to refer to again and again. Many parents do not have the time to attend workshops or to read the numerous books on parenting topics. Many times the ideas in the books conflict with each other. It has always been my job as a parent educator to filter through the various theories and present the ideas that are based on sound psychological principles and strategies that continually encourage self-esteem. In the process I have developed a philosophy of parenting that is easy to understand and implement.

There are entire books on sleep strategies or toilet learning or discipline. Parents want to learn the essence of parenting without having to read a volume on each topic. Each chapter in this unique and useful book offers real help that solves current parenting issues and gives you ways to keep a warm, loving, encouraging connection with your child.

1
Living with Your New Baby

Now your new baby is here. You want the best for your baby, and you cherish him. Here is the essence of how to care for your baby and show him how much you love him.

Building Trust

The most important task of early infancy is to learn to trust the world, to trust the family. Your baby needs to learn that the world is a safe and caring place and that his needs will be met in a predictable, consistent manner. This is the first step in personality development as outlined by Erickson in his stages of personality development: Trust vs. Mistrust. Responding as quickly and lovingly as possible to his cries helps him begin to trust in his new world.

With this in mind, demand feeding is encouraged. Feeding him each time he cries to tell you he is hungry builds his trust that you are there to care for him. Holding him when he cries to be held and rocking him when he cries to be rocked and cuddled sends important messages to the child. The message says, "I am here for you, and I'm going to do my best to figure out what you need. You can trust me."

Soon you will be able to learn what your baby is asking for when he cries. Before you figure it out, try holding, rocking, or feeding and see which response soothes and settles him. You will learn his signals as you carefully look at his behavioral cues. If you just fed him and he cries, he may have another burp or may need to be changed. If he hasn't slept in a while, he may be fussing because he is tired. You guess in the beginning and a rhythm will begin to develop until your guessing becomes more accurate.

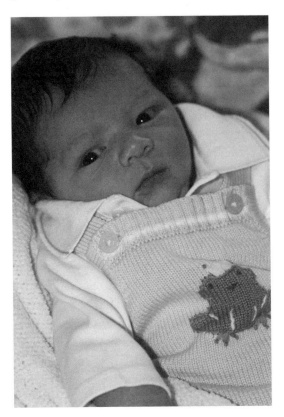

1

Crying

I have mentioned that developing a sense of trust is the most important task in early infancy—the feeling that someone will help him when he needs it. Responding to cries as quickly and as often as possible will help the baby learn to trust and to have self-confidence. Being consoled gives a sense of trust that the parent is available and *trying* to help. We cannot always figure out what the baby needs or wants. If we *try* to help, that is good enough to maintain trust.

Crying is the baby's way of communicating. In the beginning, crying is his only language, his only way to convey his needs: hunger, wetness, gas, fatigue, change in temperature, entertainment, or loving. By crying and eliciting—or not eliciting—his parents' responses, the infant begins to shape a concept of his world. The messages to the child when you respond are "You are safe here with me," "You are worthy of being taken care of," and "You are special and deserve my attention." His communication (crying) has worked. He feels empowered to change things for himself.

On the other hand, a baby who sometimes is responded to and sometimes not does not learn that communication works. He feels helpless and unimportant. You will begin to learn your baby's precry signals. In responding to these, you are teaching him to communicate effectively. The message to the child is, "I am beginning to understand your cues, and you don't need to cry to get your needs met," and he will cry less often.

Some people think that responding to every cry spoils the baby. What really spoils a child is inconsistency of handling. Responding sometimes and ignoring other times causes the baby to be confused and insecure. He may become more irritable and demanding. He may begin to mistrust his world.

An interesting study by Dr. Mary S. Ainsworth at Johns Hopkins University found that the babies of parents who responded consistently cried less by the end of one year than the babies whose parents sometimes responded. What the babies learned in the group where the parents responded was that communication works! These babies learned other ways of signaling for attention.

Very young babies learn to "call out" when they wake up in the morning instead of crying, confident that someone will come. They may reach out toward you or crawl toward you as they get older. They develop a rich variety of other modes of communication. They realize that they do not need to cry to get their needs met. Therefore, they cry less by one year old than the babies who were not consistently responded to.

Dr. Crockenberg, University of California at Davis, replicated this study with similar results. She states, "The more responsive a mother is to her baby, the less he cries, the more securely attached he gets to be, and the more readily he develops trust." These early nurturing relationships are the foundation for future relationships. If your baby feels you truly care for him by meeting his needs—caring for him, feeding, and cuddling him—he will feel a sense of trust and goodness in life.

Some people advocate not going to a crying newborn at night so she will learn not to wake at night. At what expense to the child's trust? The message to these tiny newborns is that no one cares enough to answer. She may give up trying to get a response.

At a luncheon, I saw a mother nursing her 6-week-old son and then she proceeded to place him in an upstairs bedroom. As I was checking on my 5-month-old son asleep upstairs, I heard her infant crying and went to tell her. She told me that he was all right because he had been fed and changed. She said he did not need anything. I was shocked at this. The baby kept crying in the room alone with no one responding. The message to the child was "Your needs are not important." He was learning to mistrust.

I emphasize that the important thing is that you *try* to help your crying infant. Sometimes even if you do not understand what your baby wants or needs, yet you are physically there and comforting, the baby will be comforted. I have learned that sometimes the efforts of trying to help may make the crying worse. I have a vivid memory of a teacher at one of the child care centers vigorously bouncing a crying baby on her knee. It seemed that the bouncing was upsetting the baby more.

Some young babies seem to need to have a crying spell at the end of the day to discharge the stimulation of all the sights and sounds in the environment. It is a way of handling the sensory overload. My feeling is that we need to try to soothe them by being there. Consider yourself an ally. That does not mean increasing the stimulation:

Sometimes walking or rocking works. Sometimes that makes the crying increase.

We must remember that anxiety is transmitted from human to human. The baby is upset, we get upset, and that makes the baby more upset. Sometimes it might be best to lie the baby down, or lie down with him, and sing gently or pat him gently. It is comforting for him to know you are there. You could put the crying baby in a sling or front carrier and go about your chores or take a walk. The side-to-side or up-and-down movement soothes the baby, as does the closeness to you.

This new world outside the womb can be stimulating to the newborn. In the womb, your baby had her needs instantly met. Reconstructing what it was like in the womb can be soothing to a fussy baby. The steady beating of your heart was part of her experience. Lying her next to your heart can remind her of being in the womb. Providing other rhythmic sounds can be comforting, such as singing lullabies or playing womb sounds to her on a CD. In the womb, she was warm and snug, so swaddling a newborn with a blanket can soothe her. She rocked in the warm water, so a rocking motion can be very soothing.

Pediatrician Dr. Harvey Karp, author of *The Happiest Baby on the Block* (Bantam Dell Publishing, 2002),♦ has originated the idea of newborns having a "calming reflex." He studied other cultures' nurturing techniques and found that babies cried very little. Simulating what he observed, Dr. Karp came up with the "Five S's" to calm a baby: *swaddling, side-lying, swinging, shushing,* and *sucking.*

I recommend that you read the book or watch the accompanying DVD to learn how to tightly swaddle; position the swaddled baby on his right side, supported by your forearms; swing the baby by moving your arms slightly, so that his head gently jiggles 1 to 2 inches from side to side (not shaking the baby, which can cause brain damage); shushing him loudly; and allowing him to suck on a pacifier. In the DVD, babies instantly calm and look around wide-eyed. Once calmed, babies will nurse, be alert for awhile, or fall asleep.

Many parents have said that swaddling seems to upset the baby even more, and they give up that strategy. Dr. Karp says that swaddling is only the first step of the calming reflex. The side-lying, swinging, shushing, and sucking are equally important. As the baby calms, a few S's can be eliminated. He recommends that a pacifier not be used until after 3 to 4 weeks of breastfeeding well. He also recommends that the pacifier be discontinued by 4 or 5 months, at which time the baby has learned other ways of calming herself.

The strategies to engage the calming reflex are used in the first three months, the period of time he calls the fourth trimester. The five S's replicate what it was like in the womb. Try this! Many parents have told me that this magically transforms their infants' days with much less crying.

Successfully Breastfeeding

It is very helpful to write down the time that you begin each feeding. In the early weeks, it often feels like you are feeding her so often.

A newborn nurses small amounts about 8 to 12 times per day. If you write it down, you will begin to see a pattern. Your baby usually nurses about every 2 hours in the beginning, and then begins to stretch her feedings out with a longer stretch at night lasting 4 to 6 hours.

Babies are so individual as to when they are able to sleep longer stretches at night without being hungry. One study observed 9-month-olds and found that about half of them slept around 9 hours in a day, while the other half slept about 18 hours in a day. That shows how different children need different amounts of sleep—some need twice as much as others! I've known babies who sleep 12 hours at night and take two 2 to 3 hour naps. Others may sleep a 4 to 5 hour stretch at night and take a few 20-minute catnaps during the day. I remember one mother saying that she had read that newborns sleep 18 to 20 hours a day, so she bought many sewing projects for all those hours. She smiled and said that she hadn't touched even one by the time the baby was 4 months old.

I believe that breastfeeding is best. I have believed that for 30 years, even when it was not popular. As a nurse, I researched all the benefits to the child. With my first child, I found La Leche League to be a tremendous support in a world that did not believe that "breast is best." I knew no one that was nursing, so it was a blessing to find this group that believed that it was best. I learned so much and was supported during sore nipples and two breast infections. My favorite breastfeeding books are La Leche

League's *The Womanly Art of Breastfeeding* and Karen Pryor's *Nursing Your Baby*. I would encourage you to buy a good breastfeeding book to learn the how-tos and the benefits. Once you know the benefits, it will help you through the tough spots, knowing how healthy it is for your baby. Once the sore nipples are over, you will see how much easier it is to breastfeed. The food requires no preparing of bottles, it is always at the right temperature, and you always have food on hand no matter where you are.

There are numerous other major benefits of nursing your baby. First is the frequent cuddling that goes along with nursing, with skin to skin contact. Babies need to be held close and cuddled. The breast milk is perfectly suited to the baby's needs for growing and developing. It has trace nutrients that cannot be replicated in manufactured formula. It has the perfect balance of proteins, fats, and other nutrients needed for brain, nervous system, muscle, and tissue growth. The breast also acts as an immune factory. On the spot, it produces germ-fighters to try to fight the germs that are present. For example, if mom has a cold, the breast will produce some germ-fighters to help combat the cold. When my youngest was 5 months old, his two older siblings came down with chicken pox (the immunization had not yet been developed). My pediatrician thought that the antibodies that came through the breast milk helped him not get it. It is a well-known fact that breastfed babies get fewer illnesses: fewer colds and ear infections, less diarrhea, less constipation, fewer childhood cancers, and fewer allergies, less eczema, and less asthma. Research shows that juvenile onset diabetes occurs less frequently in those who were breastfed.

Parents ask, "What if I can't breastfeed?" Most concerns about not being able to breastfeed can be resolved. Sometimes breastfeeding is not possible because there is a physiological reason that the breasts are not working correctly, or the mom has to take a medication that can be harmful to the baby. If bottle feeding, my advice would be to always hold your baby for feedings. Try not to prop a bottle, no matter how old your baby is.

Sometimes the baby needs hospitalization after birth. It is hoped that the mother will be able to pump her milk and bring it to the hospital; this baby needs the benefits of the breast milk even more. The new pumps that are available are wonderful. Many places will rent them by the month, so it is affordable. For those of you going back to work, pumping is possible during the workday. With a little luck, you can find a quiet, private place to pump.

Lactation Consultants are found in most communities, and I would encourage you to use their services if you are having any concerns. They can observe you nursing and offer suggestions and solutions to help breastfeeding go more smoothly. Sometimes the answer is something as simple as repositioning.

For those of you who are told that your baby is not gaining enough weight, and that you have to supplement with formula, with your pediatrician's permission, I would suggest going home and spending the next two days leisurely nursing the baby more frequently to build up your milk supply. *Every time* you sit down to nurse, have a large drink of water or juice nearby to sip during the nursing. "Every suck brings in more milk" is a phrase I often say to breast-feeding mothers when they are worrying that their supply is not enough. As long as the baby has a minimum of six wet diapers and he is gaining weight, you have enough milk; you could take him for daily weigh-ins for a few days to reassure yourself. The more he sucks, the more milk there will be. That is how a baby adjusts the milk supply as he grows. He sucks more frequently during his growth spurt days (usually 24 to 72 hours) to build up the milk supply; then he will go back to eating less frequently. More milk will be produced to keep up with his growth. It is a miraculous, balanced system.

If after you have tried to build up your milk supply and the baby is still not gaining, you can use a Supplemental Nursing System (SNS), a bag of formula that you wear around your neck with a tube that delivers milk next to the nipple. This way, the baby is getting formula *and* sucking on your nipple to build up the supply. You will hopefully not have to use the SNS for very long. This system can also be used to restart the milk flow in the event that nursing has to be interrupted. Pumping milk acts like the sucking in that it will cause more milk to be produced.

Initially, while you are in the hospital, it is important to ask that the baby not be given a bottle of formula. There are a few reasons for this: One is that if she fills up on formula, she will not be hungry enough to nurse. Secondly, it is much easier to suck milk out of a bottle than out of the breast, and the baby may get confused. Sucking on a bottle nipple uses a different way of sucking than sucking on the breast.

It is expected that the baby will lose up to a pound in the first few days of life, as the milk supply gets established. The first nursings are colostrum, a valuable, immunity-filled substance that is important for your baby. Within a few days, your milk comes in. Nature thinks you had twins, so milk will usually be plentiful. In the first 6 weeks, supply and demand will become balanced. I would not recommend giving a supplemental bottle in the first 6 weeks until the balance is established. After that, you could pump breast milk and have someone else offer it in a bottle if you need to be away for more than a couple of hours.

Sometimes babies balk at the bottle and refuse it. If a calm person keeps offering it at intervals, the baby will take it. Babies will not allow themselves to starve. Sometimes they prefer to wait until mom comes back. If you are going back to work, it is essential that the baby take many practice bottles over several days before you return. The Playtex Nurser nipple has the same sucking mechanism as the breast and is usually well received by nursing babies. I would strongly encourage you to give only breast milk in the bottles. We have already established the value of breast milk. Also, the bottles are strange enough to the breastfed baby. She will be much more likely to accept it if it contains something familiar.

Lastly, the longer you can delay introducing cow milk or soy milk formulas, the less likely the baby will develop an allergy to it. *IgA bodies* in the gastrointestinal system are established by 6 months that can help keep allergens in the GI tract. If you are breastfeeding, this means that giving anything other than breast milk before 6 months is not recommended, especially in those families that have allergies. See Chapter 4: Nutrition Tips for the Young Child, for the section on beginning solids.

Sometimes a newborn has a poor sucking reflex and is unable to suck at the breast. The bottle is much easier for them; the milk comes out more easily. Pumping would come in handy for this baby and mom. I had one mom in one of my classes whose baby could not suck efficiently. She was diligently pumping and asking for reassurance from the other moms to keep pumping. Her baby was tiring himself from the sucking, so the bottle was more efficient for this developmentally delayed infant. Gradually, he was able to nurse for several feedings and have the bottle when he got too tired.

Tips on Handling Pumped Breast Milk

(Excerpted from a flyer, courtesy of Marian Medical Center, Santa Maria, CA)

▶ Wash hands well.

▶ Store breast milk in sterile plastic containers. Disposable bottle liners made for freezing work well. Leave some space at the top of the container because breast milk, like most liquids, expands as it freezes. Fold the top of the bag several times and secure with freezer tape or use the bags with Ziploc-type closures.

▶ Place smaller bags in a larger bag or stand upright in a container to help protect against punctures. Mark the date and amount on each small bag.

▶ If you carefully washed your hands before pumping, the freshly expressed breast milk will be safe for up to 4 hours at room temperature, 68 degrees Fahrenheit. However, immediate refrigeration is recommended.

▶ The experts advise that fresh breast milk will keep for five days in the refrigerator at 39 degrees Fahrenheit. I recommend freezing if it will not be used in 72 hours.

▶ Defrosted milk may be kept for up to 24 hours in the refrigerator.

▶ Frozen breast milk will keep for three to four months in the freezer. Put milk in the back of the freezer, not near the door. It will keep for 12 months in a deep freezer at 0 degrees Fahrenheit.

▶ Don't defrost the milk until you need the milk, and do not refreeze.

▶ You can remove breast milk from the freezer and place it in the refrigerator overnight to thaw.

▶ For quick thawing, run the milk under warm water to defrost and to warm it. Alternatively, you could warm the milk by setting it in a bowl of warm water for several minutes. *Do not heat breast milk in the microwave.* Doing so produces hot spots that may scald the baby's mouth. Also it can destroy some of the healthful ingredients in the milk.

▶ Stored milk will separate, so gently swirl the warmed milk to mix.

▶ If you want to add more fresh breast milk to a bag that has frozen breast milk in it, chill the milk before adding it. If you add it warm, it may defrost the frozen milk slightly. It is not safe to defrost and refreeze.

▶ It is a good idea to freeze breast milk in 2 to 4 ounce batches so that there is little waste. Also, smaller amounts thaw more quickly.

▶ Discard any leftover milk if the bottle has been in the baby's mouth.

▶ To transport fresh or defrosted breast milk, place it in an insulated cooler with reusable ice packs.

Postpartum Depression

Postpartum depression is a very real phenomenon. Those around the new mother must listen to her feelings and seek help if the "baby blues" persist. Some psychiatrists specialize in helping mothers with postpartum sadness. A physiological reason for the sadness can be the dramatic drop in hormone levels after the birth. Hormone replacement for a short time can sometimes help immeasurably.

The blues can also be precipitated by the changes in the mother's life after the birth of a baby, and they can be compounded by sleep deprivation. Getting together with other new mothers is sometimes the most helpful way to discuss and work through the feelings. I highly recommend attendance at a parenting class, in this case, a postpartum discussion group. I always begin every "Living with Your New Baby Class" by saying that the most helpful aspect of the class is the sharing among moms. Sometimes the best friends of a lifetime are formed during these early parenting times. Knowing that others are having some of the same feelings can be very therapeutic, helping you realize that you are not alone.

New Fathers

Fathers can be the best support people for the new mother. Her life has changed dramatically, and fathers can offer support by listening and by doing. "Take initiative" are words I hope all fathers will take to heart. If you can foresee what needs to be done and initiate the action needed, the mother feels supported and part of a parenting team.

In my experience talking to hundreds of new mothers, they tell me that their husbands are very willing to help when asked to do something, but the mothers get tired and frustrated by always having to ask. The young mother often feels that the 24-hour psychological responsibility is on her shoulders rather than shared.

I use the following metaphor: walking down the path of life is more joyful and less stressful if you walk side by side as equal partners rather than one leading the way and the other following. In other words, fathers: "Initiate." Notice when the diaper needs changing instead of waiting to be asked to change it. Offer to take the baby for a walk so Mom can rest or make dinner. Bring dinner home or prepare it yourself. Something so small as having to ask, "Can you watch the baby so I can take a shower?" can get wearing. Instead, anticipate the need to shower, and take the baby to another room to play. These things can make a world of difference.

Fathers, your baby needs you—and so does Mom. It is wonderful that the baby has two important relationships. He will learn your style of handling him as different than his mother's and will accept it. If you can be involved in the baby's daily care from the first day, you will be rewarded with a closer relationship.

Many fathers feel displaced in the early weeks. It is so important for you to support your wife. Be supportive of her nursing; bring her water or juice every time she sits down to nurse. Change the baby and bring him to her when it is time to nurse, especially at night. After the first morning feeding on the weekend, take the baby and encourage Mom to sleep a little more. Verbally praise Mom for her efforts; every day, tell her she is doing a great job. She needs reassurance that she is mothering well. It takes a superhuman amount of energy to care for a newborn when you are tired and your body is healing and adjusting to breastfeeding. If the baby is fussy, it is doubly hard. Mom cherishes your words of encouragement.

Some fathers want a turn to feed the baby. After the first 6 weeks, having dad give a bottle filled with breast milk occasionally to give mom a break can be fine.

You will not have to wait long to feed the baby regularly, because in the blink of an eye, the baby will be beginning solids, and Mom will be very happy to turn over solid-feeding duty.

You can feel close to the baby, and he will love it, if you lie skin to skin with your baby. Take off your shirt and hold your baby close. Another way to bond with the baby is to help him go from crying to being soothed. You can do this by walking him, rocking him, or patting him. So often, the baby cries and Dad hands him to Mom to solve the problem. If he has just eaten, and he begins to fuss, try some strategies to soothe him. He will appreciate your efforts and will feel closer to you. So will Mom!

Characteristics of the Newborn

Newborns are able to interact with their environments. During the quiet alert state, the newborn will turn and look for the source of a sound. While holding the baby, move an object about 12 inches away from his eyes, and he will follow the moving object. If the baby fusses and cries, see what he does to calm himself: some babies put their fingers in their mouths, and some put their hands together to stop their movement. Some will quiet by seeing a face; some will quiet by hearing a voice. Some are consoled quickly and easily; others take longer. Some babies are only alert if they are tightly swaddled. Swaddle to keep them from flailing their arms when uncovered and frightening themselves. Swaddling reminds them of being snuggled inside of you.

Your baby can visually focus at about 12 inches distance, which is about the distance from lying in the crook of your arm to your face. Immediately after birth, the baby is quiet and alert for about 40 minutes. This is the opportune time to bond with the baby. He looks into your face and seems to say, "I know your voice. So this is what you look like!" Touch him all over, and speak softly. After this bonding time, he will probably sleep for awhile to recover from his journey. Most hospitals and birthing centers encourage rooming-in. It is best for mother and baby to be together for at least a part of the day. You begin to get to know each other and begin to find a rhythm of interaction. You can respond to his crying and comfort him. You can help him begin to sort out all the stimulation and to begin the journey of making sense out of his world.

Growth and Development

Along with your pediatrician's guidance, I encourage you to read about the baby's growth and development at each month of life so you know what to anticipate. Each baby grows at his own rate, but there is a "gamut of normal," a range within normal. For example, the average baby crawls at around 8 months, but it is within normal limits not to crawl until 12 months. Similarly, the average child walks at around 12 months, but it is within normal limits not to walk until 15 months. Some children utter their first words around 11 months and others do not speak until age 2.

Do not compare your baby to another. Your baby has her own timetable to develop.

The quiet baby may be observing and may talk first, and the active baby may walk earlier but talk later. We need the guidelines of growth and development so we know when to seek further evaluation and intervention. Cities have excellent early intervention programs that can offer means of helping your child. Several people in my classes have benefited from early speech therapy, for example, and it has made a world of difference. You are your child's advocate.

Activities to Soothe and Enrich, or What to Do When the Baby is Awake

Babies can fuss because they are bored or lonely. They cannot move themselves to interesting sights and sounds, so their only way of helping themselves is to fuss for attention. Here are some ideas:

▶ The sling or the front carrier can come in handy to carry the baby around while you are going about your daily routine. She can watch what you are doing, hear your voice, be held close to your heart, and feel her body very close to yours.

▶ Babies cannot be held, touched, hugged, or cuddled too much. Cuddle with your baby as much as you want. Babies cannot be spoiled by too much loving and holding.

▶ Touch may be the first language of love. Learning how to do a baby massage can be very soothing to your baby. Taking a class would be great, or visit http://www.lovingtouch.com. The basic idea is to warm baby lotion on your hands and then massage the baby from the center of his body out. Run your hands along his front and continue down one leg, from thigh to toes, and then down the other leg. Massage his little arms from the shoulder to his fingertips. Turn him over and massage the cream onto his little back and buttocks. How soothing. Touching and cuddling is so important to your baby's well being.

Babies without parents used to be placed in orphanages. Envision cribs lined up and only a few caregivers. The babies were fed and changed but had minimal holding or cuddling. Many of them failed to thrive. One baby kept thriving. He seemed to be receiving the same care as the others. One night, the doctor returned late to check on one of the babies and found out the reason the one baby was surviving: The cleaning lady had taken a liking to this baby and had fashioned a sling from a sheet and carried the baby in it while she did her work, singing and talking to him. The baby survived because of the loving touching. After that, babies in America began to be placed in foster homes, so that each one could get the close attention he needs. Do not listen if anyone tells you that you are holding the baby too much. Enjoy cuddling and holding your baby!

► Other places to put your baby when he is awake are the bouncy seat, the swing, or the "boppy"—a horseshoe-shaped

pillow to support the baby, with varying things to look at.

▶ To calm a fussy baby, place your hand on the baby's stomach or hold the baby's hands to her chest to soothe her. You can use Dr. Karp's Five S's described earlier.

▶ The positions most often used to burp a baby are over your shoulder or sitting on your lap with her head supported under the chin. A third possibility is laying the baby across your lap on his tummy and rubbing or patting his back. You could lift one of your heels then the other to give a rocking motion while he lies across your knees.

▶ Babies like soft, high-pitched voices. They love to see the human face, especially yours.

▶ "Tummy time" is very important for practicing lifting the head. Some babies don't like being on their stomachs. To encourage her for a few minutes, place a toy or mirror in front of her to encourage her to lift her head. Another tip is to place a rolled blanket under her chest, so she is not lying so flat. If you get down on the floor too and talk to her face to face, she may be able to tolerate "tummy time" better. Aim for 10 minutes twice a day and work up to a longer period as she gets older. From this position she will progress to making "swimming" motions, to inching along, to rocking on her knees, then to crawling (around 8 months).

▶ As the baby gets more head control, you could take a bath with your baby. Of course you must be extremely careful with your infant around water. Do not allow your baby's head to go under water. Never leave a child unattended around water even for an instant.

One way to do a bath is to fill the tub and have someone hand the baby to you. You could balance her against your raised knees while you soap her up. She will love it as you hold her floating in the water to rinse off. Support her head and shoulders out of the water, and allow her legs to float freely pointing away from you. Hand her back out to be toweled dry.

If you are by yourself, undress the baby and wrap her in a big towel on the bathroom rug. Get in yourself and reach over to bring her in. *Never* carry the baby into the tub; there is too much risk of falling. When you are finished, place her back on the towel on the rug, wrap her up, and step out *without* her in your arms. Babies usually love being in warm water because it reminds them of the comfort inside the womb.

▶ Taking the baby outdoors to see the bright sky and new objects sometimes works wonders to end a fussy mood.

▶ Babies love music. Play classical music—it will help her math skills later—or play some other soothing music.

▶ Pediatrician Dr. T. Berry Brazelton and psychiatrist Dr. Stanley I. Greenspan, in their book *The Irreducible Needs of Children: What Every Child Must Have to Grow, Learn, and Flourish,*♦ recommend:

> During the infant, toddler and preschool years, children should always be in the sight of caregivers except when they are sleeping. No more than one third of the baby's waking hours should be spent in independent activities in 10 to 15-minute increments here and there.

Brazelton and Greenspan go on to recommend that another third of the time be spent in direct interaction such as cuddling, holding, handing things back and forth, and funny face or sound games.

> Infants need four or more 20 minute or longer periods of direct interaction time....direct interaction helps babies learn to have an emotional dialogue and eventually an intellectual dialogue that facilitates focus and concentration, depth of engagement, preverbal signal reading and problem solving.

Brazelton and Greenspan recommend that the final third of the time be spent facilitating interactions with the environment. This interaction includes looking at pictures together or helping the baby explore a toy. "Ideally, all types of interaction flow seamlessly with one another."

► There has been much written about infant stimulation. I prefer to call it "infant enrichment." You are offering things to enrich his five senses. Encourage your baby to touch different textures. He will do this naturally as he touches your clothes and the surfaces he is placed upon. You could make a texture pad of different textures with fuzzy, smooth, or bumpy materials. Playing music, talking, and singing stimulate his sense of hearing.

Researchers say that brain development is encouraged by allowing your child to focus on black-and-white patterns. The black-and-white face is very fascinating to newborns. The recommendation is to hold your child on your lap, cupping his feet with your hand, and say something the same each time, such as "Johnny, are you ready to play?" Then bring a black-and-white pattern in his line of vision. It is amazing how long he will focus on the black and white.

With practice his attention span will increase. Black and white, different textures, and different sounds are commonplace in infant toys as a result of infant stimulation research.

Teething

Teething can be painful for your baby. Each tooth begins to erupt below the surface of the gums, and it may take up to a month for the tooth to fully emerge. Each time the tooth moves up, it contacts gums that have never had enamel next to them before. The body reacts as if the enamel were a foreign body, producing an inflammatory reaction. This gradual eruption has been likened to getting a splinter: The gums try to reject the foreign body—the emerging enamel—by swelling and becoming reddened and painful, just as our finger does with a splinter. You may see the gums swell, become reddened, and hurt; and then the inflammation may subside until the tooth moves up again. The gums seem to get used to the enamel being there after the initial inflammation. Once the tooth erupts through the gums, the pain subsides.

Ways to soothe the pain of teething:

▶ Teething can be a long process, so it is not recommended to give pain relief medications, such as Tylenol, each time you suspect pain in the gums. They can be given occasionally.

▶ Teething toys are helpful. Some babies find relief from chewing on a toy and toys with appendages are the best. My children's favorite was a bunny with long ears; they could get the ears toward the back when molars were coming in. Toys shaped like hands with fingers and feet with toes serve the same purpose. The teething toys that go in the refrigerator directly apply cold to decrease the swelling as they chew. However, once they spring a leak, they have to be discarded because bacteria can grow inside after a puncture.

▶ A moist washcloth filled with chopped ice and secured tightly with a rubber band can be a way of applying ice a child can chew. Freezing a moist washcloth for chewing on is another way of applying cold directly to the swollen gums.

▶ There are alcohol-free, nonprescription, topical medications that you can use for anesthetizing the gums.

▶ Sometimes a slight fever can result from teething. If the temperature is over 101 degrees, it probably is not teething and another cause must be sought.

▶ There are also homeopathic drops that parents can use; please consult with your pediatrician before using any of these drops or other medications.

Weaning

When you decide to wean your baby from the breast, it is best for you and for the baby to do it gradually. The weaning process is actually begun when the bottle or solid food is introduced. Every 2 to 3 weeks, eliminate a nursing. Start with her least favorite feeding and have someone else offer the bottle. If your breasts are uncomfortable, express a small amount of breast milk. Your body will get the message to produce less milk.

If your baby is older than a year, you may be able to skip bottles. At the eliminated feeding time, you could offer a meal or a drink from a sippy cup. Plan special outings at this time to distract her from thinking about nursing. After 2 to 3 weeks without that feeding, eliminate another feeding and substitute a bottle or a meal. Continue this way gradually, until you are nursing once or twice a day and then not at all.

You can wean from the bottle in the same manner as above—gradually, one feeding at a time every 2 to 3 weeks. Distraction

works wonders. Some parents find it helpful to wrap up the bottles to send to a baby that needs them once the last feeding is eliminated.

Weaning from the pacifier is done in much the same manner by beginning to insist that the pacifier is only used in the crib. Studies show that if toddlers walk around with a pacifier, language can be stifled. They begin to say something and find the pacifier in their mouths and begin to suck instead of speak. Also it is difficult to understand a toddler speaking with a pacifier in his mouth. Developmentally, he will find other ways to self-soothe besides sucking on the pacifier.

Parenting Tips

Over the years of teaching "Living with Your New Baby," I have collected tips for new parents.

▶ Realize that parenting an infant is more than a one-person job. Your grandmothers had extended families to lend a hand. So many of us have moved away from family and find our nuclear families isolated. Grandmothers are busy working or pursuing other activities. Dr. Kuris, a psychiatrist who spoke at the Family Resource Infant Center in Princeton, said, "You need a wife, too…someone else to do the shopping, cleaning, and preparing meals." Realize that you only have the energy of one person. He said we need a fresh, rested person to come in at 5 p.m. and take care of us, because we already worked our eight hours. Be kind to yourself. Most new parents expect too much of themselves.

▶ Mothers are often saying to me "so-and-so has such a perfect house and she always looks so put together. Why can't I do that?" My answer is that we do not know the whole story. Or perhaps she is not holding or playing with her baby very much. Babies are little for such a short time. Enjoy them! For awhile, forget about the dust bunnies under the bed. Pick clean laundry out of the laundry basket. Let your dishes soak overnight so the food doesn't dry on, and they can be rinsed in the morning.

Spend time with your precious baby—rock him, love him, and respond to him.

▶ Give yourself an extra 15 minutes when leaving the house in case the baby needs a last-minute diaper change. It is so stressful to be late.

▶ Double every recipe you prepare and freeze one. You will have two dinners, only one set of dishes to wash, and a meal for next week.

▶ Use your spare minutes to nurture yourself, not for housework. You need to refuel to be able to keep giving. Think of activities that you find interesting or relaxing, like reading, having a cup of tea out in the sunshine, perhaps taking a nap. Sleeping whenever the baby sleeps is sage advice to help you catch up on some of the sleep you are missing in the night. Please don't run around cleaning up while the baby is sleeping; try to do housework while the baby is awake. Take her with you, either in the front carrier, her seat, or her stroller as you go from room to room. Sing and talk to her as you dust and mop.

▶ Dust off that old Crock-Pot. Dinner will be warm whenever you can eat it.

▶ Use aluminum foil to line baking pans for easier clean up.

▶ Plan and prepare dinner in the morning; babies are usually more content in the morning. The 5 to 7 p.m. hour has been called the "arsenic hour," because everyone is tired and hungry.

▶ Give faucets a swipe with rubbing alcohol. They will sparkle.

▶ Set the table from the dishwasher. That saves the step of putting dishes away and getting them back out. At least it looks like dinner is on the way.

▶ Put your feet up when you are nursing; it helps you feel more rested. Or better yet, lie down to nurse to rest your entire body.

▶ If the doctor prescribes vitamins (about half do), give them to the baby at bath time, so when he dribbles, the vitamins won't stain his clothes.

▶ Put a dimmer switch on the baby's room light switch, so you can turn the light down very low. It can be made dimmer than nightlights. Another option is to place a blue bulb in the nightlight; it is not quite so bright. I used to stock up at Christmas time—the large-size Christmas lights fit nightlights.

▶ Do baby laundry separately, then it is sorted for you. Dreft detergent works great to get the nursing bowel-movement brown out of clothes. Place the baby's socks into one of those net bags made to wash lingerie in before throwing them in the washer. They will be easier to find, and they won't get "eaten" by the machine.

▶ Use tissue at the changing table to clean a bowel movement. Use a wipe as the last swipe. That way, you will not use so many wipes—they are expensive.

► Invest in an intercom. It will save many steps and give you peace of mind.

► Have warm, nurturing interactions with exchanges of vocalizations and gestures during diapering and feeding.

► For a red diaper rash, buy packets of Domeboro (in the first aid section). Put a packet in a cup of warm water. Place a washcloth in the warm water, and then place it on your baby's bottom for a few minutes. It will draw the red out—it works like a miracle. (Tip from my children's pediatrician.)

  Leaving her bottom open to the air can be very helpful. Diaper rash ointments such as Balmex and Desitin can be used for diaper rashes, too. A soothing ointment such as A and D ointment creates a protective barrier and can be used at every diaper change.

► Another tip from my children's pediatrician is a strategy to handle cradle cap. Cradle cap looks like a patch of flaking dry skin on the scalp. Place baby oil on a cotton ball and dab the spots of cradle cap. Let the oil sit for one hour. Place the baby in the football hold to enable you to shampoo. Run the water from the faucet over his shampooed head as you gently use a baby brush in circular motions over the area of cradle cap. Rinse thoroughly. Two to three treatments do the trick. Among others, there is a special shampoo from France called Mustela, which can be ordered from http://www.Nordstrom.com or http://www.mustela.com.

► In the first weeks of life, your baby may get infant acne. It looks like pimples on the face. Just keep it clean and dry; it will go away on its own. It is caused by your hormones leaving his system.

► Some babies get a plugged tear duct, in which yellowish drainage appears at the corner of his eye. Wipe with a cotton ball moistened with water, from the inside corner out. Gently massage the duct in the inside corner of the eye; your pediatrician will show you how. He will determine whether drops are needed. Children usually outgrow plugged tear ducts because the tear ducts enlarge as they grow, and therefore they drain more easily.

► Every day that passes helps make the next day better, easier, and happier as you learn your baby's ways and she learns yours.

▶ Keep a bag of diapers in your car so you always have extras.

▶ Keep your diaper bag stocked at all times. Replace items used soon after you get home so you will be ready to go the next time. Always pack a few outfits in case more than one gets soiled.

▶ Sing, sing, sing. Babies love music, and they don't mind if you can't carry a tune.

▶ Classical music is good for brain development. If you aren't familiar with classical music, Vivaldi's *Seasons* or Pachebel's *Canon* are lovely. Listening to anything by Beethoven or Mozart has been shown to enhance math skills later. Discount stores sell classical music CDs for a few dollars.

▶ Place a mirror next to the changing table, or a mobile over it, to entertain your baby while he is being changed. You can talk to the baby in the mirror or to the characters on the mobile to further encourage his cooperation with the changing.

▶ Infants cannot make sense of the images on TV, and it is not advisable to place infants in front of one, even with "educational videos." Children learn best within a relationship. They learn language by listening to you, not from the images on TV. Many pediatricians discourage parents from allowing children to watch TV in the first two years. After that, TV watching needs to be limited to educational programming for a half hour per day or less. Infants learn about the world by doing, not by watching images on TV.

▶ Make plans with a friend or meet your husband for lunch with the baby, so you have something to look forward to in the future. Feeding, changing, feeding, changing, doing laundry, feeding, changing can get quite monotonous. Be sure you take walks and have outings planned for a change of scene.

2
Building Your Child's Self-Esteem

Defining Self-Esteem

I am the only unique me that will ever be...
I have the power to make a difference
in this world—
I look forward to taking on the
grand adventure of life...
I love being me!
—*Anonymous*

This is how you want your child to feel about himself! Your interactions with your child become part of his soul, the essence of how he feels about himself and about life. Having high self-esteem makes a big difference in life. In her book *Building Your Child's Self-Esteem: The Key to Life*, Dorothy Corkille Briggs gives a wonderful definition: "the child's quiet inner feeling that adds up to 'I am glad to be me'; an inner confidence."

High self-esteem has nothing to do with bragging or being conceited. Actually, being conceited is merely a cover-up for low self-esteem and insecurity. One parent shared that her 3-year-old asked 13 times in one day, "Am I being good?" Her self-esteem was based on another person's opinion of her. She was asking for frequent reassurance that she was measuring up to her mother's expectations.

The feeling of being special and unique comes from within. It is not dependent on other people's views. This little girl needed her mom to work on increasing her self-esteem from within (numerous ideas for increasing self-esteem are coming up).

It is very important for you to understand how self-esteem is built. Every message, every response from the day of birth, is absorbed and assimilated into the self-concept. Daily messages to the child add up to a sense of self. Does she feel lovable and worthwhile? The love and responses we give to newborns begin the journey to a high self-esteem.

A child needs to feel that he is loved unconditionally. The message to the child must be "I cherish you just because you are you. I love you no matter how you behave and no matter how you look." Loving your child in each interaction is the best gift you can give your child. Once he *feels* that love, that sense of being valued and cherished, he will have the ability to develop competencies with enthusiasm for life.

In psychologist Abraham Maslow's famous hierarchy of needs (from his paper entitled "A Theory of Human Motivation"), the physical needs for food, shelter, and clothing come first. The need for safety comes next, and then the need to feel valued and cherished. This is poignantly expressed in the example of the one baby surviving at the orphanage (told in Chapter 1: Living with Your New Baby). His needs for food, clothing, shelter and safety were being met just like the other babies. Yet he was the only one thriving because the cleaning lady took a liking to him and carried him around in a sheet-constructed sling, singing and talking to him as she worked. All the babies had their physical needs met, but he was the only one who felt cherished and loved. All children have a need to feel cherished and loved.

Traits of a Person with High Self-Esteem

Studies show that people with high self-esteem are capable of making good decisions, are proud of their accomplishments, are willing to take responsibility, and are able to cope with frustration. They get along better with others and are not easily discouraged. They are also more likely to be creative, because they are willing to meet challenges and to take risks in new situations. A child with a high IQ and low self-esteem may do poorly in school, while a child with average intelligence but high self-esteem may excel.

We all want these traits for our children. The daily messages that your child receives form her feelings of self-worth. Is she getting the message that "The world feels safe and I feel worthy because people are loving me and responding to my efforts of communication"? If the messages she receives are that "you are a nuisance," "all you ever do is cry," or "you are impossible," that is the view of herself that she will develop. Sometimes, parents criticize children to try to get them to behave differently. Many times the words that are used are hurtful to the very person of the child, an attack on the child's character. Children take our words to heart. When we are angry with them, with an angry face, they think that we do not like them anymore. They have not had enough experiences to realize that you still love them even if you have a mean face and are calling them naughty, slow, clumsy, bad, or impossible. If she frequently feels that she cannot meet your expectations, she feels disappointed in herself and discouraged. Messages like these add up to a negative self-image, a low self-esteem. How people see her is how she believes she is. Each message you send shapes her image of herself.

Ways to Increase Self-Esteem

Self-esteem can always be improved. We need to improve the messages received by the child. As long as one person believes in the child and loves him unconditionally, he can develop a high self-esteem. Here are several suggestions for building your child's self-esteem daily.

▶ **Daily cherished moments.** Be open to the wonder of your child. Convey in little messages throughout your time together that you value and cherish her. Make time for a daily "cherished moment" with each child. It takes less than a minute to connect in the moment, to look into her eyes, to convey "I love you for being you" with a loving look, a touch, a ruffle of her hair, a hug, or words that say "You are very special to me." Your child needs to *feel* your love, really *feel* it. Parents can say "I love you" in many ways, but if the child does not *feel* your caring with your actions, it makes less impact.

► **Trust** in you is an integral part of unconditional love. How does your child learn to trust you? Your newborn learns trust when you consistently respond to her cries. You become reliable, someone she can count on to be there. Secondly, it is very important that you never leave a child without saying goodbye. Many parents sneak away to avoid the crying, but when the child notices that you are gone, she feels betrayed and loses trust in you. When you come home, she is afraid to let you out of her sight and clings to you. She fears that you will sneak away again.

One night at Children's Hospital of Los Angeles, where I worked as a new graduate, one toddler was crying inconsolably, and I could not figure out why. I found out that the mother said she was going to the bathroom and never returned. The next day, he clung to her and would not even let her go to the bathroom. He had lost trust in her words. It is respectful to tell your child when you are leaving the room or going outside to get the mail. Always say "I will be right back" and "I'm back" when you return. With repeated experiences

of you coming and going, she will know you mean what you say and will feel comfortable with your comings and goings. Following through on doing what you say you are going to do also helps build trust. Do not threaten consequences unless you will carry them out. Do not promise activities and not deliver. Children need to learn that they can trust your words.

▶ **Notice the positive.** Notice when your child is behaving and comment on it. Thank them for cooperating with you. Adults are often stressed and busy with the task at hand. A child may be behaving beautifully for an hour and then begins to misbehave. He immediately gets the busy adult's attention in a negative manner. The negative behavior is therefore reinforced, because it got the parent's attention. Give attention when he is behaving and cooperating!

▶ **Listening to your child** conveys the message that what he has to say is worthwhile and that he is worthy of your time. You recognize that he has needs and desires; you convey that his thoughts are interesting. What a gift to give a child! The messages to your child are "I am interested in what you have to say," "What you say is valuable," "Your ideas are important."

▶ **Acknowledging your child's feelings** conveys the message that you are validating his feelings. "You are so sad." "I see you are frustrated!" These messages convey that her feelings are accepted and important. Denying children's feelings with such phrases as "Don't cry, that didn't hurt that much" or "Don't be angry" or "Don't be disappointed by that" convey that it is not okay to have some feelings, or that the child's true feelings are not important or valued. One helpful phrase is "I hear you. I don't have to agree, but I can understand how someone might feel that way."

▶ **Giving choices** sends the message "I think you are capable of making a good decision." You are giving them the proof that you believe in them, that they are intelligent and have opinions of their own. You convey that you trust them to make good decisions and show that you value their ideas.

▶ **Convey that you enjoy being with your child.** Reflect on how it feels to have someone want to spend time with you, someone who just enjoys your company. Remember the courtship days when all you wanted was to be together; it didn't matter what you did? It makes us feel good to have a friend call up and say "I miss you. Let's set up a time to be together" or "I just called to see how you are doing."

It is a gift to find ways to be with your child, enjoying her company. Have times where you are just "hanging out," not doing much of anything but finding joy in her presence, connecting in the moment. When you are doing something, focus your attention on the child, not the task. For example, during her bath, watch how she notices the sparkle of the bubbles rather than focusing on getting her clean.

Quality time is about *connecting in the moment.* So often parents are distracted and never fully with the child in the moment. Try to take a few minutes out of your busy day to be fully present with your child. If time does not allow this connection during the week, plan a "date" on the weekend for an hour or two that you refer to the rest of the week, saying how much you are looking forward to your together time on Saturday. How wonderful your child will feel that you want to spend time with her! The message to her is "This big person that I love and depend on wants to spend time with me. I am special."

▶ **"I'll always love you; it is your behavior I don't like."** What a wonderful statement to learn to say, so that your child realizes that you still love him even though you may have an angry face or a disappointed look about something he did. Remember that he cannot yet realize that you still love him even when you are angry at something he has done. Restate that you love him unconditionally. Use nonjudgmental statements as you describe the behavior. Instead of saying "You are impossible," describe the behavior: "I would like you to wait your turn" or "Please don't interrupt me while I'm talking to your teacher."

▶ Adele Faber and Elaine Mazlish, in their book entitled *How to Talk So*

Kids Will Listen and Listen So Kids Will Talk (based on psychologist Dr. Haim Ginott's theories), help us realize **two parts of praise: describe your child's behavior, and then she will praise herself.** Become a very good describer, noticing the details of what she did, being very specific. For example, saying "You are a good girl" is a judgmental statement. The child might immediately think of something she did that was not good, or she may remember that the day before she did the opposite behavior. In both instances she may say to herself, "I am bad." It is best to describe exactly what she did: "You picked up every toy on the floor and put them in their places," or "You showed your little sister all the animals in the book with their sounds. See how you are teaching her?"

The second part of praise is that her little chest will puff out, and she will say to herself, "I am good." This is a verbal picture of herself that can never be taken away. A little boy plays the part of a rabbit in a school play. He comes up to his father asking, "Was I good?" Dad could say, "You were great!" The child may say or think, "No, I'm not. I forgot three lines, and I tripped over a cord." It is hard to live up to judgmental words like "great," "wonderful," "terrific." Much more effective is the father describing in detail, "You spoke so clearly. I could hear every word. You put so much feeling into each sentence. You seemed to really care about what happened to the other animals." Now he *knows* that his father really paid attention and thought he had done a good job. He beams and thinks, "I did a good job!" Noticing the details helps the child feel appreciated. Take time to notice and describe the details of something they made or something they did.

The second part of praise is so important: The child praises himself. Good feelings about himself come from within. Children carry these positive pictures of themselves inside, and when something happens to hurt their self-esteem, they remember these pictures and are more resilient and less affected when someone hurts them.

► **Giving responsibilities** to children of all ages helps them feel that they are valued members of the family team. They really can help: the younger child could play and sing until dinner is ready, the preschooler could help sort socks, the older child could water the plants or sweep. Remember to show your delight by describing detail, so the child can praise himself for a job well done.

► **Express interest in their days and their activities.** Children who feel this interest have more confidence; they have an important audience to live up to. Being there for their important moments is very supportive. Go to games, performances, back-to-school nights, parent-teacher conferences, and awards ceremonies. If you are unable to attend, be sure to send someone with a video camera so you can share the special moments together later.

► **Have realistic expectations in accor-**

dance with their age and abilities. "If mom or dad thinks I should be able to do that, and I can't, I feel badly about myself." Parents place pressure on children. Provide "success experiences" in which children can feel good about themselves, such as hobbies, sports (not necessarily team sports), art activities, or music lessons. Try to offer children experiences where they will find what they are passionate about. Always allow time for free play and relaxation, where they can exercise their imaginations and just be children.

► **Being respectful to your child** helps him see that you view him as worthy of respect. Squatting down to eye level to speak to your child is a sign of respect. Another way to show respect is to tell children what to do instead of what not to do. This is especially helpful when they encounter a new situation. For example, teach them how to interact with a new baby by saying "You may let the baby hold your finger, or you could rub her back" instead of "Don't touch her head or poke her in the eyes."

As adults we tend to move too fast for children. We whisk them here and there. To show respect, we need to try to slow our pace down and allow time for transition between activities. We need to let a child know we are there and what our intentions are before we pick a child up. Get in front of an infant to get his attention, and tell him what is about to happen. For example, it is a sign of respect to gain eye contact with an infant and say, "I'm going to pick you up now, and we will go have lunch." Model respect for others by saying "please," "thank you," and "excuse me." Avoid comparing, and *always* avoid sarcasm. Sarcasm confuses children, because our nonverbal behavior does not match our words. Give quiet correction. Yelling a reprimand across the room can be very humiliating and discouraging. Ask for his opinion when making a decision or when problem solving. The message to the child is "You are an important person with good ideas. I respect you."

Safe Harbor

Your relationship with your child is a safe harbor where the child feels valued and confident. She knows deep down that you love her no matter how she acts or how she looks. She is confident that you will help her learn what are acceptable behaviors, all

the time knowing that she is worthy of your love. The message to the child is "I'm glad I had a chance to share my life with you."

3
Living with Your Toddler: Tips for Daily Life

One of the most popular topics in my Toddler Parent Participation Class is the sharing of tips for living with toddlers. Parents share the strategies that help make life with a toddler go more smoothly and peacefully.

Structuring the Day

A reliable daily schedule helps your child know what to expect so there will be fewer battles of will. He will know what comes next. I am not in favor of rigid scheduling, however. If a class delays his nap one day a week, no problem. If a spontaneous butterfly hunt delays lunch, have fun. I'm referring to the general framework for the day. If he learns that nap comes after lunch, he will more willingly cooperate.

Pediatrician Dr. T. Berry Brazelton and psychiatrist Dr. Stanley I. Greenspan, in their book *The Irreducible Needs of Children: What Every Child Must Have to Grow, Learn, and Flourish,*♦ recommend that

during the infant, toddler, and preschool years, children should always be in the sight of caregivers except when they are sleeping. No more than one third of the toddler's waking hours should be spent

in independent activities in 10–15 minute increments here and there.

They go on to recommend that another third of the time be spent in direct interaction such as cuddling, holding, handing things back and forth, and joint pretend play. They believe that

direct interaction helps toddlers learn to have an emotional dialogue and eventually an intellectual dialogue that facilitates focus and concentration, depth of engagement, preverbal signal reading, and problem solving.

They recommend that the final third of the time be spent facilitating interactions with the environment. This interaction includes helping the toddler explore his surroundings by helping him look, touch, examine, and talk about the experiences. "Ideally, all types of interaction flow seamlessly with one another."

Transitions

Many toddlers have trouble changing from one activity to another. For example, if she is playing happily with her blocks, and you say it is time for her bath, she may balk.

When you pick her up at child care, she may fuss about leaving. These are called *transition times*. The most helpful strategy for transitions is to give a five-minute warning about the change. "I see how much fun you are having with your blocks. In five minutes, it will be time for your bath." This gives the child time to "change gears" and to get ready for the change. Too often parents are in a hurry and whisk children from place to place without warnings, and this sets the child up for refusing loudly. Small children need to have the adult pace slowed down to allow time for transitions.

One helpful strategy is to make a time line of the day, either in book form or on a Velcro time line. The idea is to take pictures of his daily activities and place them in sequential order to "read" periodically with the child to teach him the sequence of the day. Assemble pictures of the daily activities in time order. Include eating breakfast together, getting dressed, driving to child care, playing at child care, Mom and Dad at their workplaces, having lunch, taking a nap, being picked up, driving home, playing, having dinner together, bathtime, bedtime stories, and going to sleep. Using a little photo album makes this quite easy.

A Velcro time line also works well. You can buy a strip of Velcro, place Velcro "buttons" on the back of each picture, and place them on the line in order. The beauty of either method is that the pictures can easily be placed in a different order if things change for that day. This way the child will know what to expect and will balk less. It is also a helpful strategy for helping your child cope with any separation during the day; they visually can see

that you will be together again at the end of the day. Reviewing the schedule each day in this concrete form helps prepare your child for his day and helps him cope with transitions.

The Task of Separating

The 14- to 36-month old has the personality task of separating from you to assert her independence. She needs to move from being an infant to being a child. Negativism begins earlier than 2. In psychological terms, this process is called *individuation*: being able to function as a separate individual. The process continues through the year of being 2 and is usually completed by age 3. That is why the toddler years can be so stormy. They want to be little, and they want to be big.

You are their trust base. They will check in with their trust base by refueling on your lap or by visually checking back with a glance to make sure you are still around. Children of this age are often referred to as *mini-teenagers* because they have a similar task of asserting their independence that teenagers do.

Parents need to anticipate that the child will say "No" to nearly every yes or no request, even if that means refusing one of her favorite things. Saying "No" to her favorite cereal or to her favorite outfit gives her the feeling of asserting her independence. Realize that she is trying to control her little world by saying "No! Me do it!" Or "My way!" A parent needs to smile to herself and say, "She is really separating today!" One way to handle this is to not ask questions that require yes and no answers. Rather say it is time to do something or give the child a choice.

Separation rituals are very important at this age to ease into the separations. Going to sleep is a separation from you, so the bedtime ritual has a very important place in her life. Do the same sequence of activities each night, then into bed. It could be a bath, reading two stories, rocking and singing "Twinkle, Twinkle, Little Star," saying goodnight to each stuffed animal, three kisses, and into bed. Saying goodbye is another time for a separation ritual, whether it is when the babysitter comes for an evening out or when you drop her off at child care. Three hugs, two kisses, or a kiss in the palm of each hand for her pockets and saying goodbye could be a possible goodbye ritual.

Offering Choices

The best strategy with toddlers is to offer a choice. "Do you want to wear your blue pants or your red pants?" "Do you want apple juice or milk?" "Do you want to do it now or wait one minute?" "Do you want to walk or do you want me to carry you?" "You can come over here by yourself or I can come and get you. You decide." This small change in wording gives her a feeling of importance. The message is "I think you are capable of making decisions." Offering choices gives her the feeling that she is in control of her life and what happens to her instead of being told what to do. She chooses. Her little chest puffs out with the feeling that she has important decisions to make.

Sometimes the child is unable to make a choice. The best strategy is to restate the choice once and wait a minute or two. If a choice is still not made, you say that you will make the choice this time and that she will have another chance later with another choice. Invariably, whichever one you choose will be the wrong one, and she will say she wants the other one. Calmly restate that she had the chance to choose, but could not, so you made the choice for her. Reminding her that she will have another chance is very important. If she fusses, it is best to stick to the choice you made. Otherwise, you find yourself pouring apple juice, then milk, then apple juice, then milk. That is what Dr. Burton White, the author of *The First Three Years of Life*, calls "undue service." That means that you are going beyond what is reasonable in that situation (more about this in Chapter 9: Discipline Styles). In this situ-

ation with a young toddler, she will manage better if you give her the chance to make a choice, restate once, and then decide for her if she cannot choose. You are setting a limit. A child who is changing her mind back and forth becomes anxious; setting a limit gives her a feeling of security.

As with the juice/milk example, the young toddler can be ambivalent on occasion, which can drive a parent to distraction. The child may feel two emotions at once. For example, he may feel like a big boy and want to be a baby all at once. This collision of feelings often ends in a temper tantrum, or what some parents call a "meltdown." This sometimes occurs when he is unable to make simple choices. He may become very upset when you ask him if he would like strawberry or vanilla yogurt. This irrationality is part of being a toddler. If you accept this ambivalence, or dissonance inside them, as a form of confusion in the separation process and assertion of independence, you will be able to stay calm and support him instead of yelling in exasperation. Your staying calm will help him pull himself back together.

Handling Tantrums

What to do about tantrums is uppermost in the mind of the parent of a toddler. Most psychologists are no longer in favor of leaving the child and walking out of the room when a tantrum occurs. No matter how irrational the tantrum is, your child has a clashing of feelings inside. He is being overwhelmed by feelings. He is being flooded by emotions pushing him beyond his ability to cope. He

doesn't yet have the self-control to keep his feelings under control. With increased language and more experience, he will soon be able to verbalize about his feelings and express them in other more constructive ways (see Chapter 9: Discipline Styles).

When a temper tantrum occurs, the strategy is to first acknowledge her feelings. "I see you are so mad that we can't go outside now." "Whew! You are so angry that I can't let you climb on the dining room table." You wonder if she can hear your words. Do not despair. She sees your face and hears the calm tone of your words. Next, busy yourself in the same room doing something other than being right next to her. Moving into her space may escalate the tantrum. Respect her boundaries and move away slightly. The idea is that you are not leaving her alone with these out of control feelings.

A child caught in a tantrum does not have enough experience to know that the feelings will end. She thinks this will last forever. You are loaning her your ego; by your presence, you are saying, "I'll stay with you till you feel better." You sincerely express confidence that she can pull herself back together with your presence nearby. If she is not hurting herself, let the tantrum run its course.

If the tantrum lasts more than 10 minutes, it is time to try to help her stop. Some children get stuck and are unable to calm themselves. Your child may say, "I wanted to stop, Daddy, but I couldn't." When she does calm down, praise her: "You did it! You were able to calm yourself."

You may offer her something to calm down; the important thing is that what you offer is something that can help her calm herself down, not something you do for her. For example, you could offer her lovey—her special bear or blanket to hold. You could offer her a cool drink of water. You could get a cool moist washcloth and hand it to her to put on her own forehead. You could tell her to take some deep breaths and breathe with her. You could offer to have her listen to her favorite song.

Talk for the teddy bear you hand to her: "Teddy is sad to see you so upset. He needs a hug." You could offer her a constructive outlet to let her show you her feelings: kneading and pounding play dough, for example. You could say, "It is time to stop. You are flooded by your feelings. I have confidence that you can get yourself back under control. Perhaps you could try tak-ing deep, relaxing breaths." Offer her your lap and a cuddle when she is ready. "I have a hug waiting when you are ready."

When calm, talk to her about her feelings and what preceded her loss of control. Talk to her about how she was able to calm herself down. Cuddle her and make sure she knows that you will always love her, no matter how she behaves. Talk about words she could use to express her feelings. Teach her other things she can do to express her feelings when she feels so mad or sad. The message is that all feelings are accepted.

Using the Safe Hold

Flailing arms and legs on the ground is the usual tantrum, and the child is not harming himself. Sometimes, however, a child gets so out of control that he hurts himself or others. A child may bang his head on the ground, on a table, or against a door. Another child may try to pinch or hit his parent. When a child is hurting himself or another, the child must be physically stopped. In my experience, the most effective way is to sit down and hug the child from behind in the *safe hold* (as described in *Parent/Toddler Group* by Phyllis Rothman and Irene van der Zand). His little legs are held firmly between your legs, and both your arms are around him. If he starts to head bang your chin, you can gently and firmly hold his forehead against your chest. Hold him gently but firmly. Continually acknowledge his feelings in a calm, gentle voice.

What you are physically doing is giving him a boundary for his behavior. You are setting a limit so he cannot hurt himself or another. Remember that this strategy is *only* implemented when the child is hurting himself or another. The parent's permission for the safe hold must be given before it can be used in a child care setting.

An example of the safe hold in action: the teachers of one of the preschools in Princeton called me in to consult about a 3-year-old who banged his head on the glass door to the classroom during a tantrum that he had each day when his mother left him. Efforts at engaging him in an activity that would help him express his feelings had failed. With the mother's permission, one of the teachers agreed to try the safe hold. We could not let him continue to bang his head. Efforts to try to stop him had failed because he would run back to the door and bang his head again. The first day the teacher held him in the safe hold, he flailed for 15 minutes, and then he calmed down. The second day, the flailing lasted 3 minutes. Miraculously, on the third day, he quietly climbed in the teacher's lap for support when his mother left. With emotional support and physical boundaries, he was able to regain control. He learned that he was capable of self-control.

The key here is that the teacher held him kindly, but firmly, all the while quietly acknowledging his feelings. "I see you are sad that Mommy has left. She will be back. We have such fun planned today. We are going to finger paint, and also we will be doing your favorite activity, playing in the water."

Another example using the safe hold: a little girl threw sand at another child. The child was told that she could not throw sand, and if she did it again, she would have to leave the park. The child threw sand again and her mother took her from the park kicking and screaming. The problem was the child was 4, and the mother feared dropping her on the cement sidewalk because she was fighting so hard. They had walked to the park several blocks from home. She tried putting her down, and she ran back to the park. The safe hold would have been a possible solution until the child regained control and could walk home.

Children may have tantrums in public places because they sense that you are more vulnerable. If you can, safely remove the child to outside the place to finish the tantrum, and follow the steps above. If you cannot move them, sit down and employ the safe hold calmly. Usually store floors are cement under the tile, so a child could hurt himself. Try to feel confident, and armor yourself against "public opinion."

While you are employing the safe hold, whisper gently in his ear, rock gently, or softly sing one of his favorite songs. When he becomes calm, point out that he was able to calm *himself* down. Reassure your child by saying, "You listened to my song, you let yourself relax, and you took a deep breath." Be sure to hug and hold your child frequently at peaceful times, so the safe hold doesn't become a reward of being held.

Be aware of any pattern that leads to a child being overwhelmed by his feelings. If he is overstimulated, take him to a quiet place. If there have been too many transitions, do not make that one last stop. Find a place for him to run if he has been in his stroller or car seat too long.

Do Not Reinforce Tantrums

The American Academy of Pediatrics states in their flyer entitled "Temper Tantrums: A Natural Part of Growing Up" that temper tantrums should end when the child is 4 years old or even sooner, as they learn other skills to deal with their feelings. When children have tantrums beyond that, the parent needs to look at the situation and see where they may be reinforcing the tantrum.

The most common way to reinforce tantrums is to give in to the child's desires when he has one. For example, when a child has a tantrum because he cannot go outside, reinforcing the tantrum would be to take him outside anyway, so he will stop the tantrum.

Many parents will do anything to prevent tantrums. Do not relax your limits to avoid a tantrum; that is the surest way to make sure the tantrums continue. One parent observed the following: at his sister's ballet class, an 8-year-old brother was getting bored and began saying over and over that he wanted to go to Jack-in-the-Box. His mother said they could not go, and she listed the reasons. He continued like a chant: "I want to go to Jack-in-the-Box." Out in the parking lot, the observing parent witnessed that this boy was kicking the tires and the back of the seat in the car yelling, "I want to go to Jack-in-the-Box!" Guess what the mother did? She said, "Okay. We will go to Jack-in-the-Box."

Repeated examples of giving in throughout his 8 years taught him that temper tantrums work! You need to not let temper tantrums work for the child: Children will stop behaviors that do not work. Enforce the limit and accept the feelings that ensue. Limits from the outside will help them learn self-discipline.

"Me Do It!"

Another refrain from a toddler is "Me do it!" The drive for asserting independence is so strong. Within safe boundaries, try to let her do things for herself as much as possible. It encourages her self-esteem, helps her gain new skills, and helps her see she can do things for herself. The completion of the individuation process happens when she can do things such as dressing herself, feeding herself, getting herself a snack, learning to use the potty, and learning to use her words. At first, you need to demonstrate the steps and then allow her to do a portion of the task until she can master the whole task. What pleasure she receives from these accomplishments!

In our busy days, it is easier and quicker to do the tasks ourselves. As parents, we need to slow our adult pace down and allow time for our children to do things for themselves. When given these small ways to have control of their lives, they will be more cooperative at other times. They have been given opportunities to assert their autonomy.

"I Don't Want To Brush My Teeth!"

Brushing teeth always comes up as a challenge in our toddler discussions. Whether or not to brush teeth is not a choice; how you brush teeth can be a choice. Offering choices involves the child in the process and will hopefully encourage them to cooperate. Our brainstorming sessions offer the following solutions:

▶ Introduce the toothbrush when your child is an infant so he gets used to it early.

▶ Have your child choose a couple of toothbrushes at the store—an Elmo toothbrush or a Nemo toothbrush, for example—and each night they can choose which one to use.

▶ Do the same with two types of toothpaste. Use nonfluoride toothpaste until your child learns to spit well. Ingesting too much fluoride can cause mottling of the teeth. Your pediatrician can prescribe the amount of fluoride drops or fluoridated water needed based on your child's weight. Fluoride becomes incorporated into the enamel of the teeth—in both baby teeth and the forming adult teeth—and makes them more resistant to decay.

▶ Using a stool, let them see themselves in the mirror while brushing their teeth.

▶ Teach them to say "AH" for the back teeth so you can reach the molars and "EEE" for the front teeth.

▶ Have them copy you as you brush your teeth—front, back, inside.

▶ Use a children's book about brushing your teeth as a teaching tool.

▶ Brush the teeth as long as it takes to sing the ABC Song. That way they learn that the teeth-brushing session has an end.

▶ Have your child hold a toothbrush while you use a second to brush the child's teeth. Let him begin the brushing, and you finish up. (Remember the "me do it!" mentality.)

▶ Take them with you when you go to the dentist so they can see how important it is to take care of your teeth. (Most dentists recommend a first peek between 2 and 3 years old, unless you notice discoloring before that.)

▶ Some children tolerate teeth brushing lying down. If two parents are available, one could have the child lie across his lap while the other parent brushes.

▶ Another parent shared that her child became accepting of teeth brushing when she held him like a baby in the cradle position.

▶ Bring a doll into the bathroom and have your child brush the doll's teeth while you brush hers.

▶ Some children love the electric toothbrushes that vibrate.

Quiet Time

The transition between nap and no nap can be very tricky. If children nap, they are up late. If they do not nap, they are too cranky to enjoy the evening. Or you find them asleep right before dinner, and you have trouble waking them up.

When giving up a nap, the best idea is to do peaceful activities in the late afternoon, such as taking a walk or taking a bath, to prevent them from falling asleep in the late afternoon. Once they give up their naps, usually around 3, although it varies, they will go to bed earlier.

When your toddler gives up his nap, it is highly recommended that you have a quiet time in its place. During quiet time he plays quietly in his room, reading books, listening to music, or otherwise playing quietly. Sometimes, he will climb in bed just to rest and may fall asleep. A gate at the door can be a gentle reminder that he needs to stay in his room for the allotted time—maybe a half hour to one hour. You rest also. He needs a break from his exploring, he expends so much energy throughout the day. You need a break also. Rest yourself. Do something to refuel yourself. For your well-being, do not use the time to run around getting all your chores done.

A Peaceful Attitude Models Gentleness

In your daily interactions with your child, give him permission to feel. When he falls down, acknowledge his feeling. "That hurt your knee" instead of "That didn't hurt" or "Shake it off." Say to a crying child, "I see you are sad that Jenny has to go home now" instead of "Stop crying. You knew she would have to go home." When you are empathetic to his feelings, he learns to be empathetic and caring towards others. Telling him not to have his feelings causes him to distrust his own feelings and to not value them. Worse yet, it can cause the feelings to go underground and come out in other hurtful ways.

A side benefit of acknowledging feelings is that you are giving names to feelings. This helps him learn to identify and express his feelings more accurately. Just as you teach him other names of things in his life, you are teaching him the names for feelings. "You are frustrated that the block won't fit in the hole" or "I see how disappointed you are that you can't go with Daddy."

As your toddler explores, be available. Observe his responses. Allow him to initiate. Comment on his actions in a calm manner. Come near when he is in trouble or becoming frustrated, and ask him if he wants help. Show him how to help himself. When you want to pick him up, reach out and wait for his response. If he is attempting something new which may be unsafe, come near him and keep him safe or stop him and encourage another activity. If he seems bored, suggest other things to do. If he misbehaves, set a limit and show him how he can safely behave.

Try to stay calm as he explores and inevitably gets into mishaps. Instead of rushing over and saying "Oh no!" when his tricycle tips, and picking it up, and picking him up, walk calmly over and say "The tricycle tipped. If you push it up with your hand, you could get your leg out." He feels proud that *he* was able to handle the situation.

Staying calm in the storm of the negativism and the separation tasks of toddlerhood is your best strategy in helping your child learn self-discipline. Your staying calm will help him pull himself together sooner. If we escalate out of control out of frustration or anger, he will escalate more out of control. If we can stay calm, he will calm himself more easily.

Parenting a toddler can be joyful with his eager observation of life. He notices things that we have long taken for granted. His little sense of humor touches your funny bone. I would suggest that you keep a toddler journal of these joyful moments that you and he can share again and again. It will also help you in the more challenging times. The tasks of toddlerhood can be exhausting and patience-trying for any parent. It is one of the most joyful and most challenging times in your child's life.

4
Nutrition Tips for the Young Child

Allergies and Breastfeeding

The benefits of breastfeeding are discussed in Chapter 1: Living with Your New Baby. Food allergies in breastfed infants are not caused by breast milk itself but by foreign substances excreted in the breast milk. If allergic symptoms occur in your baby, such as eczema or a gassy stomach, you can eliminate the suspected food from your diet. To confirm that this food was the culprit, you should see a decrease in the baby's symptoms. To further confirm, with your pediatrician's guidance, you can reintroduce the food and observe for a reappearance of symptoms at a later time.

Pediatricians have shared that the most likely culprits, foods to eliminate from the nursing mother's diet, are milk products, chocolate, orange juice, citrus fruits, broccoli, cauliflower, beans (except for green beans), coffee, tea, coke, iron pills, peanut butter, and tuna. You may eliminate them all and then reintroduce one at a time every 4 to 7 days to observe for a reappearance of symptoms. It may take 4 to 7 days for the symptoms to appear; if a week passes with no symptoms, reintroduce the next food. I have seen miraculous reductions in symptoms by finding the food culprit in this way.

Why Delay the Introduction of Solids?

There are many reasons to delay the introduction of solids until 6 months of age.

► Breast milk has all the important nutrients your baby needs. Starting solids early dulls the interest in sucking and fills him up, so he does not get enough breast milk or formula.

► Analyses of infants' bowel movements show that infants do not digest the complex molecules of carbohydrates, fats, and protein in food. Food often passes undigested. Breast milk has easily digestible molecules. The breast fed infants' stools are so loose because most of the milk is utilized in growth. Introducing solids before the minimum 4 months of age taxes the undeveloped gastrointestinal system, which chugs along trying to digest the complex molecules, but it cannot.

► Avoiding allergies is the most compelling reason to delay solids until 6 months. By then, the infant is producing sufficient IgA antibodies to prevent absorption of food antigens through the intestinal mucous membranes. In other words, the IgA antibodies hold the allergen in the digestive tract for excretion in the bowel movement; the molecules that cause allergies are not allowed to go into the bloodstream and cause allergic symptoms. For example, if orange juice is offered before the IgA antibodies are established, an allergy to orange juice is established; whereas if the parent had waited to introduce orange juice until later, an allergy to orange juice would be much less likely.

▶ Early introduction of solids contributes to obesity, because the infant is sometimes given twice the calories needed.

▶ It is unsubstantiated that early introduction of solids encourages a baby to sleep longer at night.

Signs That a Baby Is Ready for Solids

At 6 months, a baby needs to begin solids to replenish iron. There is excellent absorption of iron from breast milk, yet most pediatricians agree that it is not enough after 6 months.

Remember that an increased demand to be nursed is your baby's way of increasing your milk supply. Every suck brings in more milk. By wanting to be nursed more frequently, she is building up your milk supply to meet her growing needs. We call this a "growth spurt." Infants will nurse more frequently for 24 to 72 hours and then return to the number of feedings she had before. On these growth spurt days—usually around 6 weeks, 3 months, and 5 months—it is best to cuddle in for the day and drink, drink, drink.

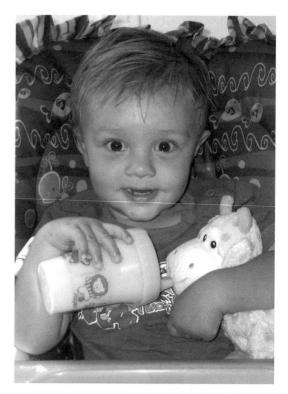

If the frequent nursing lasts for more than 72 hours and your child is over 4 months old, you and your pediatrician may decide to begin introducing solids.

Another sign that your infant is ready for solids is when he begins to grab for his parent's food off the parent's spoon or plate. He opens his mouth like a little bird when you are eating.

How to Introduce Solids

Pediatricians suggest offering breast milk or formula first until 7 months to make sure your child is getting enough milk. Try offering solids just after nursing. You could try midmorning or midafternoon, when you are not fixing other meals. Begin with one meal a day and gradually work up to three meals a day over several weeks. Little systems need to get used to the different foods gradually, so his first meals will be only a few spoonfuls once a day.

Hold your baby on your lap for his first foods, because your presence helps him be more accepting of the spoon and the new tastes. The first attempts at solids are not to fill him up but to get him used to the spoon. Put a tiny bit of food on the tip of the tiniest baby spoon, put it far back in the baby's mouth, and drop the food in. Tongue movements by which he sucks milk will probably cause him to spit the food right back out. This is called the *tongue retrusion reflex.* Scoop the food gently off his chin and place it back in his mouth. Soon he will learn how to swallow food off the spoon.

Do not put diluted food in a bottle. Babies need to learn to use the spoon, and they may ingest too many calories drinking the food from a bottle. Most babies like the new tastes and textures when foods are served separately.

Pay attention to the baby's "had enough" cues. She will tell you that she is full by clamping her mouth shut, spitting out more than is going in, turning her head, or by batting the spoon away. Respect these signals, and do not encourage her to finish up the last little bit, and do not play airplane with the spoon to distract her into eating. If she is overfed, fat cells are laid down in early childhood that the child has for the rest of her life. An area in our brain that regulates appetite has been called the "appestat." It lets us know when we are full. Many of us overeat, and our appestats are not allowed to function. Respect your baby's appestat.

Preventing Allergies

Give one food at a time every 4 to 7 days. That way, if an allergic reaction occurs, you will know exactly what caused it. It takes up to a week for symptoms to appear. If you do not allow enough time before starting a new food, and an allergic reaction occurs, you will have to begin eliminating foods all over again to find the culprit. It is so much easier to allow the time between foods in the beginning. Once you begin a new food, be sure to include it in your baby's diet at least once a week after that to encourage her with familiar tastes and to help prevent allergies.

The symptoms of a possible allergic reaction include vomiting the food; frequent and loose bowel movements; being quite fussy or gassy for several hours; a dry, scaly, red rash, usually on the face; hives; itching; wheezing; or a very sore bottom. Sometimes the area around the anus will get flaming red quickly, such as between diaper changes.

Some foods are more highly allergenic than others. Delaying introduction of these foods may prevent an allergy (remember the IgA antibodies). These are eggs, wheat, citrus fruits, nuts, and fish. Egg yolks can be given around 7 months, and the egg whites around 8 months. Wait to introduce wheat until close to 8 months. Wait until a child is at least a year old to introduce fish, shellfish, or chocolate. Because they present a choking hazard, wait until your child is 2 years old to introduce nuts and popcorn.

It is imperative that everyone who takes care of the baby take an infant CPR class that includes what to do if choking occurs.

If you have a family history of allergies, delay the allergenic foods even longer. A child inherits the tendency to be allergic, not the exact allergy. For example, you might be allergic to strawberries and break out in a skin rash; your baby might be allergic to tomatoes and have respiratory symptoms.

A child needs immediate care if respiratory symptoms such as wheezing or trouble breathing occur. Facial swelling is also an emergency, because a baby's tiny trachea can swell and occlude the airway.

Why Bother to Make Your Own Baby Food?

There are several reasons to make your own baby food:

▶ More nutritious with less processing and fresher fruits and vegetables.

▶ More economical: The cost of baby food is mainly in the processing and the jars, not the food inside. For example, you can buy a pound of carrots for under a dollar, and the equivalent number of jars of commercial baby food would easily be double that. With meat, it may be triple the cost!

▶ Improved taste, color, and texture by far: Make your own peas and taste them, then taste the jarred peas. There is a big difference.

▶ You can make the food chewier and lumpier as the child gets older. Many children get so used to the smooth texture that they refuse foods with any other texture. I have known children who refuse any food other than pureed food and are still eating baby food at 2 years old!

▶ Children can begin finger foods around 8 months, as soon as they develop the *pincer reflex*—the ability to use their thumbs and forefingers to pick things up. (That means that making baby food lasts only for a very few months.) A realistic goal is to have your child on all table food by 1 year old.

▶ When you make your own food, you can build around the foods that your family eats.

▶ The shelf life of food in a jar can be years. Glass jars allow light in to destroy some B vitamins, so sitting on the shelf for months can decrease the vitamins inside.

▶ Chemically modified starch (tapioca or corn) has no nutritive value. It is often added to jar foods to prevent separation of the foods and to thicken the food. Giving jar foods is giving highly processed foods.

How to Make Your Own Baby Food

With tools like the food processor or a blender, making your own baby food is very easy. Steaming vegetables is the most healthful way of cooking them, so the nutrients do not go into the water. Bake or boil meat and cut it up. Place the meat or vegetables in the processor, with a little of the cooking liquid or water, and puree. Pour the puree into an ice cube tray and place the tray in a Ziploc bag in the freezer. When the cubes are frozen, break them out into the bag. Voila! You have a week's worth of carrots, green beans, peas, chicken, or turkey. (Two filled cubes equal one jar of food.) When your baby is just beginning a new food, fill the cubes only a quarter to half full. These little cubes are wonderful, leaving little waste. When you open a jar, it has to be used within 24 hours, and many beginning eaters consume very tiny amounts.

The frozen cubes can be heated in a warming dish or in the microwave (as long as you stir it and test the temperature before serving; hot spots can develop). Another way to warm the frozen cubes is to place them in a Pyrex dish, place the dish in a pan of water, and heat on the stove (like a little double boiler). Heating cubes directly in a pan causes them to stick. Fruits do not need to be cooked, but most fruits need to be peeled before pureeing.

Important tips:

▶ Always wash your hands before preparing food.

▶ Larger amounts of food puree better, such as a pound of carrots peeled and steamed rather than one or two carrots alone.

▶ The little baby-food grinders are good for small amounts, for use at a restaurant, or someone else's house; the grinder can be used right at the table.

▶ Tupperware has tiny containers that just fit one cube, for use when you are out.

Place the frozen cube in the container in the morning, and it will be defrosted by mealtime. On a long plane flight, I decided to bring jars of food, and my daughter refused them! She was used to the richer color, taste, and texture.

▶ When your baby is 7 months old, you may boil an egg and mash the egg yolk with a little water or breast milk. Use the egg whites in your salad. After 8 months, with the introduction of egg whites, you have many possibilities: scrambled eggs, French toast cut into "fingers," or pancakes. No more than three eggs a week are suggested due to the cholesterol.

▶ Always spread peanut butter on a cracker or bread, never eat it off a spoon—even for adults. If a person chokes, the pea-nut butter sticks to the trachea, and the Heimlich maneuver will not work. Peanut butter and peanuts should be delayed until after age 2 because they are highly allergenic.

▶ Be sure you add only a small amount of puree liquid at first. Puree, check the consistency, and then add more as needed. I ruined several batches of food by adding too much liquid.

▶ As you add more and more vegetables to your baby's menu (remember, one new food every week), you could make vegetable soup and puree it all.

▶ Cook more of what you are having for dinner, so there is no extra cooking time. For example, cook four extra chicken breasts plain as you bake your

own chicken dinner. Cook two packages of vegetables, eat some for dinner, and puree the rest. If you are cooking tacos, reserve some cooked, unseasoned meat cut to puree before adding the seasoning.

Tips for Using Jar Foods

If you have not been convinced to make your own baby food, here are a few considerations when using jar foods:

▶ Avoid combination meals. Modified starch can equal one-quarter of the total solids in some of the combination products according to Consumer Reports studies. Meat content in jars is low, and children need good sources of protein for growth. One test showed 12 to 13 percent protein in plain meat jars and only 1.3 to 2.4 percent protein in combination meals.

▶ Be sure the jar has an indented jar lid, and be sure it pops when opened. People have been known to open a jar to see and smell the contents and then put it back on the shelf. Bacteria are sure to have grown in it.

▶ Avoid the "desserts," like Blueberry Buckle or Apple Pie. Babies do not need sugary foods.

▶ Be sure to wash the jars in hot, soapy water before opening them. Dust and other foreign matter can collect under the edge of the lid during the months on the shelf. When the jar is opened, and the vacuum seal is broken—whoosh!— the dust is drawn into the food.

▶ If you notice a grating noise as you are opening the jar, discard it. Some jars are broken in the box during shipping, and shards of glass can collect under the jar lid. When breaking the vacuum seal, the same "whoosh!" can suck in the shards of glass.

Foods to Begin With and Foods to Avoid

You may begin with banana as the first food. Buy a fresh banana with black specks on the skin. Cut off an inch, peel, and mash with a fork. The more you mash, the more liquid it becomes.

Some pediatricians suggest beginning with cereal. Use the regular, single-grain baby cereal, not mixed grains in the beginning. The iron is very bioavailable in regular baby cereal, meaning that it is easily absorbed. Do not introduce cow's milk yet; use rice cereal mixed with water or breast milk. Pediatricians recommend formula or breast milk for the first year and then whole milk until age 2. You could give a small amount of banana once a day for a week, then add rice cereal to the one meal a day. You could then introduce a vegetable such as carrots or sweet potatoes.

Keeping in mind that we are replenishing the baby's iron stores, meat could be next. Meat used to be left until last, when solids were started earlier. Now that you have waited until 6 months to begin solids, he can digest meat. Meat has iron and protein that is so important for growth. You may choose chicken as his first meat. Now you have a balanced variety of foods that you can give him.

If he is enjoying the food and learning to use the spoon, you could go to two meals a day. You could give banana and cereal for breakfast and carrots and chicken for dinner. I prefer this method, which works toward a balanced diet, instead of trying all the vegetables, then all the fruits, and then adding meat. It is best to introduce mostly vegetables first, however. If babies have fruits before they try vegetables, they may prefer the more sweet fruit and not accept the vegetables.

For those of you who want to raise your babies as vegetarians, it is very important that children get complete proteins. Balancing the amino acids is tricky but essential. Because there is such a need for protein for brain growth in the early years, you must work closely with your pediatrician or a dietician to make sure you know how to balance amino acids and otherwise give your child a balanced diet.

Keep in mind that a baby's tummy is very tiny, so it is important that every morsel of food be nutritious. Babies do not know about desserts, so they can be avoided. You must avoid filling her tummy with empty calories, which reduces her appetite for more nutritious food. Parents tell me that their children will not eat the foods they offer, and then I see them giving their children an endless supply of crackers between meals. The crackers are filling them up, so when it is mealtime, they are not hungry. My adage is to give as snacks anything you would give as a meal; do not give traditional snack foods. For example, give infants cooked carrots or pureed peaches for a snack.

Children can be given finger foods when they are able to use a pincer motion to pick up tiny things, usually around 8 months. It is ideal to have babies on all table food by 1 year. Yes, even if they do not have any teeth! As long as the foods are soft and small, infants with no back molars can gum their foods.

Babies love to feed themselves. Place a variety of soft, cooked vegetables on the tray, cut up about the size of the carrots in peas and carrots, or matchstick size, to make them easier to pick up (remember the rule of one new food every 4 to 7 days). Pierce peas and blueberries with a fork so they will flatten; they fit in the trachea (windpipe) and can cause choking. The trick is to offer your child variety and only a few pieces at a time. If too many pieces are placed on the tray at once, the children may fill their cheeks like little chipmunks and not be able to swallow so much.

Use only whole grains, which contain important trace nutrients and offer variety. Once you have worked up to several types of food, offer a variety at each meal. For example, offer a meat, a vegetable, and a fruit instead of only one type of food. Different foods have different trace vitamins and minerals essential for health. Focus on variety not quantity.

Keep in mind that as your baby becomes a toddler, she will eat less volume because her growth rate has slowed down. A toddler may eat much less than she did at 10 months. Parents worry about this. As an infant, she may have gained 2 pounds and 2 inches a month. As a toddler, her growth may be a quarter of that. As long as you offer a variety of foods with no pressure or cajoling, and do not fill your baby up with nonnutritious snacks, she will eat what she needs.

Avoid nitrites and nitrates that are found in hot dogs, bologna, other deli meats and bacon. They are known to cause cancer. Keep in mind the weight of the child. If an adult eats a hot dog, it is spread over 100+ pounds. When a child eats a nitrate containing food, it is more concentrated in his body, because he weighs much less. Hot dogs are not nutritious anyway, and they are a choking hazard.

If you give your child deli meats, check the package. A few kinds are nitrate and nitrite free. Spinach or carrots grown with chemical fertilizers may contain nitrates. Beets, too, may have too many. Organic fruits and vegetables grown without pesticides are healthier for little bodies.

Cathe Olson, author of *Simply Natural Baby Food*—an excellent book about feeding infants and toddlers—talks about letting children go after the food instead of having the food forced on the child. A common refrain of toddler parents is that he is not eating enough: "We have such a battle of wills over mealtime." Refer back to the tasks of toddlerhood and striving for independence. Do not allow eating to become a battleground. Just offer the food. If he refuses it, let him down from his chair. When he is hungry, he will eat. Offer pieces of meals as snacks, nothing else.

Sometimes toddlers are so busy exploring the world they do not want to take time to eat. This is short-lived. Offering small, frequent meals can be a helpful, temporary measure. Just be sure he isn't filling up on crackers!

In her book *Child of Mine: Feeding with Love and Good Sense,* dietician Ellyn Satter gives wonderful advice: parents are responsible for giving a variety of nutritious foods at regular intervals, and children are responsible for how much they eat. Allow children to eat as much and what they want off their plates. Young children's appetites can vary widely from day to day, depending on how they are growing and how active they are.

Try to eat as a family as much as possible. Insist on the child sitting in her high chair or at the table to eat; walking around eating can be a choking hazard. When purposeful throwing or "windshield wipes" occur, the meal is done. The typical serving size is 1 to 2 tablespoons of any given food, increasing to 2 to 4 tablespoons for 2-year-olds.

Only water should be given between meals and snacks. Limit juice to one serving a day and dilute it with water (half water, half juice). Do not allow her to walk around with juice in a cup or bottle because that bathes the teeth in sugar and may cause decay. Many pediatricians recommend no juices because children get more nutrients from the original foods (apples, grapes, etc.).

There are a few creative ways to hide vegetables if your child will not eat them or only likes one kind. Vegetables can be pureed and placed in tomato sauce, in pancakes to make special green or orange pancakes, or in smoothies. They can also be minced in the processor and added as "flecks" in rice or pasta. They can be added to meatloaf pureed or minced. Cathe Olson calls kale the "king of vegetables." She suggests mincing it in the food processor after it has been washed and dried thoroughly. Freeze it and break off a chunk to add easily to smoothies, sauces, or soups. Olson freezes peeled, quartered bananas and uses them in delicious smoothie recipes.

In addition to the books already mentioned are two wonderful books with creative ideas for hiding nutritious foods:

▶ *Deceptively Delicious: Simple Secrets to Get Your Kids Eating Good Food,* by Jessica Seinfeld (Collins Living, 2007). For example, she purees vegetables that are the same color as the favorite food and adds them, such as adding pureed carrots under the cheese in a grilled cheese sandwich!

▶ *Sneaky Chef: Simple Strategies for Hiding Healthy Foods in Kids Favorite Meals,* by Missy Chase Lapine (Running Press, 2007). She hides nutrition in favorite foods such as "Maxed Out Meatloaf," "Bonus Burgers," and "Grilled Cheese Muffins."

Healthy Finger Foods

Please refer to the previous section on suggested ages to begin foods containing milk, wheat, or eggs.

Cooked vegetables, soft and diced
  Peas, pierced with a fork
  Carrots
  String beans
  Sweet potatoes
  Potatoes
  Broccoli "trees"

Fresh fruit, soft and diced
  No citrus until after one year old
  Peaches
  Plums
  Grapes, quartered
  Blueberries, pierced
  Apple or pear, grated
  Bananas, sliced

Soft natural cheeses, diced, cut in thin strips, or grated
  Muenster
  Mozzarella
  Monterey Jack
  Mild Cheddar
  Avoid American cheese due to high salt and processing

Whole grain or vegetable pasta cooked
  Cut up, served warm or cold
  Spirals, elbows, butterflies
  Ravioli or tortellini with meat, cheese, or vegetable filling

Eggs (no more than three per week)
  Scrambled eggs
  Diced French toast
  Diced pancakes—veggies can be pureed and hidden in pancakes

Soft ground meat or shredded meat
  Spread pureed meat on whole grain bread to make finger sandwiches

Cubes of tofu

Tahini (sesame seed paste spread on whole grain bread or put in soups instead of cream)

Pieces of whole grain cereal
  Unsugared (read the box)
  Cheerios

Children's Books about Healthy Foods

The library has books that teach children which foods are healthy and help them grow big and strong. What a great teaching tool! It is not only you telling them what is good for them. They are not the only ones that are asked to eat healthy foods. Books provide a wonderful way to discuss which foods are healthy. Sometimes nutrition books are too difficult to read to small children, so embellish and add your own words. Talk about healthy foods as "growing foods." Some examples of books to read to children on nutrition are:

Eat Healthy, Feel Great by Dr. William Sears, Martha Sears, R.N. and Christie Watts Kelly. Little, Brown Young Readers, 2002.

The Colors We Eat Series: Blue and Purple Foods, Black Foods, Pink Foods by Isabel Thomas. Heinemann Educational Books, 2004.

Eating the Alphabet: Fruits and Vegetables from A to Z by Lois Ehlert. Voyager Books, 1993.

The Vegetables We Eat by Gail Gibbons. Holiday House Publishers, 2008.

The Green Eggs and Ham Cookbook by Georgeanne Brennan and Dr. Seuss. Random House Books for Young Readers, 2006.

Fruit (On Your Plate), Vegetables (On Your Plate) by Honor Head. Franklin Watts Ltd, 2007.

Meat and Fish (What's for Lunch) and *Dairy and Eggs (What's for Lunch)*, by Honor Head. QED Publishing, 2007.

5
Encouraging Language Development

Beginning Language

Children are communicating with you from the day of birth. They feel the love in the ways that you care for them, smile at them, and cuddle them. Nonverbal "language," or body language, is the language learned first. They learn to "read" your face, watching your expressions. The gentleness of your voice, your touch, the warmth of your smiles will be understood by your baby as love.

When she makes noises in the morning and you come, she is using vocalizations to call you. She learns many other ways to communicate nonverbally. She may point for something she wants or raise her arms to be picked up. Learning baby sign language is an enjoyable way to expand your ability to communicate with each other.

Children begin to understand the spoken language at around 8 months. This beginning understanding is called *receptive language*. A parent begins noticing that the child responds to actual words in small ways; for example, she lifts her foot when you say, "Let's put on your shoes." Or she may demonstrate "bye-bye" by waving her hand or "so big" by raising her arms over her head. This is evidence that receptive language is developing.

It is amazing how many words are in your child's receptive vocabulary by age 1. Parents often do not realize how much a child understands before he or she ever speaks a word.

Talk to Your Baby

Talking to your baby as you go about your daily activities is an excellent way to encourage receptive language. Studies show that the size of the child's vocabulary is directly related to how much the parents talk to their child. You are encouraged to talk, talk, talk throughout the day—from day one. Children begin absorbing the cadences and sounds of language.

Label items that you encounter in your activities with your child: *nose, truck, dog,* or *camera*. That is the way a child learns the names of objects in the environment. As I would toss toys into the bathtub, I would say "boat," "duck," or "cup." One day, I forgot to name the duck, and my son uttered his first word—"DUCK"—clearly and loudly. He would not have known the name if I had not labeled it over and over. Narrating the day is a wonderful way of helping you think of things to talk about. You can talk about feelings, the things you are doing, the things you see, and the things you hear. For example, talking about feelings, you could say, "I see you are so sad," or "I feel happy when you cuddle with me." Talk with your baby about everyday activities you both do, such as "You are touching the yellow ball," or "I am making a salad with lettuce, tomatoes, and cucumbers." Talk about the things you see: "The little bird is sitting on the branch," or "The ball is rolling to you." Talk about things that you hear, such as "The rocking chair is squeaking as we rock back and forth," or "The big truck is making a loud noise."

Reinforce Your Child's Language Attempts

The second most important way to encourage language development is to respond to the attempts at language made by your baby. Your baby will make sounds, and it is important to listen to the sounds and try to repeat the sounds back to your baby. Copying his actual sounds is immediate reinforcement for his efforts. He says "ah" and you repeat "ah" and pause.

At 6 weeks old, my youngest son had a "conversation" with my uncle. My uncle repeated my son's sounds back to him and then paused for him to respond again. The immediate positive reinforcement kept the conversation going for an amazing 45 minutes!

Listening, repeating the sounds, then pausing for a response is the way to teach the child that language is reciprocal, that conversations have a rhythm of give and take. Too many parents talk to a baby but do not give the expectant pause to encourage the baby to make another sound and teach him the rhythm of a conversation. I read that a deaf couple had a hearing baby. She babbled as expected, but the parents could not hear the sounds nor repeat the sounds back. By 4 months, the baby was silent with no babbling sounds. Reinforcing your baby's babbling sounds is so important for language development.

Studies show that only "live" language encourages language development. In other words, language is learned in relation to ongoing events and interactions. Watching people talk on TV or hearing language on the radio will not teach language; it is learned *within a relationship.*

Language specialists encourage some characteristics of "Parentese," or baby talk, such as higher pitch, short utterances and repeating words your child uses, assuring her that she is understood. Parentese is using simple language, putting expression in your voice and on your face, and speaking slowly in a singsong voice.

It is important to use pronouns and to enunciate when speaking to a child. Use "I" and "you." Instead of "Does Tommy want a cookie?" say, "Do *you* want a cookie?" Instead of saying "Mommy is fixing your lunch," say "*I* am fixing your lunch." The child will learn to use pronouns when you use them.

Expanding on Her Words

Expanding on her words is a simple, effective strategy to encourage language development. For example, if she says "ball," the parent can say, "Ball. The ball is round." Or if she says "duck," you can expand her words and say, "Yes, duck. The duck is yellow and fluffy." This builds her vocabulary and understanding.

Children need to understand what they hear. There are many activities to encourage and practice the understanding of sounds. You can call your child's attention to sounds and then show or explain what made the sounds, such as airplanes flying overhead, a dog barking, a truck horn beeping, or a bird singing.

Giving Directions

Giving children directions, such as "Bring me the shovel," is another way of encouraging language. Practice in following directions can also be given by having her point out her body parts: "Where are your toes? Where are your eyes? Nose? Mouth?" Use other things that are familiar to her, and praise her for her efforts. Songs with actions are wonderful tools to encourage language understanding, such as "Pat-a-Cake" or "Itsy-Bitsy Spider."

Reading Encourages Language

Reading to a child is another excellent way to encourage language development. He will learn new words with each book and will also benefit from the repetition of words in familiar books.

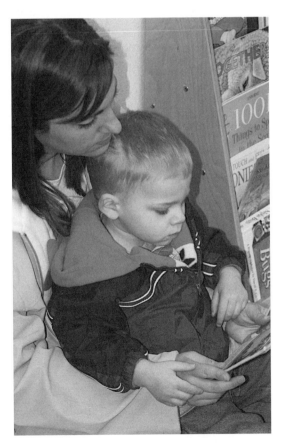

Two Languages

Language specialists encourage children to learn two languages simultaneously. Languages learned in the first 3 years are learned in the language center of the brain, whereas languages learned later are learned in the cognitive centers of the brain.

It is much more difficult to learn a language later in life. Many of us marvel at Europeans who can speak five languages fluently. Probably two languages were spoken to them from birth. When a child learns two languages, he can more easily learn other languages later. Several families in my classes are speaking two languages to their children. One very effective way I have seen to teach two languages at once is for one parent to speak one language to the child and the other parent to speak the other language. Most children, barring any learning disabilities, can sort out the languages by age 3. Before that, the two languages may be intermingled in sentences. One mother of a 3-year-old spoke only Spanish to him and the father spoke only English. The child would translate for his mother into Spanish when the father spoke to them in English! What a gift to give your child. Of course, the person speaking must be fluent in the second language.

Stuttering

Sometimes children's thoughts are coming faster than they are able to speak them, and they begin to stutter. This can be normal nonfluency. Times of stress, excitement, illness, or rapid language development can increase the tendency to get stuck on the beginning sounds of words and cause stuttering.

Speech pathologists recommend that you do not bring attention to such difficulty by saying things such as "Slow down," "Speak more slowly," "Take your time," or "Say that over again." These comments draw attention to the stuttering and make him realize that something is different about the way he speaks, and he may react in ways that lead to serious language problems. Point this out to everyone in his life. Find ways to make talking a pleasant experience for him, and give him the time to express himself without supplying words. Stuttering usually passes in a month or two if handled in this matter-of-fact way.

Variable Timing of Language Development

Keep in mind that language development is highly variable. Some children say their first words at about age 1, while others wait until they are nearing their second birthdays.

For language to develop properly, it is important to make sure your child is hearing well. With repeated ear infections, sometimes children fail to hear sounds clearly and do not pronounce words well. It has been said that children with chronic fluid in their middle ears hear words muffled, as if they were spoken under water. Seek a hearing evaluation if your child does not turn toward you when you call his name or does not startle at a loud noise. With widespread newborn hearing screenings, doctors are finding hearing problems early, and with treatment, are minimizing effects on language development.

Indications for a Referral

When a child can follow simple commands such as "Come here," or "Open your mouth," or when he can point to objects when asked, you know language is developing. Referral for a speech and language evaluation is indicated if any of the following difficulties are noted:

► Between 1 and 2 years, he is unable to point to pictures that you name in a book or understand simple questions such as "Where are your shoes?"

► She is unable to follow two requests between 2 and 3 years old, such as "Please pick up the book and put it on the table."

► The child is not talking at all by the age of 2. Some speech specialists will evaluate a child if he is not speaking 50 words by age 2.

► She is not using two- to three-word sentences by the age of 3 such as "Pick me up" or "I want juice."

► His speech is unintelligible after 3 years of age to people outside the family.

► She is unable to answer simple who, what, and where questions between 3 and 4 years of age.

► Word endings are missing after the age of 5.

► Incorrect sentence structure is used after the age of 5 such as, "Jean runs wants to."

► Her voice is monotone, too loud, or too soft.

► He speaks nasally, as if he has a cold.

Several children in my classes have been referred for a speech and language evaluation and have benefited immeasurably by early intervention programs, available through the local county Office of Education or the county Health Department. Before a child is 3, a speech pathologist visits the home for treatment and also teaches the family things they can do to encourage language development. At 3, children are usually enrolled in group therapy classes one or more times per week; I have witnessed remarkable results with speech therapy.

6
Encouraging Your Child to Learn How to Share

Parents are eager to learn ways to teach a child to share. As you play with your child, she is learning the "give and take" of relationships. This rhythm of interaction is called the *social dance*. You smile, your baby smiles back. He says "Maaaa," you wait for him to finish, and you repeat it back to him. You roll the ball, and he pushes it back to you. You have a make-believe tea party and pour tea and pretend to eat cookies together. You talk about what each of you did that day to further teach the give and take of conversation. Playing simple board games teaches taking turns. In all your interactions you are teaching the social dance, and your child will begin to learn that others have needs and desires too.

Teaching Empathy

In lovingly responding to your child's needs, your child is learning empathy. Empathy is showing that you care how other people feel. As your child develops empathy, you will notice her patting you on the hand if you are sad. She may bring another child a toy or her own special lovey to comfort him. She may show empathy by talking quietly to her teddy in comforting sounds.

You teach your child to be empathetic and caring by being empathetic and caring toward her. Acknowledging her feelings will teach her to do the same for others. Teach your child how to recognize feelings in others and to care about what others feel. Notice the look on another child's face and comment on it: "Tommy looks sad. Let's see if there is anything we can do to help him."

Distraction for Toddlers

The scene of two children pulling on the same toy is common. When an infant or toddler under 18 months grabs a toy away from another child of that same age, it often helps to wait a moment to see the reaction of the other child. If the other child seems unconcerned and moves on to something else, no intervention is necessary. If the child wants the toy and shows distress by a frown or by crying, the parent can return the toy and distract the one who grabbed it with another toy. An older sibling can be taught to hand his younger sibling another toy before taking the one he wants from him.

Two Schools of Thought about Encouraging Sharing

After 18 months, when distraction is no longer effective, you may approach sharing in one of two ways: One school of thought is that sharing should never be forced, and the other school of thought is to use time limits to help children take turns.

The Not Forcing Sharing Philosophy

The first philosophy believes that sharing is giving of oneself from inside and should never be forced. Toddlers have difficulty with this because they view themselves as the center of the world and have not learned delay of gratification. They want what they want now, and they have trouble thinking about another's feelings or point of view. If and when children are made to share, they become angry, not loving.

In this view of encouraging sharing, a child should be able to play with a toy until he is ready to give it up on his own. The parent can return the grabbed toy and acknowledge the feelings of the child who wants the toy. She could say, "I know it is hard to want something that someone else has. When she is done playing with it, you will have a turn." Make a suggestion for another activity.

One solution for a play date is to have your child choose the toys she is unwilling to share and put them away. One parent told me that there is no fighting over toys at her daughter's preschool, because they have the rule that a person needs to finish with something before another child can play with it. Each child learns that her own things will not be taken from her and that she cannot take something from someone else. The atmosphere is respectful.

There are several ways to encourage sharing rather than forcing sharing. Praise

the child when she shares spontaneously, and point out how good the other child feels by describing the other child's facial expressions and feelings. For example, the parent could say, "I see how you are sharing the farm animals with Susie. You are playing so nicely together. See how she is smiling? She is happy that you let her play with you." The child who shares also feels good. It is this pleasure that encourages more sharing.

Comments such as "Timmy will let you know when he is ready to share" gives the child who has the toy time to think and process. It gives him a few minutes to think through allowing the other child to join his play or have the object he is playing with. When sharing is forced, he clings more tightly to the object, and he feels his rights have not been respected.

Another way to encourage sharing is to emphasize the value of sharing as you go about your daily activities. You have one oatmeal cookie and one chocolate chip cookie. Both children want the chocolate chip cookie. What an opportunity for learning the benefits of sharing! "If we break each cookie in half, you can share the chocolate chip cookie. You will each have half an oatmeal cookie and half a chocolate chip cookie." Talk about how you can share your lap or a hug. Use the word "share" often, so the child begins to understand its meaning by your examples.

Take opportunities to thank your child whenever she shares on her own. Show her how much you appreciate that she shared something with you or with someone else. "I appreciate that you shared your cookie with me." Take every chance to praise her for her efforts.

Your child will begin to learn to share best by your own example. From infancy talk about sharing. Model sharing. Your children will copy you. Say things like, "Would you like to share my cookie?" or "Come sit on my lap and we will share this new book together." When you have more than one child—a playmate or a sibling—set up situations to encourage sharing. For example, you could buy one container of play dough and help the children figure out a way to share it. Modeling sharing and practicing sharing is the best way to help your child learn how to share.

The Time Limit Sharing Philosophy

The second philosophy about sharing is to return the grabbed toy to the child who had it first and ask the grabber to make another choice after acknowledging his feelings. A time limit is set for the one with the toy, and then the other child gets his turn. This is a way of teaching taking turns. For example, a parent can say, "I see how much you want that toy. In 2 minutes it will be your turn."

It is important to follow through with offering the object to the child when the time limit is up, even if he found something else to play with. This way he knows that you mean what you say, and that he truly will get a turn. Knowing this will help him accept the time limit without becoming upset.

Using a timer to mark the time limit can be very helpful. It acts as an impartial "third party." Some preschools use an egg timer with sand sifting down to mark 3 minutes. If a child wants the toy that someone is playing with, he places the egg timer near the other child and waits for it to sift through. This is a visual way to mark the waiting time. A side benefit is that it gives the child waiting something to do as he watches the sand sift down.

When the timer signals that the time is up, wait a minute to see if the two children manage the switching. If not, take the child with the toy to find the other child when the timer goes off. Between 2 and 2 and a half, the children will need help with the timer. By 3 the children can learn to set the timer. Of course, you can use your watch when a timer is not handy.

A helpful strategy is to support the waiting child by saying something like "I'll hold your hand while you are waiting." To help the child wait, you could also say "Come sit on my lap and we'll look at a book until it is your turn," or "By the time we finish singing *Old McDonald*, it will be your turn." The waiting, when he wants it *now*, is the hard part. He may not be developmentally ready to be able to share without outside help and support.

Sometimes it might be prudent to remove the toy that the children are fighting over. The trouble with this approach is that the person having the toy first is unjustly deprived of the toy. If they both approach the toy at the same time, and a literal tug of war ensues, you may want to remove the toy

and tell them they will get another chance to play with it later. However, removing the toy also takes away the opportunity to learn how to share.

You can empower your child by teaching her words to use if another child tries to take the toy she is playing with. Teach her to say something like, "Don't take my toy," or "I am playing with this right now." To the other child you could say, "I see how much you want that toy. Please ask, 'May I play with that toy?'"

It is important for the adult to move close to prevent hurtful actions. If one child is about to be hurtful, you can move your body between the children to prevent the hurtful action or stop the child's hand from hurting. Children learn from getting angry and then being able to work things out. Help them find words for their feelings and choices for their actions.

My suggestion would be to use the first philosophy in most interactions, except for certain instances in which the time-limit strategy works best. For example, when outside time begins and the preschoolers rush the bike area and try to grab the available six bikes, it would be best to set up a time limit strategy so everyone gets a turn. Or at the park with only two swings and four children waiting, a time limit would be the fair thing to do.

Supporting the waiting children is most important in both strategies. They will learn that you respect their wishes and will be more able to learn ways to cope with not getting what they want immediately.

A book that may encourage your child to learn to share is *Share and Take Turns* (Learning to Get Along Series), by Cheri J. Meiners (Free Spirit Publishing, 2003).

As your child approaches the age of 4, there will be fewer conflicts over sharing because she will understand. She has developed greater self-control and has found effective words to use.

7
How Your Child's Temperament Shapes Behavior

It is no surprise to parents that children, even in the same family, can be very different. Children show a distinct individuality of temperament in the first few weeks of life. Your child's temperament has an active influence from birth onward in parent–child interactions. Some newborns quietly observe their environments, others are very intense as they try to learn to organize their environments, others seem to adapt easily to their new environments.

A child is born with a specfic temperament. Recently, researchers have suggested that the origins of temperament are largely genetic. Yet, clearly, environmental circumstances can diminish, heighten, or modify the associated behaviors. Specific nurturing strategies for each temperament type can have a lasting impact on how your child's temperament affects his behavior and life.

Temperament can be described as *the behavioral style* of a child. Three main types of temperament are outlined in the hallmark study by Stella Chess and Alexander Thomas:

1. Flexible, easy

2. Fearful, slow-to-warm-up

3. Feisty, difficult, strong-willed

Chess and Thomas outlined nine temperamental traits associated with each temperament type:

1. **Activity level**—low to high

2. **Biological rhythms**—regularity and predictability of sleep and toileting

3. **Approach or withdrawal to new situations**

4. **Adaptability to a new or changed situation**—how quickly the child adapts to a change in routine

5. **Quality of mood**—happy or sad, positive or negative

6. **Intensity of reaction to various situations**—what is the energy level of a response?

7. **Sensitivity or threshold of responsiveness**—to things like bright lights, noises, or touch

8. **Distractibility and attention span**

9. **Persistence**—how stubborn is the child?

To determine what traits your child has, keep track of his reactions to daily routines. Ask yourself questions such as:

▶ Does he go to sleep at about the same time at night and for naps (within one-half hour)?

▶ Is there a regular pattern of eating and sleeping?

▶ What is his initial reaction to new situations—does he accept them or not? Does he accept new foods by swallowing without fussing, or does he cry and refuse new foods?

▶ How easily does he calm himself?

▶ How sensitive is he to movement and touch?

▶ What is the intensity of his reaction to things such as falls?

Three Clusters of Behaviors

1. *The Flexible or Easy Child*

Chess and Thomas in the New York Longitudinal Study of Child Development found that temperamental traits or characteristics fall into three clusters of behavior. They found that 40 percent of the children in the study were flexible or easy with regular feeding and nap routines and a generally happy, positive mood. Such a child has low intensity reactions and low sensitivity to bright lights, noise, or touch. She is quick to adapt and positive in a new situation.

Nurturing strategies for the "Easy" child are to be aware that she is the most susceptible to having her needs overlooked. She needs special attention, because she shows her needs in quiet ways. When noise or bright lights overwhelm her, she may quietly fall asleep to block them out. She will appreciate your attention and will be resilient in new situations.

As all children do, the easy, flexible child needs interaction for emotional and physical development. It is easy to leave the happy and content child on her own, because she fusses little and does not often ask for attention. Initiate interactions with her. Talk to your quiet baby, comment on things she is playing with, and give her things to look at and play with. Dr. Brazelton and Dr. Greenspan, authors of *The Irreducible Needs of Children,*◆ recommend that you facilitate her interaction with her environment for about one third of her waking hours. This includes helping her "look, touch, examine, vocalize and eventually verbalize about her experiences." Another third of her waking hours can be in independent play with you in sight. The last third of her waking hours should be spent in direct interaction with you or another caregiver. Brazelton and Greenspan suggest a minimum of four 20-minute or longer periods of continuous communication with you: "holding, cuddling, comforting back rubs, hugging and kissing, caressing, imaginative play and direct conversations." They discuss a "seamless flow" between all three types of interaction throughout the day.

2. The Fearful or Slow-to-Warm-Up Child

Fifteen percent of the children in the study were fearful or slow-to-warm-up. This child is described as being shy or timid and needing time to warm up to a new situation. He is slow to adapt, withdraws from new interactions, has a low activity level, and a low intensity of reaction to situations. He has a relatively negative mood but is less intense than the feisty or strong-willed child. The fearful child checks things out from a safe distance or from his parent's side.

Such a child observes from a safe distance until he feels comfortable to join in. This may happen each time he enters a situation, even a situation he has been in before; for example, a child may stand by his mother's side each time they go to his weekly playgroup. It may take 20 to 30 minutes of watching from his mother's side before he feels comfortable enough to join in.

Helpful nurturing strategies include avoiding a confronting style by allowing him to stay close until he is comfortable. He will enjoy activities if allowed time to adjust. If pushed into joining the group too soon, he will cling more tightly.

Slow-to-warm-up children need to be offered practice to try new situations. The tendency is to avoid new situations with this type of child, because it can be difficult for both of you. As a parent of such a child, you may sometimes feel that other parents are looking at you, seemingly saying, "What is wrong with her? Why doesn't she go play with the other children?" Your child senses this criticism also. She feels like she is not doing something right. If people say, "She is just shy," it feels like something negative.

Continue to offer new situations to this child, such as library story hours, play dates at the park, and so on, and allow her to stay close for a few minutes. Support her in being comfortable in a new situation. Role-playing before a new situation can be very helpful. With guidance, she can learn to adapt. Her emotions will change, from caution to enjoyment.

The best strategy is *going with, being with, staying with, and then stepping back.* Perhaps you could say, "Look what Rachel is playing. Maybe you'd like to join her." Let others approach your child. The key is not to reinforce the fear by holding them close and giving the feeling that it is not safe to join in.

Sometimes parents inadvertently give the message, "You can't be safe unless you stay by my side." These children never venture far from Mom and do not join in at all. The healthy slow-to-warm-up child will stand by your side for a few minutes then join in with interest and enthusiasm.

It is helpful to structure situations so the child can master them. Finding things in the same places in her environment can be helpful. Having a similar structure to each day can also be helpful.

She will need special handling in many situations, including beginning a new child care situation or having a new babysitter. Enable her to have time to gain trust in the new person by accompanying her for a few days for a few hours each day. Gradually wean yourself out of the situation.

One possible "phase-in" strategy would be for both of you stay for 2 hours and then both of you leave. The next day, you could stay with your child for an hour and leave her for an hour. The third day, you could stay for an hour and leave her for 2 hours.

Your presence places a "stamp of safety" on the new caregiver. "Mommy seems to like this person; if she feels safe with this person, then I can too." The side benefit of "phasing-in" is that you, as the parent, can also gain trust in this new person caring for your child.

3. *The Feisty or Spirited Child*

Children of the third cluster of behaviors made up 10 percent of the study and are called feisty, difficult, high need, or strong-willed. I actually prefer calling them the more positive "spirited." This group has intense reactions; high intensity of expres-

sion; high sensitivity to noise, lights, and touch; and irregular rhythms. They withdraw from new things, are slow to adapt, cry more than they laugh, and are forceful. They may initially object strongly to almost everything and later show exuberant joy. They are active, intense, distractible, irregular, and moody. Their irregular rhythms are manifested by one day sleeping or eating a lot and the next day sleeping or eating very little.

These children are the most challenging for parents, yet they can be the most joyous also. They seem to have a zest for life that is exuded in their enthusiasm for the small things they notice that many of us miss. They can be joyful about noticing a little bug or a newly blooming flower. They have wonderful imaginations and are the most creative people. They become the actors, singers, dancers, artists, inventors, and entrepreneurs.

Nurturing strategies can have a great impact on how the spirited child learns to become socialized and able to live among us peacefully. Mishandling of the spirited child can lead to problems in group interactions and to people labeling him "hyperactive" and "disruptive."

The spirited child needs steady, consistent, and patient care. The positive aspects of his temperament need to be emphasized. Encourage his creativity and imagination. He needs to know the boundaries for his behavior, and they need to be consistently applied (see Chapter 9: Discipline Styles). Within these boundaries, the child needs to have freedom to be himself. Be very sure and specific about what is important to you, and let the other things go. Do not demand too much immediately; he needs to be helped to enjoy activities.

With his irregular rhythms, it is helpful if you are flexible and if *you* adapt. Understand that some days he will not sleep very much. Understand that on the days he eats very little, you will not make an issue of food. Using empathy and redirection can help a spirited child move on to another activity.

Routines can be invaluable. If a child knows that a nap comes after lunch day after day, he will be more able to accept it. Prepare a picture book about the daily schedule: place photographs in the book in the sequence that activities will occur. Review this with him each morning so that he is reassured. If the schedule is changed for that day, rearrange the photos and review them with him. Prepare him for any change by talking to him ahead of time.

Spirited children need special care with transitions. Give 5-minute warnings before activities change. "In 5 minutes it will be time to get in the car seat to go pick up your sister." A timer can be used to tell him the time is up, so there won't be a battle.

Use empathy with each change. "I see how much you want to keep playing with your cars. It is hard when you have to stop and come eat lunch." "I see you are so angry that we have to go inside now to fix dinner."

Limit the number of new adjustments at any one time. Spirited children need daily opportunities for active, vigorous play. One mother told me that if she did not take her three boys to the park every day to run and

play, their evening was ruined. She would even put raincoats and boots on them for rainy days. Sometimes spirited children have strong reactions to group care. There will be a worse reaction if the situation is overcrowded, noisy, and brightly lit. A smaller setting with a calm, peaceful caregiver may be successful. A phase-in, as described with the slow-to-warm-up child, is often helpful.

Your perceptions and reactions can make a tremendous difference in how the child views herself and how others see her. Remember how imaginative, exuberant, and delightful she can be. Try not to feel that the child is being deliberately negative. Do not take it personally when she exhibits spirited behavior. You did not cause her to have this temperament.

Try to give lots of gradual repeated exposures to things. Expect loud protests, but do

not give in to initial protests. Keep yourself calm so she can better keep herself calm. When you escalate out of control by yelling, she will escalate out of control. Verbalize confidence in her that she can soon regain control.

Help others revise their views of your child. If someone says, "She is hyperactive, she never stops moving," say calmly, "Yes, she has enthusiasm for life! I wish I could bottle her energy and use it for myself." I recommend three books to read more about the spirited child: *Raising Your Spirited Child,* by Mary Sheedy Kurcinka, *The Challenging Child,* by Stanley I. Greenspan, M.D., and *The Difficult Child,* by Stanley Turecki and Leslie Tonner.

Two-year-olds often have many of the characteristics of the spirited child. He is truly a spirited child if he has been like this from birth, not just when he nears 2 years of age. See Chapter 3: Living with Your Toddler—Tips for Daily Life for strategies for the 2-year-old.

The remaining 35 percent of children in the study exhibited a mixture of traits. Nurturing strategies can be pulled from each cluster of behaviors, and each child must be seen as an individual with his or her own unique ways of responding.

8
Creating a "YES" Environment

Saying "Yes"

Parents frequently find themselves saying "no" to crawling infants and toddlers as they explore their worlds and get into things. One study followed toddlers for the day and found, on average, that they were told "no" 336 times and "yes" only 32.

What does this mean to the child? For one thing, it places the child in a negative atmosphere. Your child thinks most things he wants to touch and feel to learn about are not acceptable to Mommy. She gets a frown on her face or raises her voice and says "no." Children at this age have what is called *touch hunger*. They want to touch and feel everything to learn about their world. Dr. Burton White, psychologist and author of *The First Three Years of Life,* finds that restricting children's ability to explore their environments can squelch curiosity. He feels that their touch hunger should have free rein as much as possible.

The most frequent message to the child needs to be, "Yes, you can touch that to learn about your world." With a frequent "no," the child begins to reach toward something and "checks back" with Mom by looking at her with a questioning look: "Can I touch this?" This may seem desirable to some parents, but Dr. White feels that this is a sign that

the child's curiosity is already being diminished with the frequent admonitions. He completed a longitudinal study on parenting styles that encouraged the maintaining of curiosity. He observed parenting styles and then followed the children into the first few school years and found that certain parenting styles encouraged children to maintain their curiosity and to be good learners. Setting up the "yes" environment is the best way to encourage curiosity.

Childproofing for Safety and Curiosity

Childproofing your home for safety and for curiosity means removing the "no" as much as possible. In the "yes" environment, you are able to let the child explore freely. "Yes, you can touch that" is the affirming message. This means removing or placing out of reach the things that you do not want your child to touch. I call this "environmental control." Moving or physically blocking something that you do not want them to touch removes the issue. One parent came to me for advice about her toddler playing with the stereo knobs. It had become a daily issue. She would move him or try to distract him, and he would head in a beeline straight to the stereo knobs again. Saying "no" and then moving him exhausted her. It had become a battle of wills between them. I advised that she had two choices: to continue shadowing him and saying "no" or to "environmentally control" the stereo by moving it or blocking access to the knobs. She returned to tell me that she placed the stereo on a high shelf and it had become a nonissue. Both mother and child could be comfortable in the room.

Many safety gadgets are available to help parents set up the "yes" environment. Gates can be very helpful. Devices to block the TV controls or the DVD player opening are available. Other examples are included in the chapter on safety, along with Web sites for ordering safety devices.

Some who give advice, such as grandmothers, say "But he has to know what no means!" He will learn it, because some "no's" cannot be removed, such as no running in the street, no touching the hot stove, no riding in the car without being in your car seat, no ice cream instead of meals—and the list goes on.

Coffee table objects are often in dispute. Grandma says he has to learn not to touch her favorite knick-knacks that are perfectly positioned for touching and feeling. So what happens? Mom has to consistently say, "No, don't touch" and shadow him to make sure he does not harm those or other knick-knacks. Mom cannot sit and chat, she has to be up and on guard, following the child. Why bother visiting? If she leaves the child with Grandma in an unchildproofed house, how will the child feel with repeated reprimands?

I liken this negative situation to the Charles Schultz character of Pig Pen with the black cloud following him around. The child who lives with frequent "no's" and "don't touch thats" is enveloped in a negative cloud. He does not enjoy his day. Not only is his curiosity dampened, his self-esteem suffers. He feels like he cannot do anything right. At my mother-in-law's house, I would move the myriad of valuable knick-knacks and place them on the mantel when we arrived. I would try my best to memorize the positioning and return them to their places as we left.

One mother shared that she was living with her in-laws when her husband was on disability, and her mother-in-law refused to childproof. Her two little girls were constantly reprimanded for touching things that could have easily been environmentally controlled. The mother said she would stay in their bedroom most of the time when she was home to prevent them from being in such a negative environment.

The ideal situation for an exploring child is to have as much of the house to safely explore as possible. For example, if you have a family room and a living room, a gate can keep the living room out of bounds and the rest of the rooms can be childproofed. If you have a smaller home, try to childproof as many rooms as possible. Placing children in playpens also restricts their exploring ability, so they are not recommended.

A side benefit of childproofing for curiosity is that it lessens the need to shadow your child, so the parent does not have to follow physically close behind the child to continuously reprimand. Children explore less with a parent hovering over them. Of course the parent needs to make sure the child is safe by being watchful. A child-proofed kitchen still has counters, and children have been known to crawl up on them and then onto the top of the refrigerator. Some dangers cannot be removed, but thorough childproofing can eliminate many dangers—and saying "no."

When Your Child Ignores Your "No"

Many parents have noted that their children stop responding to "no" when they hear it too much. It soon becomes ineffective with overuse. Children may even smile and touch the forbidden item anyway, waiting for a reaction. Each time you say "no" and your child does not respond, an action is required. If you do not stop him, "no" will mean nothing. In a "yes" environment, there are much fewer reasons for parents to reprimand. Therefore, a "yes" environment is easier on parents, too.

Depending on your child, you can begin to reintroduce objects into the environment around 2-and-a-half to 3 years of age. Childproofing is not forever. At about 3, your child begins to have the cognitive ability to have better judgment, and he

is not interested in touching and feeling *everything*. If he shows an interest in some breakable knick-knack, you can go over to it with him, pick it up yourself and admire it together. You can explain that only grown-ups can pick it up. Most 3-year-olds can understand this; he has more self-control and has the beginning of self-discipline.

Keep in mind that if "no" is used only for hurtful or dangerous situations, "no" will be meaningful to the child.

9
Discipline Styles

It is my hope that this chapter will offer loving solutions that enhance your relationship with your child. The word *discipline* means *to teach,* not to threaten, punish, or humiliate. You need to teach your child to engage in acceptable behavior, to be considerate of other's feelings, to be responsible for himself, and to express his feelings.

Setting Limits

Setting limits on behavior is very important. Dr. T. Berry Brazelton, in his book *Touchpoints: Your Child's Emotional and Behavioral Development,*♦ states that setting limits is the second most important thing for parents to do next to loving their child.

Many parents are reluctant to set limits, especially when they have little precious time with their child. Limits are *firm expectations of behavior.* Having firm boundaries for your child gives her security. In other words, a child without limits is an anxious child. She will frequently use testing behaviors to find where the limits are.

A child needs boundaries from the outside before she can develop self-discipline. A young child has a feeling and acts on it immediately; she does not have the self-control to stop herself. Dr. Brazelton explains that a limit is saying to the child,

"I have to stop you until you can stop yourself." No matter what topic you are discussing that needs some limits set, the phrase "I will stop you until you can stop yourself" can have amazing effects. It gives the child a clear message that the behavior is not acceptable and that her parent will set a firm limit and stop her. Yet there is hope in this statement: "One day soon, you will be able to stop yourself. I have confidence that you will learn this." Using the statement "I have confidence that you can learn this" is a valuable phrase to use to empower your child.

Setting reasonable, age-appropriate limits can be envisioned as a circle, or boundary, drawn around your child at some distance. Within this boundary are all the acceptable behaviors your child can decide to have. Outside the boundary are behaviors that the parent must limit or not allow.

Another way to view limits is that in the circle or boundary are the family rules. When a behavior occurs that is outside the boundary, a consequence needs to occur. For example, if the child is a climber and climbs to the top of the kitchen table, the parent must set a limit by removing him from the table with a clear message, "Tables are not for climbing. I have to stop you until you can stop yourself." Offer an alternative where the child could climb safely, perhaps the stairs with you nearby to help, or perhaps on some equipment at the park.

If the kitchen table climbing continues after repeated removals, perhaps the child's consequence would be to not be able to be in the kitchen for a prescribed period of time (consider using a gate). At the end of that time, a half hour for example, she would be given another chance to show that she understands the family rule. I tease and say that it sometimes takes 106 repetitions before it becomes self-discipline. In other words, you have to teach acceptable behavior over and over until the child internalizes it and is able to stop herself.

Parents often ask, "Can a 16-month-old or a 2-year-old understand what I am teaching?" Yes. Children begin to learn receptive language at around 8 months old, and they understand a lot of what you say to them. A toddler understands most of your words. Also, many times setting limits includes moving the child or physically stopping him from doing something, so he understands.

Another question I often pose when concerns are brought to me is "Who is in charge?" Many parents need guidance on how to set limits on behaviors. Children feel more secure and less anxious when parents set limits and are consistent with them. Then children know what rules to integrate into their self-discipline. When rules change or are nonexistent, children do not learn the boundaries for their behaviors.

One mother shared that the only way she could get her child to fall asleep was to walk around the dining room table with the child in the stroller for 30 minutes. This type of behavior is called *undue service,* which means going beyond what is reasonable. The child was in charge. We problem solved to think of other ways to help her child fall asleep without such measures (see Chapter 10: Sleep Strategies for the Weary Parent). She was thankful to know that her child would feel more secure with limits.

Another example of undue service came from a father who told me that he could not get anything done because his 18-month-old wanted to be held all the time. Not only did he want his father to hold him, but he would fuss if the father would sit down to do it. To keep him from fussing, the father had to hold the child standing up! The father said that he was exhausted and felt helpless: The child was in charge. The child was also anxious. He did not really feel comfortable being in charge of his father. He wanted his father to be in charge.

It took a few days of fussing, but the father was able to place the child on the ground and calmly talk to him as he washed dishes or watered the plants. The dad would alternate with periods of holding and special one-on-one time. Soon the child calmed down and felt less anxious. The child needed to know how much his father loved him, and he loved spending time together, but he also needed to know that he could be safe without his father holding him standing up.

When a child is beginning to internalize the limits, she may walk by something and say, "No touch" and touch it anyway. She is beginning to see the correlation. She may say, "No rip books" and rip the page anyway. She will get it soon. She needs another teaching limit, and maybe another, until she can stop herself. In the case of the ripped page, you could show her how you have to repair the page with tape, teach her how special the books are, and give her only board books for awhile. You could tell her she will have another chance later to show you that she knows how to treat books nicely.

Setting limits takes more energy initially, as your child learns the boundaries. When she has been taught the boundaries, and consistent consequences are in place, she will begin to develop self-discipline and behave within the boundaries. It will become easier to keep the limits in place when your child knows they are consistent. The key is to maintain the limits, even when it is 5 o'clock and you are exhausted. Do not say "Oh, okay, you can have 3 cookies before dinner!" because you are too tired to state and enforce the limit.

Young mothers with infants often say to me, "But I can't stop her because I'm busy with the baby." If the older child thinks she can cross the limits when you are busy, you are not being consistent. Muster your energy now for a more peaceful tomorrow; she will begin to know you mean your words and abide by the limits.

Picking Your Issues

Picking your issues is a very important part of discipline. A child can only learn a few behavior changes at a time. If a parent is setting limits on nearly every action, the child becomes discouraged (review Chapter 8:

Creating a "Yes" Environment).

If the safety of the child is in question, you know a limit needs setting. If he is about to hurt himself or another, a limit has to be set. Outside of these essential considerations, choose your issues carefully. For example, it was 7 p.m. at one of the children's centers and one 2-year-old had not been picked up. When the parent arrived, the teacher said that the child had to put the puzzle they were working on back together before she could go home. The child had seen all the other parents pick up their children and was tired and hungry. She crossed her arms and said "No."

The teacher picked an issue that should not have been chosen. She had backed herself into a corner that was hard to get out of. Parents frequently find themselves in situations where they wish they had not set a limit; now they have to follow through. In this example, perhaps the teacher could have completed the puzzle herself, due to the circumstances, or saved it for the next morning for the child to complete.

Encouraging Cooperation

Children respond best when you assist them with a chore. Many parents ask, "How can I get her to pick up her toys?" Age must be taken into consideration. For younger children—under 5 years old—you can get the best results by making a game of it. "You pick up the blue toys, and I'll pick up the red toys" or "Let's sing a song and see how many toys we can pick up before it ends" or "What song shall we play on the CD player while we pick up all the toys?" Positively reinforce her efforts, especially when she sorts the toys into their proper containers.

Environmentally controlling the storage system can help immeasurably. What that means is to be sure to have sufficient bins and shelves for easy storage. One excellent suggestion is to put away one-third of the toys and rotate them each month. Each month, the third they have not seen in a while will have new play interest.

As children get older, they can put away one set of toys when they finish playing with them before they take out another set. If the older child refuses to clean up his toys, one consequence could be to tell him that any toys left out would be taken and put in a bag and stored. As children show you they can clean up other toys, they can earn back the toys from the bag. Many times children have so many toys that they will not miss the first or second batch of toys removed. Soon, without toys to play with, they will learn to be responsible for cleaning up.

Another possible strategy could be to remove the toys for a prescribed period of time, such as a day. The toys can be given back after one day saying, "Here are your toys back. You have another chance to show me you can pick them up when you are finished playing with them." If your child has a friend over, it is a good rule of thumb to make a habit of the children picking up toys together a few minutes before the play date ends.

Consequences

One mother said, "I wish we could have a class just on consequences, because it is difficult to think them up!" Children learn best when the consequence is related to the misbehavior. If they come home ten minutes late, they will have to be home ten minutes earlier the next day. If they dawdle at bedtime, you may have time for only one story, or they have to go to bed that many minutes earlier the next night. If they spill something, ask if they want a rag or a paper towel to clean it up. Let them try to "fix it," what Faber and Mazlish, in their book *How to Talk So Kids Will Listen,* call "making amends." If a child knocks over a plant and dirt is everywhere, show him how to clean it up.

Children take great pride in being able to right a mistake. If they break something, let them do extra chores to earn money to pay to replace the object. Try your hardest to have the consequence be related. Taking away a video game for hitting another child is not as effective as restricting him for a time period from playing with that child or, if old enough, having him write a letter of apology stating that he is sorry and will not hit again.

The child needs to know that "sorry" means behaving differently. He could write that he understands that each person in the family is safe and will not be hurt. This clear no-violence policy must be restated many times.

Parents ask, "Should I make my child say he is sorry for something he has done?" It seems to be the right thing to do, but I want you to consider a few things. First of all, in the heat of the moment, the child probably is not feeling sorry, so to make him say it then is asking him to be dishonest. I have heard of children who say "Sorry" with each hit; they think that saying they are sorry erases the hit as it falls!

Another consideration is the fact that you cannot force a child to speak words. If you tell your child to say she is sorry, and she just stands there looking down, you have backed yourself into a corner. The best strategy is to model the desired behavior, saying you are sorry. That means to say something like, "Johnny would feel better if you told him you are sorry" or "When you are ready, you could tell Johnny that you are sorry for hurting him." Another strategy is to have your child notice Johnny's feelings by saying, "Johnny's face is sad. Your hit hurt him. It would make him feel better if you told him you are sorry."

When a consequence is stated, it can be helpful to add, "You will get another chance." It gives the child the hope that he will have another opportunity to behave differently and more acceptably. "You cannot have your bike for 2 days because you are not riding it safely. In 2 days you will have another chance to show me that you can ride it safely." "You cannot play with your sister for an hour. After an hour, you will have another chance to show me that you can treat her gently."

Listening

Parents often ask how to get their child to listen. We can model listening as we listen to their words. We can be sure we have their attention by looking in their eyes. We can do all the things we are discussing in this chapter. However, we have to follow through on what we say, so the child knows that we mean our words.

I witnessed a father telling his 4-year-old son to not walk on the rocks beside the path but to walk in the path. The little boy ignored him. The father stated it again, a little louder. The little boy acted as if he didn't hear the words. The father shouted the command at the little boy, who acted as if he were deaf to his father's words. The path ended and nothing more was said or done.

What happened? The little boy had experienced repeatedly that the father would tell him what to do and then not follow through with action. Why listen? It did not make any difference. Why not do what *I* want to do? The father had taught him not to listen.

In this instance, I would not have chosen to make an issue of this because the 4-year-old was sure-footed on the rocks. If, however, the father chose to make an issue of this, he needed to go over next to the child, state the request, and, if it was not heeded, set a limit by guiding the boy off the rocks. If he went back to the rocks, the child's hand would need to be held to keep him on the path.

Overuse of Time-outs

Time-outs have been overused. When used too much, they become ineffective. The National Association for the Education of Young Children (NAEYC) has stated that time-outs are not recommended in preschools. The reason is that time-outs take a child out of the situation that she needs to be learning to deal with. Misbehaviors are a time for teaching, not for isolating the child. Many families use time-outs as the only consequence for misbehavior. It is best to match the consequence to the misbehavior for better learning.

If you do use time-outs, they need to be followed by talking about what happened and what she could do differently in the future. Time-outs should be limited to one minute for each year of the child's age. In other words, if your child is 2 years old, the time-out should last 2 minutes. It is best not to use your child's crib for a time-out place. The bed should be associated with rest and peace; it can have a negative association if used for time-outs, which can later cause sleep issues.

I hear parents threatening children with time-outs frequently: "If you don't stop, I am going to put you in time-out!" It is so much better to state your firm expectation for behavior and then *act* when your child does not cooperate. If he continues to throw toys after you have clearly told him that toys are not for throwing, you act. Take the toy he is about to throw out of his hand and offer an alternate behavior. You have given him a clear message: Toys are not for throwing. An alternate choice could be throwing a ball outside or throwing his beanbags into a basket. You have stopped his misbehavior and have shown him how he can safely throw. Another consequence could be that the toys he is throwing are taken away for a period of time, such as an hour or a day. Clearly state, "You will have another chance in one hour to show me you know how to play with these toys safely. For now, they are going to be put away." You have *acted* to teach your child how to behave in that particular situation. A time-out is not nearly as effective.

Handling Hurtful Behaviors

Clear limits are set on hurtful behavior. Hurtful behaviors are always outside the circle or boundary you have set. Handling harmful actions—like pushing, hitting, and biting—involves stating the limit very clearly. "No hitting (or biting or pushing) people. I have to stop you until you can stop yourself."

It is best if this message is delivered in a firm voice, squatting down, looking the child right in the eye with your hands on your child's shoulders. The consequence could be removing the child from the play situation for a short period. The message to the child is that he cannot play with the child he hurt right now. He will have another chance to show that he knows not to hurt another child. Ideally, the parent moves in closely if a harmful action is anticipated and physically stops it.

One parent had little bruises on her neck and upper chest, and I asked what had happened. She said her toddler was pinching her! I told her she needed to stop the pinch before it happened by actually catching his hand before the pinch. She needed to give him a clear message: No pinching. Pinching hurts. If pinching attempts continue, she needs to set a consequence. She could say, "I can't hold you right now if you are going to pinch me. I will give you another chance in 5 minutes to show me that you have learned not to pinch." This sequence may have to be repeated.

The goal is that children will learn acceptable ways of handling their feelings and actions with the parents' guidance. "I will stop you until you can stop yourself." In other words, "I won't let you hurt anyone. By giving you limits, I am helping you learn self-discipline."

Teaching children *what to do* instead of just saying "Don't do that" is a very effective behavior strategy. It shows that you respect the child. For example, a child may try to poke his new sister in the eyes. He is stopped and told that he cannot do that but could be shown that he could place his finger in the newborn's fingers (that helpful grasp reflex) or that he could rub her back or show her a toy.

A child who bites can be given a clear message that he cannot bite people but he can bite a teething toy and then pin one to his shirt. Small children respond to this because they may bite out of frustration. That way they can bite to release the frustration as long as it is an inanimate object. Usually the child begins to find other more constructive ways to release frustration in about a week and no longer needs the biting toy. This strategy has often been successfully used in the toddler rooms at children's centers. (Sixteen to 24 months is often when this behavior surfaces).

Of course, the child who bites must also be shadowed when with other children. Follow closely whenever he nears another child so an adult can be in a position to prevent the bite and offer the alternative. More examples of offering alternative behaviors are included in the Communication Discipline Style section that discusses helping your child express her feelings in a constructive way.

The Importance of Consistency

The importance of the consistency of limits cannot be overemphasized. The child can learn more easily if the rules stay the same. She needs to know what rules to internalize into her self-discipline system.

Both parents and anyone who lives in the house with the child need to be consistent with the child. If two parents are giving mixed messages, which rule does the child internalize and learn to live by?

Children seem to be able to distinguish between two sets of limits if the limits are in two different settings. For example, home and school may have different rules, or home and grandmother's house may have different rules. One place may allow the child to play with several different sets

of toys before cleaning up, and the other may expect the child to pick up one set of toys before going on to another toy. One place may allow drinks in the living room; the other one may not. In different settings he can learn the differing rules. But if the mother says drinks are not allowed in the living room and the father allows drinks in the same living room, which rule does the child learn to follow? If parents disagree on limits, they are responsible for working out compromises beforehand.

Why Spanking Is Not Advised

It is my hope that you will learn effective discipline styles so that you will not resort to spanking. Many parents say that they do not know what else to do. Many of them were spanked as children and say, "I turned out okay." Many grandparents say, "All that child needs is a good smack and that will teach him!"

Spanking does not teach a child what behavior you would like to see. Rather, it teaches the child that hitting is a way to get others to do what you want them to do. Studies show that children who are spanked are more aggressive to their peers. A child who wants a turn on the slide may push or hit the child ahead of him to get him off the slide. He seems to say, "I want that child to get out of my way. Mommy hits me when she wants me to do something else. I will hit him so he does what I want him to do."

Spanking teaches a way of getting what you want. When you hit your child, you are teaching him to hit. I have seen parents hitting their children saying, "No hitting. You hurt him. You know better than to hit your brother!" Also, spanking models that when you are angry, you hit. A child may say to himself, "He took my toy. That makes me angry. I will hit him. I see that when Mommy and Daddy get angry with me, they hit me."

One parent shared that she spanked her 4-year-old for the first time. She said the child's reaction would forever prevent her from spanking her again. The child backed away from her mother, her eyes widened, and she said, *Why would you want to hurt me?* She had always been taught never to hurt anyone.

Another parent shared that he had heard that another parent would tell his child to go into the yard to find a stick to be spanked with when there had been misbehavior. One day, his little boy came back into the kitchen sobbing, saying that he could not find a stick. He said, holding out his hands, "Here are two rocks you can throw at me instead." It was all about hurting. The little boy felt fear.

We don't want our children to fear us. We don't want our relationships to be based on fear. We don't want the message to be: "You will do what I want because you are afraid I will hurt you if you don't."

At a workshop, one parent said nearly inaudibly, "That is why my brothers never visit my father anymore." She explained that her father had frequently spanked her brothers to get them to behave. The fear of their father hurt their relationship with him. They did not build loving relationships with him; the relationships were built on his power over them. Using power over another person to get them to do what you want them to do does not establish a loving connection. The child views the relationship as frightening and unsafe.

If you have ever had another person be mean to you, belittle you, or "melt down" over something that you did, it is very hard to be around that person for fear of upsetting them again. It is like "walking on eggshells" when you are interacting with that person. Any moment they may turn on you for reasons you may not understand.

Children take time to learn which behaviors are acceptable and which are not. Many times they are spanked for behaviors they have not yet internalized into their self-discipline system. Perhaps they were unable to stop themselves from doing it. Hitting them makes them afraid and anxious anytime they are in the presence of the person who hits them.

Families need to have a clear no-violence policy in their homes: No one gets hurt. We learn to work out our problems. No one needs to fear that he or she will be hurt in the safe haven of home.

As mentioned in Faber and Mazlish's *How to Talk So Kids Will Listen and Listen So Kids Will Talk,* spanking crosses the interpersonal boundary saying, "your body does not belong to you," "I don't respect your body," "I can do whatever I want to your body."

In this day and age, children need to be empowered to say "no" to any infringement on their bodies that feels uncomfortable or hurtful.

Spanking also teaches that "people who love me, hit me." It sets the stage for accepting domestic violence in later years. One study found that men who were spanked as children were twice as likely to hurt their wives, and women who were spanked as children were twice as likely to accept abuse. They learned at a young age that "Mommy and Daddy hurt me, even when they say they love me." Loving and hurting are associated. "This person says he loves me, so I think it is okay if he hurts me sometimes."

Spanking may stop the behavior temporarily, but what happens when the parent is not there to witness the misbehavior the next time? The child may not act out the behavior in front of the parent for fear of being hurt, but when the parent is not around to mete out punishment, he may repeat the misbehavior.

Pediatrician Dr. T. Berry Brazelton and Child Psychiatrist Dr. Joshua Sparrow, in their book *Discipline the Brazelton Way,*♦ state that

> when parents use corporal punishment, they are also saying to a child, 'You will have to behave because I can make you.' These messages do not prepare a child for the day when a parent is absent or can no longer discipline them. In today's violent world, we can no longer afford to teach our children violent behavior. We can no longer afford to discipline them without giving them better and longer-lasting reasons to take responsibility for their behavior.

A child does not begin to internalize the limit with spanking. The goal is for the child to learn how to control himself, not to have someone else control him by hurting him.

Positive Discipline

Positive discipline is the most effective discipline style. Noticing positive behavior is the most powerful reinforcement. A smile of approval, a tousle of the hair, a pat on the shoulder, a hug of approval, or words of praise—all go a long way toward encouraging acceptable behavior. You are teaching desirable behavior by noticing it.

So many parents do not want to rock the boat when things are going smoothly. They are afraid that if they make a comment when children are behaving, the children will start misbehaving. A common example is when siblings are playing together beautifully in the next room. Parents are afraid to go in, smile, and say, "Look how nicely you are sharing the farm set." Instead, they go in only when there is trouble.

The old adage that negative attention is better than no attention is very true. Misbehavior may continue because you are reinforcing it by your attention, however negative.

Keep noticing good behavior. When your child is cooperating with dressing or with running errands, tell her how well she is cooperating. Children want to please you. Showing pleasure and appreciation for the behavior you want to see will increase that behavior.

One school tried an experiment. They took one or two boys from each of the fifth grade classes who had been labeled as troublemakers for behaviors like calling out, getting out of their seats, and not completing their work. They placed the boys in one class together with several teachers—about a 1:3 ratio. The teachers were instructed to notice the positive and to praise or otherwise acknowledge desirable behavior as they taught. In 2 weeks, with this positive reinforcement, the boys were behaving!

Rapport, or a feeling of connection with your child, encourages your child to care about what you say. Keeping that feeling of warm closeness, of feeling you are on the same wavelength will encourage desirable behavior. This warmth and harmony is built from birth with cuddling and warm conversations. Your child *feels* the love you have for him. You have cherished moments everyday (refer to Chapter 2: Building Your Child's Self-Esteem). Rapport is developed when you convey to the child that you enjoy

her company; you just like *being* with her, no matter what you are doing.

Conveying how much you like being with your child can be invaluable. Carve out one to two hours with your child on the weekend—do something fun together. Tell him all week how much you are looking forward to your time together. It is a time to focus on the child and be with him. If you have more than one child, plan it every other week or so. One parent shared that she tried this with her little girl who was misbehaving after the birth of her sister. She said it caused a miraculous change; the child was reassured that her mother liked being with *her*.

Developing trust between you and your child is another important part of positive discipline. Meaning your words and following through on what you say helps engender trust. If you say you will take her to the park after her nap, do it. If you say she cannot go outside to play until the toys are picked up, do not let her go outside until they are picked up. All your interactions impact the trust between you. Keep her trust by telling her when you are leaving. Tell her when something will hurt. Be honest.

Creating a positive behavior chart is another way to reward desirable behavior. State the behavior you want to see from a positive viewpoint. Instead of "Don't hit your brother," the heading would read "Get along with your brother." Instead of "Don't dawdle in the morning" it would be "Get dressed on time."

I like relationship awards instead of material rewards. You could draw a key to the chart. For example, if he earns two stars, he can choose to play a board game; place two stars next to a picture of stick people playing a game. Three stars could be a trip to the park; draw a little swing set, and place three stars next to it. Four stars could be lunch with Daddy on Saturday; put four stars next to a big stick person and a little stick person at a table.

You know what your child likes to do with you. Your child will soon internalize the desirable behavior and will no longer need the reward chart. The behavior chart offers motivation to improve behavior; focus on one or two behaviors at a time until they are learned.

The Communication Discipline Style

The communication method of discipline teaches the child to communicate her feelings, and it teaches acceptable outlets for her feelings. Showing empathy when a child is upset for any reason is a way to show the acceptance of his or her feelings. So many times we try to talk a child out of being angry or sad or otherwise upset. We want to immediately make them cheer up and feel better. *Empathy is being with the person in the feeling.* This is extremely hard for parents. "I see you are so sad" shows empathy. "Don't be sad" denies feelings. Many parents have been amazed when they tried empathetic comments. The child feels comforted, and often that is all that is needed.

Too many times, children are told, "Don't be angry," or "Don't be sad," or "Go to your room until you can show me a happy face." All these comments are communicat-

ing to the child that she cannot trust her feelings, and her feelings are not okay. Isolating an angry child is saying, "I don't want to be with you when you are angry. I only want to be around you when you are happy." Children need to know that all feelings are accepted. It is the behavior associated with the feelings that needs to be limited.

As parents, we need to teach children acceptable activities to do with the *energy* of the feeling. Misbehavior can be prevented if feelings are expressed in a constructive way. For example, a child is angry with his brother for knocking down his tower and the mother says, "Don't be angry at him. He is little and doesn't know any better." Where do the feelings go? Many times they are "pushed down" or "swallowed." They may come out later as a hit or other hurtful behaviors. Rather she could say, "How frustrating to have your tower knocked down!"

What else can happen to these feelings that are not allowed expression? The physical energy of the feeling can cause physical symptoms such as stomachaches, headaches, high blood pressure, ulcers (yes, in children too), depression, and even physical tics. I worked on a Child Psychiatric Unit for 3 years. In that time, three children came in with psychological tics. One little girl jerked her head to the right side from the moment she woke up to the moment she fell asleep. The energy of the suppressed feelings was expressed in the tic. Once the psychiatrist, psychologist, and other therapists helped her learn to express her feelings, the tic disappeared.

As parents, you can help your child express her feelings constructively at the time they arise so they will not be pushed down and come out later as physical symptoms, hits, bites, or pushes. The first step is to acknowledge the feeling by saying something like, "I see you are angry," or "You are so sad that you can't go outside before lunch." Sometimes such an empathetic response will soothe the feelings. For example, a little girl was sitting in the back seat with her grandmother and her balloon burst. She cried, "My beautiful balloon! My beautiful balloon!" Trying to cheer her up, her grandmother denied her feelings by saying, "Don't worry. It is only a balloon. We will buy you another one." She continued to cry "My beautiful balloon! My beautiful balloon!"

Mom, in the front seat, said to herself: Acknowledge her feelings. And then she said, "I see you are so sad that your special balloon broke." The little girl said, "Yes" with a sigh and calmed herself.

A child whose feelings are being denied will try to convince the other person how badly she feels, and she gets stuck in the feeling. When someone shows empathy by acknowledging her feelings, she can sometimes let the feelings go with a sigh. Whenever a child is upset for whatever reason, even an unreasonable one, the first thing to do is to acknowledge the feeling: "You are so frustrated!" or "I see you are sad" or "It is hard to be little."

Another way to acknowledge feelings is to use "I wish" statements. Think of what the

child might wish right then and state it. "I wish we could spend our whole day outside but we need to go in for lunch now." "I wish we could eat a big mound of ice cream for dinner, but our bodies wouldn't be healthy if we didn't eat vegetables." "I wish Grandma could stay all day, but she has to go home and fix dinner for Pop." "I wish we could play all day until it gets dark, but we need to go wash the clothes so we have clean clothes for tomorrow." A simple "I wish" statement acknowledges feelings and helps a child accept the inevitable. It shows that you understand how much they wish things were different.

A side benefit to acknowledging feelings is that you are labeling her feelings for her. Just as you would teach her what a shoulder or a chin is, you are teaching her the name of the feelings she is experiencing. Labeling feelings as they arise is an immeasurably helpful strategy to help children begin to organize their feelings into manageable behaviors. Aside from the empathy of saying, "I see you are so angry (or frustrated or sad or disappointed)," naming the feeling will bring it into their awareness: "Oh, that is the name of how I am feeling." One mother told me that this was so helpful to her son. One day, instead of having a tantrum, he said "I am upset!" And that was the end of that. He was able to use his words to work through the feelings.

It will be a great day when your child can say, "I am frustrated!" instead of acting out her feelings by screaming or throwing something. Encourage her to use her words to tell you how she feels. Teach her to say, "I am angry that you ripped my drawing!" instead of hitting the perpetrator. Role-playing can be most helpful. Help her practice her words in imaginary situations. Reconstruct a real situation and teach her the words she could use next time. You could reverse roles to help her learn. So many times parents tell children to use words, but the child has no clue what words to use. We need to teach them what they could say.

Many times children cannot find the words to express the magnitude of a feeling. Constructive feeling expression can be encouraged by saying, "I can't let you hurt your sister. Show me with the doll how you feel," or "Show me how you feel on this pillow." The key piece is that you hold the doll or the pillow or the teddy and say, "Show me." In showing you, the child feels your acceptance of the feelings. A parent could hold beanbags for the child and hand them one at a time saying, "Show me how angry you are by throwing the beanbag into the basket. That angry? Show me some more," and hand him another beanbag. Usually by about the third beanbag, the child has worked out the energy of his feelings and is able to move on with his day, smiling.

One little boy would hurt someone within the first 10 minutes of arriving at school each day. He came to school with angry feelings. We drew an angry face on an old pillowcase and when he started getting upset, the teacher would hold the pillow and say, "I can't let you hurt your friends, but you can show me how angry you are on the pillow." He would ball up his little fists and pound on the pillow she held. She would say, "That angry! Show me some more." He would pound a few more times and run off, feeling better that he would not hurt his friends. One day he noticed two children beginning to argue and he ran to get the angry pillow and said, "Show me how angry you are. I don't want you to hurt my friend."

That boy did not want to hurt anyone; he needed an outlet for his feelings. Setting the limit of not allowing him to hurt his friends and showing him what he could do instead was therapeutic. It prevented future hurtful behaviors.

A parent could suggest a physical activity that could release the energy of the feeling, such as shooting a basketball, punching a punching bag, pumping a swing very high, riding a bike, or running around the backyard.

Encouraging children to draw a picture of how they feel is another way to encourage feeling expression. Children can put their feelings into drawings. Many parents have brought me pictures that their children drew to express feelings. Sometimes they include fire and explosions. Do not judge whatever they draw; their feelings are expressed in the drawings instead of in hurtful actions or internalized as physical symptoms.

A teacher once brought a sobbing 5-year-old child to my office and said, "I can't get him to stop crying and he is disrupting the class. He won't tell me what is wrong." I tried encouraging the child to express his feelings with words with no success. I then gave him some crayons and paper and asked him to draw me a picture of how he felt. He drew a very detailed figure of a little boy. He drew tears streaming from his eyes by pressing into the paper about 50 small, deliberate circles in a line below the figure's eyes, crying all the while. By the time he got to the fiftieth circle streaming from the second eye, he brightened, stopped crying, and said he was ready to go back to class. I never figured out what was causing him to be sad—he may have not known. But he was allowed to express his feelings and was able to go on with his day.

Another child drew a picture of his mother and sister holding hands in the center of the drawing in a child's swimming pool with grins on their faces. He drew himself very tiny up in the right-hand corner of the picture. From his drawing, it seemed that he was feeling left out and needing more attention.

You could buy a journal for your child and explain that writing your feelings down in a journal can be very helpful. Explain to your child that she can express all her feelings, and that the journal is only for her, and no one else will read it. This would be good practice for all of us. Usually a child over 8 years old is able to do this. Writing a letter to the person they are angry with—but not sending it—can be very therapeutic. They can let all their feelings out without restriction. Notes that tell a person how they feel can be given and are helpful. For example, a child can write, "Do not borrow my markers without asking me first" and tape it to the markers; or "Do not borrow my favorite yellow sweater, but you could borrow my blue one." The child feels empowered.

Using play dough is an excellent way to work out the energy of feelings. Play dough—called "clay" for the older children—can be kneaded, rolled, poked, pulled, and pounded. I was called in to consult at one of the Princeton children's centers when a 3-year-old boy was knocking off an entire shelf of toys every morning to show how upset he was that his mother had left him. I suggested giving him some play dough with some tools each morning when his mother left. He was told that we could see how upset he was that his mother had gone and that he could show us how he felt with the play dough.

It worked miraculously. His feelings were acknowledged, and he was given a constructive alternative. Every day for the rest of the year when his mother left him, he pounded, poked, and kneaded the play dough for 10 minutes and then went on about his day without ever knocking toys off the shelf again. Allowing him to express his feelings in an accepting atmosphere prevented misbehavior. Kneading, poking, and pounding the play dough was a constructive alternative to knocking toys off the shelf. The teachers respected his feelings by allowing their expression in an acceptable way.

One parent shared that she took her little girl to buy a gift for an aunt. The little girl came running up to her with a little bird gently held in both hands, as if she cherished it. "Mommy, can I have this beautiful bird? I love him so much!" Her mother said no, they were there to buy a gift for someone else. The child asked again pleadingly, and

the mother again said no firmly and told her daughter to put it back. A week later, when the mother was cleaning, she found the little bird under the child's bed.

The scenario could have been so different if the mother had acknowledged the little girl's feelings. "Oh what a beautiful little bird! It has tiny shiny eyes and lavender and pink feathers. I see how much you love it. I wish we could buy it for you, but today we are shopping for a gift for Aunt Sue." Her feelings would have been acknowledged, and she may have been able to put the bird back.

Another great idea in such a circumstance could be to have an ongoing wish list for your child. When you are shopping, and she sees something she wants, or she sees a commercial of something she wants, or a friend has something she wants, you could jot it down to add to her wish list. Genuinely keep the wish list updated. Show her. What it does is offers hope that they may be able to get their wish one day. When it is her birthday or Christmas or Hanukkah, pull the list out and have her choose a few items from the list.

Delay of gratification is hard to teach, and the wish list concept helps. It also gives her hope. In the case of the stolen bird, the mother rightfully took the child back to the store with the bird to return it with an apology. For an older child, a letter of apology could be written also. If the item was not returnable, the child could do extra chores to earn the money to pay for it.

If a child is taught how to express his feelings as they arise, the feelings will not be tucked inside and come out later as physical symptoms, hurtful actions, or other misbehavior. This strategy actually prevents misbehavior. It teaches lifelong skills for managing feelings.

"I" Messages

"I" messages are so helpful in all our interactions. It is fine to let your child know how you are feeling as long as you phrase it as, "I feel frustrated when your toys are all over the floor" instead of "You never pick up your toys," or "You make me so mad." Starting a sentence with "you" places the person on the defensive, and he may feel as though you are attacking his character. When you state your feelings with an "I" message, he may be willing to cooperate, because he wants to please you and not have you be upset.

The Five-Minute Warning

Children have trouble with transition times, those times when things change from one activity to another. They are playing with their cars, and you say it is time for lunch; or they are playing with a friend, and you say it is time to come in for dinner. You take them to school, and they do not want to go; you go and pick them up, and they do not want to leave. The best strategy is to give them time to regroup, to prepare themselves for change. Whisking children from place to place can cause arguments and tears.

Respecting the child and allowing time for them to process the change can eliminate misbehaviors. The 5-minute warning is an excellent strategy. "In 5 minutes it will be time to pick up your cars and go have lunch," or "In 5 minutes it will be time to have your bath."

Many parents find a timer very handy, in that it is not *you* telling them that the 5 minutes are up; it is the "third party": the timer. Even toddlers respond to the 5-minute warning, even though they have no idea what 5 minutes are. They get the message that things are about to change. It is helpful even to infants to let them know that you are picking them up to go and change their diapers, or it is time to get in the car seat.

Giving Choices

Giving a choice and saying "you decide" is a very effective discipline strategy. Choices allow a child to determine what happens

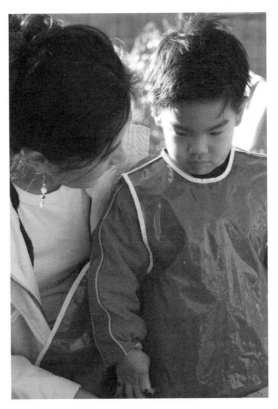

next. He learns that his choice of the next behavior is his responsibility and learns to be responsible for his behavior.

The consequence or what happens next is up to him. For example: "You can use the markers correctly, or they will be put away. You decide." "You can stop jumping up and down in front of the TV, preventing us from seeing the movie, or you can play with your trucks in the other room; you decide."

If he continues to jump up and down in front of the TV, you say, "I see you have decided to play in the other room with your trucks." He will probably have to be guided there. Say to him, "You can have another chance to show us that you can stop jumping up and down. You can come back when you are ready."

If he tests you and returns with the misbehavior, you do it all again. Perhaps setting the scene differently might be another option. Ask "Would you like to bring your trucks or your farm into the room to play with while we watch our movie? You decide."

Your little boy is running his tricycle into your legs. You could say, "You can ride your tricycle properly, or you can play in the sand with the shovels; you decide." He runs into your legs again, and you say, "I see you have decided to play in the sand. Your tricycle will be put away until tomorrow morning. You will have another chance to show me you can ride it properly then." Remember to let him know that he will have another chance to show you he can do it correctly. This helps him accept the limit better and realize that you have confidence that he can do it better next time.

Choices also give some control back to a child who is struggling with his autonomy. It is the personality task of the 2-year-old to become independent, to individuate, to feel like a separate individual that feels he can care for himself somewhat by the age of 3. They have a "me do it" mentality; they do not like being told what to do.

The more choices you are able to give your child, the fewer battles you will encounter. "Do you want to wear your yellow dress or green dress?" "Do you want Cheerios or Rice Krispies?" The child feels your confidence that he can make a good decision.

All this practice with little decisions prepares children for making bigger decisions as they get older. Giving choices can sometimes prevent meltdowns. You are not saying, "Do this now." You are giving your child some control over what happens next. The trick is to offer two choices that are equally acceptable to you.

Sometimes it is hard to think of a choice. If you are having difficulty, think about *how* or *when* something could be done. "Do you want to take your bath with plain water or bubbles?" "Do you want to take your bath before or after your stories?" "Do you want to get changed now or in one minute?" You could ask if he wants to get wherever he has to go using giant steps or baby steps. "Do you want to walk to the car, or do you want me to carry you?" If he insists on a battle of the wills, all is not lost. Refer to Chapter 3: Living with Your Toddler, to learn how to handle tantrums.

Learning to Make Behaviors Not Work for the Child

Children will not continue a behavior that is not working for them. In the workshops, I often ask, "How is that behavior working for your child?" Then we brainstorm ways to make it not work any longer. One scenario that often comes up is tantrums that continue past 4 years of age. The American Academy of Pediatrics states that tantrums are normal until then. Parents often inadvertently reinforce tantrums by giving in or offering extra attention during the tantrum, which encourages more tantrums.

Whining and screaming can be problematic behaviors that can work for the child. They may be getting lots of attention from these behaviors, even though most of it is negative attention. Parents may even give their children whatever they want to get them to stop. (Remember the adage that "negative attention is better than no attention.")

First of all, you need to positively reinforce the behavior you *do* want by praising when a child uses his voice to ask for something nicely. Notice it by commenting: "You asked me so nicely," and say it with a big smile. When whining or screaming occurs, you need to give the clear message that you want to help them with whatever they want, but your ears cannot hear well when she whines or screams. Just refuse to respond other than calmly saying, "If you can say it in your regular voice, I will help you." They will soon realize that whining or screaming is not working. It is not getting a rise out of you, and they are not getting whatever it is they are whining or screaming about.

Talking back is another problematic behavior that shows disrespect to the parent. Make it not work for the child. Stay calm and state that you will not listen to disrespectful words. Ask the child to rephrase: "Please rephrase what you said, showing respect." Of course the word "rephrase" will have to be explained. Role playing some suggestions of how the comment can be rephrased is very helpful. For example, a child is asked to do something, and he talks back and says, "I won't!" You could calmly say, "I hear how much you don't want to take your bath. I will not listen to your talking to me like that." You could rephrase it with respect and say, "I'm busy playing. Could I take it in a half hour?" or "I wish you would give me 10 more minutes."

Parents often tell me that when a limit is set, the child smiles or laughs as if they could not care less what you are saying. It is best at the time to ignore the smile or laugh and proceed as if they were not smiling or laughing. You do not want the behavior to work. You do not want it to rile you up and get you distracted from the limit at hand. It pushes our buttons, but stay calm, ignore the smile or laugh and firmly restate the limit.

Children do this to try to "win you back." They may say to themselves, "When I smile, she usually smiles back at me. Maybe I can make her smile, too, and stop showing me that angry face." Laughing or smiling can also be a sign of discomfort. They do not know how to respond, and they are nervous that you are displeased. Make it not work. The same strategy goes for covering their ears with their hands when you are disciplining them. Ignore it. Make it not work. They can hear you through their hands.

Sometimes children will shout "I hate you" or "You are a bad mommy" when you are disciplining them. The strategy is to look past the words at the feeling. Say "I see how angry you are that we have to pick up the toys before we go to the park."

Many parents respond to the words with something like "How can you hate me? I have been taking care of you for years. I stayed up at night when you were sick and changed thousands of diapers," or "Don't use that word." Unfortunately, children do get behavior reinforced by us getting upset or displaying behavior that says, "I have had my buttons pushed!" Ignore the words now. Later, when you are having a quiet moment, explain that her saying "I hate you" hurt your feelings. Reassure her that you love her very much and you know that she loves you. Use a big hug to reconnect. You should be proud of yourself for not letting her push your buttons and making you feel frantic.

Tattling can be a troublesome behavior. You do not want to stop it altogether, because you can get some important safety information that way. The best strategy is to calmly take the child back to the child she is tattling about and say, "I have confidence that you can tell her how you feel about what she did." Perhaps you could help the children find a solution they can work out themselves for next time, so tattling will not recur. This makes tattling not work for the child.

Using bad words is another behavior that upsets us. The more dramatic the response, the more reinforcement we are

giving the behavior. Calmly say, "That word is not nice." Tell him that using that word offends you. If it happens again, explain that you see that he needs help remembering not to use that word. Tell him you will continue to remind him and ask him to rephrase.

Talk-Aheads

I have created the term "talk-ahead." Simply, it is explaining to the child what is about to happen or what is about to change. It can be very helpful in preparing a child for a new situation. For example, when visiting, the child can be told ahead of time what the place is like and what behaviors are expected. A trip to the doctor could be described and the child told what might be expected of him.

It is a very effective, behavior-changing strategy to prepare and forewarn a child. It is another way of showing respect for your child. It helps prepare the child when parents' actions are going to change in order to help the child learn new behaviors. Parents have told me over and over that this strategy paved the way to a smooth change in behavior. It conveys a clear message to the child: We are in this together and I will help you. You can visualize figuratively that your arm is around the child's shoulder with the attitude "We can do this." You can convey "I have confidence that we can do this together." So many times a child is told to change his behavior without feeling the support of the parent in making that change. A talk-ahead can be used in introducing such things as toilet learning or a new bedtime strategy. Parents tell me that this strategy has eased the way to new behaviors.

"I Will Always Love You"

When children see an angry face and hear angry words, they often feel that the parent doesn't like them anymore. They have a hard time realizing that the parent is upset with the behavior, not the child himself. I remind parents that it is perfectly acceptable to show angry feelings—all feelings are accepted—but we need to clarify that we are angry about the behavior, not the child. "I will always love you. It is your behavior that I do not like" is a most helpful phrase that comforts a child and helps her cope with reprimands. She knows her parent still loves her and that she can learn new ways to behave.

"What is the message to the child?" Ask this to clarify how the child is receiving the parent's words, actions, and strategies. The goal is for children to understand that the parents unconditionally love them yet want to help them change specific behaviors that have become troublesome for the family. Many times the delivery of the message is misconstrued, or the manner of delivery frightens the child.

Keeping Calm

If you can keep calm when disciplining a child, the child will be able to better hear your words and pull himself back together. If a parent yells or screams, the child will escalate out of control also. We are modeling behaviors for our children every day. If we yell when we are upset, so will they. I suggest some deep breaths to keep in control or a *reverse time-out*. A reverse time-out is when you remove yourself from the situation for a few moments to calm yourself. One mother shared that she tried stating limits in a calm, controlled voice and she was amazed that Andrew began to sometimes say, "Okay, Mommy" and stop the behavior.

If your child gets you very upset, it gives her too much power, and that can be frightening. She wants you to set firm limits. Firm limits help her feel safe. As she is building her own inner limits, it may require sometimes tedious and frustrating efforts on your part. Keeping yourself under control is one of the best strategies.

I would encourage you to use a firm voice when setting limits; I have heard parents say, "It is not nice to hit your friends" in a voice that could be saying, "Wouldn't it be nice if we went to the park?" We want them to listen. Speak to them at their eye level, and place your hands on their shoulders. Be firm, not harsh, and try not to raise your voice.

Often a parent in a workshop will bring up a concern, and the entire group will brainstorm solutions; we come up with amazing lists of suggestions. Toddler tooth brushing is one thing that many parents have problems with, because the child struggles. Brainstormed solutions are shared in Chapter 3: Living with Your Toddler—Tips for Daily Life. Another problematic behavior is when a toddler struggles at diaper changing time. One mother was quite pleased by using one of our brainstormed strategies; she did a talk-ahead explaining that they would sing a favorite song during the diaper change. When the song was over, so was the diaper change. It gave the child a sense that there was an end to laying on his back. The mother shared that her son lay quietly, and when diaper changing was over, he said "More!" One little change transformed their days together.

The Problem-Solving Approach

The problem-solving approach can be used when the suggestions already mentioned are not working. It is used in business when an impasse is reached, and everyone is asked to brainstorm strategies to solve a problem. It is used in science to prove a theory. It is used in families to help brainstorm strategies to change behaviors to make for a happier, more peaceful family. The message to the child is "I have confidence that if we put our heads together, we will be able to brainstorm ideas that will be acceptable to both of us." The child is viewed as part of the solution, instead of as the problem. It respects the child, saying to them, "I think you will have some good ideas for helping us." It is the most powerful strategy in working out difficult issues.

1. *The child expresses her feelings* about the issue.

2. *The parent expresses her feelings* about the issue.

3. *You both brainstorm solutions* and write them down.

4. *Agree on two or three solutions to try* and shake hands on it.

5. *Meet again to talk about the results* and discuss new solutions as necessary.

It is very important to write things down, even if the child cannot read. Writing the solutions adds significance to all the ideas. Write down every idea, even outlandish, impossible ideas. From some of the outlandish ideas come some very creative solutions. For example, one solution for stopping a little boy from hitting his brother was "Have him go live with Grandma." That wasn't a possible solution, but it brought Grandma up. One of the solutions that did help was to have each child spend individual time with Grandma on alternating Saturdays. This helped the little boy get a break from the ever-present little brother.

To further illustrate the problem-solving approach, let us discuss the recurring issue of the little boy hitting his brother despite all the efforts outlined in the above discipline strategies:

1. The child expresses his feelings: he might say that he feels that his brother is always in his way, too close, getting into his things, or actually hurting his things, like ripping a drawing or knocking over a tower. He says he gets so mad and feels like hitting him. He doesn't know what else to do.

2. The parent expresses her feelings: She states that she feels disappointed when the boys do not get along. She says it gets too noisy when they are fighting so much. She wants the family to be safe, and for home to be where no one gets hurt. She needs to find ways to help when her son gets mad and to find other ways to express his feelings.

3. You both brainstorm solutions: "Let's put our heads together and try to figure out a way to have a happier, more peaceful family." The parent actually writes down all the ideas. Possible solutions could be listing all the acceptable ways he could show his feelings in a constructive way without hitting his brother: use his words, show how he felt by hitting a punching bag, poking, pounding or kneading play dough, drawing an angry picture, or writing his brother a note.

Perhaps Mom could entertain the brother for awhile each day to give the older boy a chance to build or draw without interference. Have Mom put a gate across the hall so he could do his things on one side and the little brother could watch him and talk to him but not be on top of his work.

Set aside a time each day for the boy to play with his brother at his level, to give the little brother the attention he wants so much from his big brother.

4. Decide which solutions to try and shake on it.

5. Meet again to see how things are improving.

Let us try another scenario: a little girl is dawdling in the morning, making everyone late to school and causing pandemonium in the morning.

1. The child expresses her feelings: she says that people are hurrying her too much and she feels tired in the morning and cannot move as fast as everyone wants. She also likes to watch her TV shows in the morning.

2. The parent expresses her feelings: the parent says that she gets worried that everyone will be late. She feels upset and nervous and does not like shouting. She wishes they could all have more peaceful mornings to start their days.

3. You both brainstorm solutions: write down all the solutions the two of you come up with. Possible solutions could be go to bed earlier so you are not tired in the morning. Get up 15 minutes earlier, so you do not feel so rushed. Get dressed and have your breakfast before you can watch any TV. Lay your clothes out the night before "like a person"—shirt first, then pants, socks, and shoes. Get your backpack together the night before with all notes signed and all homework inside. Play a favorite song on your CD player, and see if you can get dressed before the song is over.

4. Decide which solutions to try and shake hands.

5. Meet again to review how the solutions are working.

The examples show how the parent is taking the child's feelings into consideration. Sometimes the child comes up with a brilliant solution that the parent had not thought of. Solutions that the child offers are often the most effective. Here is another instance of figuratively or actually placing your arm around the child's shoulders and saying, "We can figure this out together. We are working together to come up with solutions to make us all happier."

If more than one child is involved, this approach can change into a family meeting, where each child and each parent state their feelings and possible solutions. In step one and two, the person who is talking can hold a toy microphone or a wooden spoon to remind the others not to interrupt. Each person will have the opportunity to share his feelings. Everyone puts their heads together to come up with the solutions and agrees on what to try. Everyone shakes hands and everyone evaluates. What a powerful tool!

Children's Books Can Encourage Desired Behaviors

Keeping in mind that discipline is teaching the behaviors you want, books are a wonderful tool to use. Many of the following books teach children what to do instead of the hurtful behaviors. Several books encourage identifying feelings and show ways of expressing them.

The Way I Feel by Janan Cain. Parenting Press, 2000.

Hands Are Not for Hitting (Best Behavior Series) by Martine Agassi, Ph.D. Free Spirit Publishing, rev. 2009.

Words Are Not for Hurting (Best Behavior Series) by Elizabeth Verdick. Free Spirit Publishing, 2004.

Feet Are Not for Kicking (Best Behavior Series) by Elizabeth Verdick. Free Spirit Publishing, 2004.

Teeth Are Not for Biting (Best Behavior Series) by Elizabeth Verdick. Free Spirit Publishing, 2003.

Tails Are Not for Pulling (Best Behavior Series) by Elizabeth Verdick. Free Spirit Publishing, 2005.

Feelings by Aliki Brandenburg. Harper Collins, 1986.

Manners by Aliki Brandenburg. Harper Collins, 1997.

How to Be a Friend: A Guide to Making Friends and Keeping Them by Laurie Krasny Brown. Little, Brown Young Readers, 2001.

Talk and Work It Out (Learning to Get Along Series) by Cheri J. Meiners. Free Spirit Publishing, 2005.

Be Polite and Kind (Learning to Get Along Series) by Cheri J. Meiners. Free Spirit Publishing, 2004.

Know and Follow the Rules (Learning to Get Along Series) by Cheri J. Meiners. Free Spirit Publishing, 2005.

Listen and Learn (Learning to Get Along Series) by Cheri J. Meiners. Free Spirit Publishing, 2003.

Respect and Take Care of Things (Learning to Get Along Series) by Cheri J. Meiners. Free Spirit Publishing, 2004.

Join In and Play (Learning to Get Along Series) by Cheri J. Meiners. Free Spirit Publishing, 2004.

10
Sleep Strategies for the Weary Parent

Facing the Day with Joy and Enthusiasm

Well-rested parents and well-rested children face the day with joy and enthusiasm. The cumulative effects of sleepless nights take their toll in feeling stressed, less patient and less able to be the parent you want to be. Well-rested children are better able to enjoy their days, cope with frustrations, and follow limits.

Many different philosophies about handling night waking abound, and many theories are diametrically opposed to each other. At one end of the continuum of solutions is the idea to let the baby cry it out: shut the door, and do not go to your child. Some say your child will develop self-soothing strategies and eventually fall asleep. At the other end of the continuum is the philosophy to parent during the night as you do during the day, by answering your child's cries and doing whatever it takes to have the child fall peacefully back to sleep.

We will be discussing some middle-of-the-continuum approaches that offer specific strategies to help both you and your child get the sleep you need. Understanding sleep physiology is the place to start to help you understand night waking.

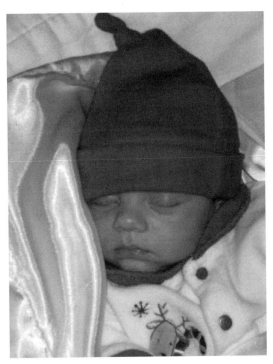

Sleep Physiology

Sleep experts have studied sleep patterns by hooking sleeping subjects up to electro-encephalograms (EEGs) and noting brain wave patterns and the ability to be aroused. Dr. Richard Ferber, director of the Center for Pediatric Sleep Disorders at Boston Children's Hospital, states in his book *Solve Your Child's Sleep Problems*♦ that there are four levels of sleep, from drowsiness (Stage I) to very deep sleep (Stage IV). Each of the stages has a distinct brain-wave pattern.

Most people have one to two cycles of deep sleep, from Stage I and then deeper to Stages II, III, and IV, and then back up from Stage IV, to Stages III, II and I. Then REM, or rapid-eye-movement, sleep occurs. REM is an active state in which there is more blood flow to your brain, more oxygen is used, and your brain waves become more active again. There are bursts of rapid eye movements and increases in the blood pressure, heart rate, and respiratory rate.

If you were awakened in the REM stage, you would most likely report that you were having a dream. Some researchers believe that the eye movements are you actually "watching" the action in the dream. Sometimes your occasional muscle twitching will match some of the action in the dream. Your spinal cord normally blocks signals from the brain to the muscles, except for the slight twitches. If it did not, you might dangerously act out the dream.

Some sleep experts think that REM sleep has a psychological function, allowing us to process emotional experiences and transfer recent memories into long-term storage. Adults spend about 25 percent of sleep in REM sleep, newborns about 50 percent. Premature babies spend 80 percent of sleep in REM sleep. Interestingly, this information leads specialists to believe that the REM sleep provides the maturing brain with adequate stimulation for establishing connections.

What this also tells us is that infants spend more time in light sleep and therefore wake more frequently. Newborns are able to sleep for only a few hours at a time. By 3 to 4 months, the sleep pattern begins maturing, and sleep cycles consolidate into about four or five sleep periods with two-thirds of their sleep occurring at night. By 6 months, the continuous nighttime sleep has increased; they are developing more mature sleep patterns. Therefore, we expect newborns to wake up for feedings every few hours because they need the nourishment, and their neurological systems are not mature enough yet to allow long periods of sleep. Our expectations are that small babies will wake up at night.

After REM sleep, there is a brief period of arousal in which you will move about, change positions, adjust your covers, check to see if everything is all right, and then go back to sleep. If something is amiss, such as you lost your pillow or you smell smoke or you hear an unusual noise, you will wake all the way up to investigate. *This information is key to understanding why a child may wake frequently at night.* As she arouses to check her environment, she finds something amiss. Where are Mommy and Daddy? I can only fall asleep if Mommy nurses me or Daddy rocks me or I have my pacifier to suck on.

Whatever it was that helped her fall asleep needs to be reinstated, for her to be able to fall asleep again. She has not learned to fall asleep on her own and needs outside help to fall back to sleep. Whatever it is that helped her fall asleep is called a *sleep association*; she calls you to give her back her sleep association. Aside from sucking and rocking, common sleep associations are twirling a piece of Mommy's hair, pulling on Mommy's ear lobe, or lying with Mommy or Daddy.

Another issue that arises is your child not going into a deeper sleep cycle as you are lying with him. In the past you got up and were no longer lying there when he awoke. Therefore he stays in a light sleep cycle to easily awaken if you begin to get up. If someone were taking your pillow every time you fell asleep, you would keep yourself in a lighter stage of sleep to be alert to stop someone from taking your pillow. In the same way, a child stays more alert so his sleep association will not be taken away.

The length of cycling through the sleep stages begins at 50 minutes for the newborn and progresses to the adult sleep-cycle length of 90 minutes. That is why some children awaken themselves every hour or so. It is the post REM arousal and checking that wakes her all the way up, because something does not feel right to her. Something is missing.

Parents can become part of their children's sleep cycles. As your child arouses after the REM sleep, she needs to call her parents to provide whatever it was that got her to sleep in the first place. If she had learned how to fall asleep without sucking or rocking, she would slip back into sleep after this normal arousal and not be aware that she had checked her environment. Therefore, one goal you have is to help your child fall asleep from awake on her own. Then, when she normally arouses during her sleep cycle, she will easily be able to fall back asleep.

Learning a new set of sleep associations with the parents' support is an important aspect of helping a child sleep through the night. That way, the parent will not need to be called in the night to reconstruct the associations that got the child to sleep at the beginning of the night. The child learns that he can get himself back to sleep.

An issue to consider is that when your child awakens at night, normally at the end of the REM stage, he senses something is different and not right if he is not in the same place as he fell asleep. If he fell asleep in your arms as you rocked or walked him, or in your bed, and then was placed in his bed when he fell asleep, the last thing he remembers was being asleep in your arms. He awakens in his bed but does not remember being put there. He wakes himself all the way up instead of drifting back to sleep. "Hey, this doesn't feel right. I don't know where Mommy or Daddy went!"

Encouraging Your Child to Fall Asleep on Her Own

Gently encourage your child to peacefully fall asleep on her own as often as possible from day one. If you can get in a routine of feeding, playing, then sleeping—instead of feeding, sleeping, then playing—you can avoid the "sucking-to-sleep" issue. This is not easy and maybe it will only happen once a day in the beginning, but encourage it when the opportunity arises.

I know from personal experience that there is nothing more peaceful than nursing a baby to sleep. It is so loving and cozy for you both. As the months go by, give the baby the opportunity to learn to fall asleep on her own. When you get the chance, lie her down when she is drowsy, before she falls asleep at your breast or with the bottle. She may need two to three night feedings before she is 6 months old and one to two feedings up to 1 year. Most doctors consider sleeping through the night to be 5 consecutive hours of sleep during the night. Take care of yourself during the night feedings by having a comfortable, cozy place to nurse. Have a padded chair with a footstool and a little table for your water glass. Have a pillow handy to support the baby's weight while you are feeding. Relax yourself with deep breaths and relax your shoulders. Enjoy this time with your baby.

Elizabeth Pantley, in her book *The No-Cry Sleep Solution*, introduces the idea of the "Pantley Gentle Removal Plan." ♦* She suggests watching for the sucking on the pacifier or nipple to slow down and gently breaking the suction with your finger to gently remove the pacifier or nipple before the baby is asleep. She goes on to say that the baby will probably root, mouth open to reclaim the nipple. She suggests to gently hold his mouth closed with your finger under his chin while rocking or swaying him. If he fusses, allow him to have the nipple, but "repeat the removal process as often as necessary until he falls asleep" without the nipple in his mouth. This is a creative way to break the sleep association of sucking to sleep.

*Adapted from *The No-Cry Sleep Solution: Gentle Ways to Help Your Baby Sleep Through the Night* by Elizabeth Pantley, copyright 2002, McGraw-Hill Publishers. Used with permission of The McGraw-Hill Companies.

The same gentle removal plan could be applied to other sleep associations. Remember the goal is have the child drift off to sleep without the sleep association, so that he will get himself back to sleep when he rouses after the REM sleep. What you are hoping for is that he will arouse himself, look around, see that all is well, and fall back asleep without calling for you. For example, if the sleep association is rocking, rock him until he is drowsy but not quite asleep. Gently lay him in bed, sway his body slightly, and keep your hands around him until he settles. Repeat as necessary until he falls asleep on his own.

The same strategy could be used for the sleep associations of lying with him or having him twirl your hair or pull on your ear lobe. Lay with him until he is drowsy then gently get up, place him in his crib, and place your hand on him for a moment until he settles. Whisper "You did it. You fell asleep without sucking, rocking, twirling my hair, or lying right next to me." The removal plan may take two or more repetitions at each waking, but over time, your baby will sleep for longer and longer stretches without calling you.

Your Child's Sleepy Cues

If we miss a child's sleepy cues, she may become overtired and have a difficult time settling down to sleep. An earlier bedtime may encourage a better night's sleep.

Pay attention to your child's sleepy cues and place her in bed when she is exhibiting them. Cues may include: quieting, rubbing her eyes, decreasing activity and movement, looking away, losing interest in people and toys, yawning, lying down on the floor, fussing, looking glazed, or caressing her lovey.

Loveys and Bedtime Rituals

At the crux of sleep problems is a separation issue. Many children have a difficult time saying goodnight and letting the parent go. Encouraging loveys and establishing bedtime rituals can ease the separation.

Loveys, such as a blanket or teddy bear, are symbolic replacements for the parent, transitional objects that help a child transition from being with you to being without you. It cannot take your place. Penelope Leach, author of *Your Baby and You*, calls a lovey "a piece of your love." It eases the transition to sleep and comforts the child.

To encourage a lovey, you can have it with you when you read or cuddle with your child. To let the lovey have your scent, you could "wear" it under your shirt for a day or sleep with it as a pillowcase. You can pull the lovey close to the child when she is in her bed about to fall asleep. The lovey can become one of her sleep cues; when the lovey is gathered, it is nearing bedtime. When she arouses in the night, she can pull the lovey close, feel comforted, and drift back off to sleep without calling for you.

The same bedtime ritual each night is a comforting separation ritual that eases the child into bed. This close personal connecting time is something to look forward to. This could include a bath, reading to your child, singing *Twinkle, Twinkle Little Star*, saying goodnight to all the stuffed animals, getting a big hug, and then climbing into bed. The familiar sequence is helpful, so the child knows that the next step is into bed.

Using the talk-ahead concept (described in Chapter 9: Discipline Styles), prepares your child for what is about to happen. You could make a bedtime ritual poster that illustrates the steps in the ritual process with drawings or photos. This could be hung at the child's eye level and reviewed before the ritual begins. The poster shows your child, in a concrete way, that this happens, then this, then this, then into bed, preparing him for the separation. A one-picture-per-page photo album illustrating the bedtime ritual could be used in the same way, as her "book" to read before bed.

Limits need to be set on the bedtime routine to decrease your child's opportunity to keep calling you back into the room. For example, you could put a sippy cup of water near the bed so he can manage his own thirst. If he is toilet trained, be sure he has used the toilet before the bedtime ritual. Decide ahead of time the number of books you will read and stick to it. It is hard when a child is asking, "Please Mommy, one more book."

Perhaps part of your ritual is lying with your child for a few minutes. Stick to the number of minutes with a timer or by watching the clock. Do not respond to more requests. Use cue words to reassure and quiet him: "I love you very much. It is night-night time now." Repeat the words if he continues his delay tactics. Monotonously repeat the same phrase and nothing else. If he climbs out of bed and comes to you, calmly and repeatedly escort him back to bed and say your cue words. By doing this you are making his behaviors not work. Minimize eye contact and talking as you escort him back. He begins to realize that he consistently ends up back in bed each time, and that it is not worth the effort to keep coming out.

Eliminating Night Feedings

Children learn to be hungry at night with night feedings. Most children are still having night feedings at 6 months and some up until 12 months. After that, it is time to gradually eliminate the feedings at night.

Learned hunger may trigger waking. Calories at night stimulate the digestive tract, which needs to be dormant at night. Hormonal balance may be interfered with. After 12 months, you can offer a snack or a bottle at bedtime and then brush her teeth. If she wakes for night feedings, replace an ounce of milk with an ounce of water in the bottle each night (breastfeeding strategy is described next). For example, if she usually drinks an 8-ounce bottle at night, fill the bottle with 7 ounces of formula and an ounce of water. The second night the bottle will contain 6 ounces of formula and 2 ounces of water and so forth.

When you get down to all water, you know she has unlearned being hungry at night. She will take those calories during the day now, and you can stop with the night feedings. If you eliminate the bottle all at once, it is too hard. She probably has learned to be hungry at that time. Some parents tell me that their child wakes like clockwork at a specific time for a bottle. This is learned hunger, just like our hunger at noontime.

You do not want to leave her hungry in the night. You want to reassure yourself that she has been weaned off the feeding instead of eliminating it "cold turkey." It is hoped she will begin sleeping through the night on her own. If not, you can use all the other strategies in this chapter to help her learn to sleep through the night.

If you are still breastfeeding at night after 12 months, you can begin to eliminate the feedings by decreasing the nursing by a minute per side per night. A child can empty a breast in 7 minutes. You will nurse her 6 minutes per side the first night, 5 minutes per side the second night, and so forth, until you are down to *no* minutes per side. Use the other strategies to help her learn to sleep through the night if she does not do it on her own, now that you know that she is not hungry anymore. Your child will begin to eat better during the day to make up for the calories she used to have at night.

Brushing Teeth

At 1 year, it is imperative that your child's teeth are brushed before going to sleep. Going to bed with a bottle can cause "baby-bottle caries" which is severe tooth decay. I have seen children having to go under general anesthesia to have all their teeth capped. As they suck and doze off, the milk pools around the teeth and causes decay. Do not let your child have a bedtime bottle filled with anything other than water. Milk, or any food for that matter, left on the teeth overnight can cause decay. Make a habit of brushing teeth after eating. See Chapter 3: Living with Your Toddler for many suggestions on helping teeth brushing go smoothly.

Evaluating Daytime Sleeping

Daytime sleeping must be evaluated when there are sleep issues. Dr. Ferber states that a 6-month-old will have settled into two naps, one midmorning and one in the afternoon, of about 1 to 2 hours each, with 10 to 11 hours at night, usually interrupted by a feeding. By age 2, the typical child sleeps 11 to 12 hours at night and takes a 1- to 2-hour nap in the early afternoon. By age 3 many children give up their naps, but some still nap until age 5. These are average numbers. One study of 9-month-olds found that several slept 9 hours per day total while others slept 18 hours a day. That means that some slept twice as much as others! Your child will have her own individual sleep pattern.

Is she sleeping too long or too late in the afternoon? Dr. Brazelton, in his book *To Listen to a Child: Understanding the Normal Problems of Growing Up,*♦ suggests that naps be started early, by 1:00 p.m., and last only 1 to 2 hours at most. If the child is over 2 years old and waking at night, he recommends that the nap be eliminated. He also states that "any rest or nap after 3 p.m. will decrease the need for continuous and deep sleep during the night."

Giving up a nap is a difficult transition for both parent and child. You need to evaluate for your family what is the better trade-off. Some parents are reluctant to give up the nap, because the child is too fussy by 4 or 5 p.m. without it. Some parents feel that they and the child both need the rest at naptime.

The pace of a day with a small child, as they explore, discover and test limits, can be very tiring for both parent and child. Naps can continue if the child goes to sleep at a reasonable hour for your family and he sleeps well at night.

Sometimes children who nap stay up too late. For some parents this is not an issue, because they like the extra time with the child. Yet for some, they feel like they have no evening and no time to relax or to spend time together as a couple. You have to determine what feels right for your family.

Adjusting Your Child's Sleep Schedule

If you would like an earlier bedtime, Dr. Ferber suggests that you gradually make the bedtime earlier in ten-minute increments for 2 days at a time. For example, if your child's bedtime is 10 p.m. and you want it to be 8 p.m., the first 2 nights put him to bed at 9:50 p.m., on day three and four at 9:40 p.m., the next 2 nights at 9:30 p.m., and so forth.

This gradual transition is necessary to readjust his biological body rhythm. If you were to put him to bed at 8 p.m. that first night, he would lie awake and not be able to fall asleep until later. As he is lying awake in the dark unable to sleep, he may develop fears of the dark or complain of body discomforts, like stomachaches.

During his awake time, he will probably continually call you or otherwise engage you. Notice what time he wakes up on his own: If he wakes up naturally at 10:00 a.m., you will want to wake him 10 minutes earlier every 2 days, until you have reached the desired bedtime at night. You are gradually taking away morning minutes of sleep to add to night minutes for an earlier bedtime. With a little effort, his natural waking time will be something you can happily live with. Dr. Ferber suggests that you keep his natural waking time the same even on weekends so that his biological rhythm is maintained. He will be able to fall asleep at his new 8 p.m. bedtime without struggles.

If you are having difficulty waking your child in the morning, and she seems cranky and tired, she probably has a late sleep cycle. That is, she would naturally wake up much later if your schedule permitted. To avoid this morning crankiness, keep waking her at the time needed for your schedule but make her bedtime earlier by 10 minutes every 2 days as described above. After about 2 weeks, she should begin to wake up on her own at the time you want her to wake up, eager to begin the day.

On weekends she has to get up at her weekday times to keep her biological rhythm. If allowed to sleep in, her rhythm will again shift to a later natural wake-up time—and crankiness in the morning. That may explain why many of us have a hard time getting out of bed on Monday mornings!

A similar strategy can be used for an early riser, to help your child sleep longer in the mornings if she is rising too early for your schedule; for example, at 5:30 a.m. Say her bedtime is 6:30 p.m. Putting her to bed later at night only causes crankiness, and she would awake at 5:30 a.m. anyway. The trick is to put her to bed 10 minutes later every 2 days, until she is waking on her own at the time you wish.

Her eating and napping times would need to be gradually shifted also. This is a gradual change of her sleep–wake rhythm. In 2 to 3 weeks, she should be waking at 7:00 a.m. and going to bed at 8:00 p.m. You are shifting her sleep–wake cycle by taking minutes away from one end of the cycle and adding them to the other.

The same strategy should be used to gradually give up naps or to shorten naps. Take 10 minutes off every 2 days, so the biological rhythm can adjust. That means waking him 10 minutes earlier from his naps every other day. For example, if your child is taking a 3-hour nap in the afternoon and waking frequently in the night, you may decide to gradually cut the nap to an hour by gently waking your child 10 minutes earlier every two days. If he sleeps from 1 to 4 p.m., you would wake him at 3:50 p.m. the first 2 days, at 3:40 p.m. the third day, and so forth. The hope is that the extra time taken away from the naps will be added to the night. Remember that this is a gradual process to gently change the biological rhythm.

As children give up naps, foresee the fussy period between 4 and 7 p.m. and plan for it. It will improve day by day as your child adjusts. Perhaps dinner can be prepared in the morning or the night before so that it is ready to put in the oven during this difficult time. Take a walk with your child or do an early bath. Engage him in the preparation of dinner, and engage him in conversation about what you are both doing. Get out the play dough or markers or otherwise set him up with an activity. Be careful about letting him watch TV in the late afternoon, because he will invariably fall asleep watching, get a "second wind," and want to stay up late.

As your child is beginning to give up naps, a great suggestion is to incorporate a *quiet time* for both of you in its place. Explain that she does not have to sleep but that during quiet time she needs to play quietly in her room, and you will do the same. At first she will need suggestions as to what to do; suggest she read books, listen to quiet music, or play with her blocks. She may need a "reminder gate" at the doorway to remind her that it is quiet time.

In the transition between nap and no nap, the child may actually fall asleep a few times a week during quiet time. You need to take the quiet time for yourself, too, to rest and refuel. Modeling relaxing is very important for your child. Many experts have said that children never see parents relaxing and therefore do not learn relaxing for themselves. Most times parents relax after their child has fallen asleep, so she never sees it. We need to teach relaxing. Their little bodies go, go, go—and they need a rest during the day. The length of quiet time can be a half-hour or an hour, whatever works for you and your child.

Darkness and Quiet at Night

An excellent strategy is to keep the sleeping room as dark as possible at night to cue your child that it is still nighttime. A dimmer switch can easily be installed in your child's bedroom to be able to turn the light down as low as possible and still be able to see well enough to maneuver. Most nightlights are too bright. You could put a blue bulb in the nightlight to dim the light (available in stores at the holiday season). Keep the lights down while feeding or changing at night.

Another nighttime cue is to not talk to your child during the night. Keep conversations to a minimum so that she learns that night is not time for fun and conversations.

You could think of a word cue to cue him that it is still night. Use the same phrase night after night. You could say, "I love you very much, but it is night-night time."

If your child slept all night, you would not change her diaper in the night. Of course, newborns and young babies need changing in the night because their skin is more sensitive and prone to diaper rash. Keep all things handy so the diaper changing can be quick and quiet. Warming baby wipes ahead of time can be helpful. If you do not have a wipe warmer, hold the wipe in your hand for a few seconds to warm it.

Changing a baby is a sure way to cause her to be more awake. Use overnight diapers, and sometimes you will not need to change her as she gets older. Assess her diaper area for rashes, and determine the need to change her.

You want your child to stay in a sleepy state at night and drift off to sleep, so darkness and quiet are helpful. However, daytime naps should be in a lit room, near the noise of daily activities.

Misunderstandings about "Ferberizing"

At one end of the continuum of sleep strategies, some pediatricians recommend that a parent shut the door and let the child *cry it out alone.* This is a behavior modification approach that is too difficult on the child. The child may be genuinely frightened and fear abandonment: "Where are you? You always came before! Are you ever coming back?" What this approach can do is violate the child's trust. You have consistently met her needs before, and she is frightened that you are not responding in your usual way.

She has come to count on you and trust that you will be there when she calls. When she cries for you in this circumstance, it is a frightened cry. I have had several parents tell me that this has worked for their children, but at what cost? Did their children become disheartened and give up calling? Perhaps they lost some trust that they would be taken care of.

I remember one distraught parent that followed her pediatrician's advice to let the child cry it out alone. With each hour of crying that passed, she felt she couldn't go in to him because it would negate the previous hour of crying and send the message, "If I continue to cry long enough, she will come." This little strong-willed child cried for 5 hours—until it was morning and his mother got him up for the day. He did not give up.

In the middle of the continuum is Dr. Richard Ferber's approach, from his book *Solve Your Child's Sleep Problems.*♦ This approach has been misunderstood: parents call it "Ferberizing" or "the crying-it-out method," but the "crying-it-out method" is what has been described in the previous paragraph. The Ferber method involves some crying, but the child's trust is not violated. The great value of the Ferber method is that it gives the child loving limits on what the parent is willing to do to help the child fall asleep, *and* it maintains the child's trust.

Ferber suggests that you go in to your child at increasing increments of time to reassure her that she has not been abandoned. The message to your child is "I have confidence that you can learn to fall asleep without my lying with you or rocking you or twirling my hair or sucking (whatever the sleep association has been). I am here to support you as you learn. I have not left you all alone to figure it out for yourself. You can trust me. I am coming in to show you I have not left you. You can do it."

The goal is to help the child learn to fall asleep on her own so that when she wakes in the night, she can get herself back to sleep without waking her parents. The chart entitled "Helping Your Child Learn to Fall Asleep with the Proper Associations—The Progressive Approach," in *Solve Your Child's Sleep Problems* by Dr. Ferber, describes the increasing intervals of going in to comfort the child, beginning with a 5-minute increment, then a 10-minute increment, and then stay at 15-minute increments until the child falls asleep.

The intervals lengthen on successive nights. Ferber says to go in briefly for 2 to 3 minutes "to reassure him and you but not to help him fall asleep. The goal is for him to learn to fall asleep alone, without being held, rocked, nursed or using a bottle or pacifier." You may lie him down with his lovey, rub his back a few times, and say, "I love you very much. It is night-night time." Do the same thing each time you go in.

Many years before Ferber, author Penelope Leach, in her book *Your Baby and You* advocated going into the room in 5-minute increments to comfort the child. Ferber thinks increasing increments work best. He says that the child will begin to see what you have planned. He finds out quickly that you are around and still responsive to him. As you gradually increase waiting, he will learn to expect this also. He will learn that it is no longer worth it to cry for 15 or 20 minutes, when you only come in briefly and do not reinstate the sleep association.

Dr. Ferber states that progressive learning keeps the crying to a minimum. He knows you will come, but there is little else to gain. He suggests doing the same at naptime. If your child does not fall asleep after an hour, that naptime is over. It is setting limits on what you will do to get him to sleep, but you are there for him. He can trust you. You have not left him.

Dr. Ferber was featured on a *20-20* segment on TV, advising parents of a 20-month-old, Michael, who was rocked to sleep. Michael awakened three to four times each night wanting to be rocked to sleep again. The first night, he cried for long periods with his parents going in to reassure him at increasing intervals. He slept for 2 to 3 hour stretches in between. The second night, on the video set up in his room, you could see him trying to exert some control as he rearranged his blanket and stuffed animals. He cried for shorter periods and slept longer stretches. On the third night, he woke up, whimpered, covered himself, and drifted back to sleep. All the nights after that he slept through.

I have seen many parents have this kind of success with Ferber's method. One 2-and-a-half-year-old, Kristin, was waking two to three times at night wanting to play. Her parents would take turns staying up with her as she played for 1 to 2 hours in the middle of the night. They said they would do anything to help her learn to sleep through the night. They decided to "pull an all-nighter," as they had done in college while finishing a paper or studying for a test. They knew it would be hard for Kristin. They got popcorn and pizza and rented videos. They would spell each other for naps the next day (that is why it is a good idea to begin this on a weekend).

The first night was difficult, with Kristin sleeping only one-and-a-half hours, twice in the night. Kristin's parents followed the Ferber chart exactly, going into her room in increasing increments. The next day, they were all tired and cranky. The second night she cried for 20 to 30 minutes at a time and fell asleep for longer periods. By the third night, she slept through as she did all the nights after that. Kristin learned that her parents were available to her and responsive, but they would not let her play in the middle of the night anymore. They set a limit on her at night. Her mother happily told of their progress, and she noted that Kristin was following their limits better during the day also. She had learned that they meant their words. They lovingly supported her in learning to sleep through the night.

Try not to go beyond what is reasonable. Many parents go beyond what is reasonable in trying to help their children get a good night's sleep. One mother walked her child around the dining room table in her stroller for 30 minutes to get her to go to sleep for naps and bedtime. This is an obvious undue service, as are many other scenarios. Laying with your child until she falls asleep for an hour can be an undue service, especially if you inadvertently fall asleep, too, and miss your evening. The message to the child is that the child is in charge of the parent's behavior. This makes the child even more anxious: Children want parents to be in charge. They feel more secure when reasonable limits are set.

Ways to Soften the Ferber Method

I was thankful when Ferber shared his innovative strategies to help children learn to fall asleep. Over the years, I have developed ways to soften his approach so parents could accept his basic ideas of maintaining trust while teaching their children new behaviors:

▶ Talking ahead of time to the child about the steps to help her stay asleep at night is very helpful. It is best to talk ahead earlier in the day, not when bedtime is imminent.

▶ Include how it will help everyone have happier days and not be grumpy. You could say, "I love being with you during the day. We will have more good times together if I am not so tired." Convey how important a good night's rest is to stay healthy.

▶ Give your child suggestions of what she can do if she wakes up during the night: "You can talk to your stuffed animals,

cuddle with your lovey, and think of all the fun things you are doing tomorrow. I have confidence that you can learn to fall back to sleep in your bed."

▶ Develop your individual plan during the daytime and write it down. At night your resolve disintegrates, and you may be less able to cope.

▶ You must *want* to change his behavior. You must *want* to help him learn to sleep through the night. If you like lying with him, or you like him nursing to sleep *and* don't mind getting up in the night to do the same thing to get him to go back to sleep, do not begin. Half-hearted attempts will not work. Your child will sense your ambivalence easily. If the method does not work, you are conveying in your eyes that you are not sure this is the right thing to do.

▶ Dr. Ferber says the approach can be used from 4 months of age, but I think it is best used when a child better understands language. Receptive language, or being able to understand your words, begins around 8 months old. By 10 or 11 months, a child can understand your cue words. Her cognitive development has progressed so that she understands that you are not far away and will respond.

▶ Lessen the number of minutes between intervals. It would have been too difficult for me to wait 10 or 15 minutes to go in to reassure my child. It could be 1 minute twice, 3 minutes twice and stay at 5 minutes until your child settles. The message to the child is "I am here for you, but I want you to learn to fall asleep without my assistance."

► If your child lies next to you to fall asleep, you could instead sit next to the bed to wean him away from actually touching you. You could start by holding his hand or patting him while you sit. Then you could gradually increase the distance between you and the bed by moving your chair further and further away each night, until you are at the doorway and then out of the doorway. He will see you are right there but that you will not do whatever the sleep association is. This may make him mad, and he may cry even with you right there. You will recognize that it is a mad cry, not a frightened cry.

► Another strategy is to make a bed next to your child's bed with a pillow and blanket. After your bedtime ritual, and after you have cuddled him with his lovey, you explain that you are going to lie next to his bed. Each night, you move your makeshift bed further and further away until you are out of sight.

► Whether sitting in a chair or lying on the "bed" on the floor, you are still in sight. Try to limit eye contact and avoid talking to your child. Busy yourself either by closing your eyes or reading something. One way you could limit the talking is to say reassuring words in increasing increments. Use your cue words: "I love you so much, but it is night-night time."

► Realize that the crying is a mad crying, not a scared crying. Your child is mad that you are not reinstating the sleep association. He is not scared that you have left him because you keep coming back.

► When a child wakes in the night, I would suggest that you go to her right away instead of waiting the first interval as Ferber suggests. If something is wrong, such as she has vomited or has her arm stuck in the bars, you can help her immediately. Being responsive helps her know that you are nearby and available. Then begin the increasing increments.

► Ferber mentions that your child may vomit and that you should clean him up and keep on going. Understand that he has vomited because he is so mad that you are not doing his sleep association. Of course if he were sick, you would start another day.

► Understand that illness, vacations, and moving can disrupt sleeping. Do whatever you can to comfort the child. When the illness, vacation, or moving is over, slip right back into the Ferber Method or your softened approach. So many sleep habits have been developed under these circumstances, and parents perpetuate them after the illness, vacation, or moving is over.

► Increase your touching and cuddling during the day when you are teaching him to fall asleep without his sleep association.

▶ Remind your child to tell you or ask you anything he wants before you leave the room. If your child continually calls out to you after you have said goodnight, remind him once that you are not answering. If you chose to answer him, use only your cue words.

▶ If your child is already in a "big-boy bed" and keeps running out of the room during the increasing intervals, you have a few options: you can walk him back calmly and use your cue words every time or you can put a gate at the door as a reminder to stay in his room. If he can climb one gate, put another one above it.

My favorite solution is to cut the door about two thirds up and make a Dutch door. One dad, with his son's assistance, made the Dutch door very cute by placing a shelf on top of the bottom portion and putting molding crisscrossed on the front. With a Dutch door, the top is open and the bottom is locked, so the child has the reminder to stay in his room. Inexpensive doors can be bought so you do not have to ruin your decorative door. The reminder gate or door is only needed for a short time until he is sleeping through the night.

▶ Developing a sticker or star chart with relationship awards can sometimes magically help your child not disturb you at night. Tell her she will earn a sticker or a star every time she is able to make it through the night without waking you. You can make a key to the chart with pictures of the relationship awards she can earn. You know what your child likes to do with you; for example, if she earns one star, she gets to play a board game of her choice; two stars could be a trip to her favorite park, and three stars could be going to lunch on Saturday with Daddy. Parents have told me that they have peeked and seen the child come to the doorway and begin to step into the room then pull back. They could almost see the child's thought; "I really want my star!" And they turn and go back to their rooms.

▶ Use all the other strategies discussed in previous paragraphs, such as loveys, bedtime rituals and talk-aheads.

Ferber's method and the softened Ferber method are at the middle of the sleep strategies continuum. At the other end of

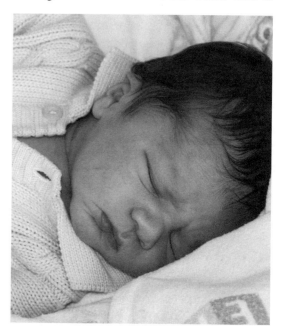

the continuum is Dr. William Sears who, in his books *Nighttime Parenting* and *The Attachment Parenting Book,* advocates parenting at night as you do during the day, answering the child's needs lovingly and consistently. In his books he addresses my main concern with this approach: Parents become exhausted without getting enough sleep. Sleep deprivation is cumulative. Parents become so exhausted that they are not the parents they want to be in the daytime, with less patience and enthusiasm for life. Sears states, "If you resent something, change it." He offers brilliant suggestions on handling parent exhaustion.

Alternatives to All Night Nursings

(From The Attachment Parenting Book *by William Sears, M.D., Copyright © 2001 by William Sears and Martha Sears. By permission of Little Brown & Company.)* ◆

Dr. Sears gives alternatives to all night nursings when your child is nursing from habit not need:

- Nurse more frequently during the day. Toddlers are often busy and do not take time to nurse, then they nurse all night long to make up for it.

- Increase other cuddle times with lots of touching, including back rubs and massages.

- When you go to bed, wake your baby for a full nursing. It may help him sleep for a longer stretch.

- When he does nurse during the night, make sure it is a good nursing, not just a snack.

- Use other ways to ease to sleep besides nursing, such as patting, singing, and so on.

- Make the breast less available by covering up after nursing.

- Tell the child that "Nummies go night-night. We will nurse again when the sun comes up. The daytime is for feeding."

- Offer a substitute, such as a "daddy neck nestle" (the child snuggles next to Daddy's neck).

- Increase the sleeping distance between you, perhaps by placing his bed next to yours.

The Family Bed

Since the beginning of time and in all cultures, children have slept with their parents. I have had no problem with this as long as everyone in the bed is happy with the arrangement. If Dad sleeps elsewhere because he wakes up all night long being kicked in the back, or Mom is not getting her sleep because the toddler is lying across her neck, the needs are out of balance. Several dads have said that they miss sleeping next to their wives and want the child out of the bed.

My other concern has developed since research about Sudden Infant Death Syndrome (SIDS) has shown that children should sleep on their backs and should not sleep with pillows, comforters, or blankets. The research points out the danger of entrapment in the spaces between the headboard and the mattress or between the mattress and the wall. How many parents can sleep without a pillow or blanket? Dr. Sears, in his book *The Attachment Parenting Book*,♦ has a long list advising about safe co-sleeping guidelines. By following these guidelines, and by knowing the risks, you can decide for yourself if co-sleeping is right for you and your family. Some of the guidelines include:

▶ Place your baby on his back to sleep.

▶ Remove all pillows and blankets from the bed.

▶ Do not allow your baby to sleep on a soft surface, such as a couch, a waterbed, or on a pillow-top mattress.

▶ The safest place for your mattress is on the floor to prevent the possible entrapment hazards and to prevent your child falling off the mattress.

▶ If your bed is placed against a wall, make sure the mattress is pushed against the wall every night to prevent the baby from getting trapped between the wall and mattress.

▶ Placing the baby between the mother and the wall is recommended because fathers, grandparents, and babysitters may not have the same instinctual awareness of the baby's location.

▶ If you only wake up when the baby is crying loudly, you may be sleeping too soundly to co-sleep.

▶ Do not sleep with your baby if you are overweight. A dip in the mattress may pose a hazard. A large body and breasts may pose a smothering hazard.

▶ Do not wear any nightclothes that have ribbons or strings, and don't wear jewelry to bed; both may entangle a child.

▶ Fitted sheets need to be secure so they cannot be pulled loose.

This is only a partial list of guidelines. Consult with your pediatrician and do your research if you decide to co-sleep.

A co-sleeping crib is available that attaches to your bed securely, so the child cannot slip into the crack between beds. It is open on the side facing you so you can reach the baby with ease for nursing. This may be a safer alternative for you.

Sleeping in My Own Bed

It is very important that everybody be happy sleeping together. Some rare children decide on their own that they want to sleep in their own beds. If Mommy or Daddy are not getting a good night's rest, it may be time to move your toddler from your bed. Toddlers can be very restless, sleeping sideways, or kicking Daddy in the back. If you are out of balance and need to make the change, there are ways to gently get your child into his bed.

You want your child to feel cozy and comfortable in her bed, so it is very important not to have negative associations with it. It is recommended that you not use the crib for time-out or any other discipline.

You want your child to feel that his bed is a peaceful place. To encourage her to like her crib, have her spend two to three happy times a day playing in the crib. Encourage her to watch a mobile or play with a toy, and slowly step back out of sight. She needs to be very familiar with her crib so that when she awakens, she will know where she is and feel happy there.

Several parents tell me that their children hate their cribs and scream when put in them. Others say they do not want their children "behind bars." Many resort to a toddler bed or "big-boy bed" too soon. Use the strategies described to help them feel comfortable in their beds.

I feel strongly that children should stay in a crib until age 3 with two exceptions: they are too long for the crib or they are climbing out of the crib. A child younger than 3 has limited judgment and can get into trouble if they get up at night. They may get out of bed in the middle of the night without you knowing and do something harmful to themselves. In the crib, you have them contained at night, so you do not have your toddler frequently getting out of bed after goodnights are said. If they do climb out, you have two options: take the crib down and place the mattress on the floor and a gate at the door, or use a mesh canopy to keep them in bed. If a new sibling arrives before your older child is 3, keep him in his crib and use a bassinet or portable crib for the baby in the early months. You will want to know your new baby and toddler are safe at night.

There are several ways to ease a child from your bed to his own bed. One option is to begin by placing his crib next to your bed. Gradually, night by night, move the crib further and further away from your bed until it is in his room. Continue to respond to him when he awakens so that he learns that you are available to him even though he is in his own bed and in his own room.

Another option is to place a mattress on the floor next to your bed and tell him this is his special bed. You could lie next to him for a few minutes as he settles there. Babyproof your bedroom and close the door or use a gate.

A third option is to put him in his crib in his room and you lie next to the crib with a pillow and blanket until he falls asleep. Each night, you move further and further out of the room. Keep talking to a minimum, using your cue words of reassurance. Once you and your pillow and blanket are out of the room, be sure to respond quickly if he does awake so that he learns you are still nearby and ready to support him in this change.

Your child may cry even if you are in sight, either from his nearby crib or from his crib when you are lying right there. Your goal is to wean him from your bed without frightening him. He needs to feel safe and confident that you are nearby. He is crying because he wants to lie next to you, not a foot or more away. He is angry that you want to change what he is familiar with.

Be sure that you are ready to have him out of your bed or he will sense your ambivalence. If he senses your resolve, he will settle more easily. Reassure him that you love him very much but that it is night-night time. For more ideas, see the earlier section, "Ways to Soften the Ferber Method."

A Word about Colic and Acid Reflux

Discomfort from colic or acid reflux can disrupt sleep. Colic or discomfort from gas can be the result of an immature digestive system. Pediatrician Dr. Harvey Karp, author of *The Happiest Baby on the Block* (Bantam Dell Publishing, 2002),♦ describes how most colic is not due to digestive upset but to the inability of the baby to trigger his calming reflex. Karp studied other cultures' nurturing techniques and found that babies cried very little. Simulating what he observed, he came up with "five S's" to calm a baby: *swaddling, side-lying, swinging, shushing, and sucking.* I recommend that you read the book or watch the accompanying DVD to learn how to tightly swaddle; position a swaddled baby on his right side supported by your forearms; swing the baby by moving your arms slightly so that his head jiggles 1 to 2 inches from side to side, not shaking the baby which can cause brain damage; shushing him loudly; and allowing him to suck on a pacifier.

Acid reflux occurs when your baby's stomach acid rises into his esophagus, causing a burning sensation. Your doctor can help you determine if your baby has this condition. Mothers have told me that acid reflux medication treatment has changed the amount of discomfort and crying miraculously. They come to class smiling and saying that they now have a different baby. It is worth exploring if your child cries for long periods.

Sleep Disruptions from New Developmental Steps

Sleep disruptions can occur right before a developmental step. The child may be more irritable and demanding during the day also. For example, before a child takes her first steps, she has a dissonance or discomfort in her body as she gathers her energy. All her energy is focused on practicing cruising around furniture, with little time or interest left over for eating and sleeping.

You may find her standing up in her crib half awake several times in the night as she exhibits this drive to be upright. She may call for you, because she has no idea how to get back to lying down. You may need to teach her how to get herself down to a sitting position by gently placing your arm behind her knees, exerting gentle pressure, and bending her legs. This inner discomfort is usually gone when she comfortably toddles around. Similar discomforts may arise before a burst of language development or before learning to crawl or run.

Nightmares

Yes, children have nightmares. Before they have the language to tell you what they dreamed, it is so difficult to know whether night crying is a nightmare or another discomfort, such as teething or illness. Children's nightmares usually involve their experiences of daily life. They may fear motorcycles, big dogs, or big trucks, and they may dream about them.

Images from TV or videos can also frighten children and cause nightmares. Children are frightened of the dreams because they cannot realize that they are not real. If they "see" a big dog in their dreams, they are not realizing that the dog is not there in the room.

If the child is moaning or complaining in his sleep, there is no need to wake him up. You could stroke him gently, lightly kiss him, and stay with him until he is peacefully sleeping. If you wake him, he will remember the frightening images and be afraid. If you let him sleep, he will not remember. Remember that we all dream each night but that we usually do not remember each dream.

If your child wakes crying and you suspect a nightmare, be calm, reassuring, and loving. Teach him that dreams are "stories that we tell ourselves" and that they are just pretend. If he is verbal and tells you what was frightening him, try to finish the "story" with a happy ending. If he dreams of monsters chasing him, make up a happy ending by saying that all the monsters took off their masks and he played ring-around-the-rosy with them. Some wonderful books are available to help dispel fears, such as *There is a Nightmare in my Closet,* by Mercer Mayer, and *Where the Wild Things Are,* by Maurice Sendak. Making up a happy ending will make it less likely that the nightmare will begin again when the child falls asleep. Has that ever happened to you? You wake up with a start from a nightmare and are thankful to be safely in your bed, only to slip back to sleep and enter that same dream again!

The recommendation is that you *not* shut the shades or the windows so the imagined bear or dog or motorcycle cannot get in. That action makes it seem that the scary things are really out there and could get in. You need to focus on the fact that she is safe and that whatever scared her is only pretend. This also applies to checking the closet or looking under the bed for monsters before she is tucked into bed. Those actions make it seem that they could be under there!

Since a child's cognitive ability increases as he matures, he may develop fears of the dark or of being alone. His increased imagination may be picturing monsters in the shadows in the corners. We all cope less well at night when we are tired. Dr. Ferber calls this a "regressed state at night where we think about worries, thoughts run out of control and we have less control over fears and feelings." The following are some strategies that could help with nighttime fears:

► A nightlight can dispel fears of the dark. When your child awakens, she can reorient herself to her room.

► Do not dismiss or belittle fears. Listen, reassure, and give plenty of hugs.

► It is better for her to stay in her bed instead of coming into your bed, because bringing her into your bed may give her the message that her bed is not safe. Perhaps you could sit with her for a few minutes of reassurance.

► Increase her confidence during the day by discussing her fears or reading books about her fears. If bears are in her nightmare, read books about bears, have her cuddle with her teddy bear, and visit the zoo to show her where bears live. If motorcycles are in her nightmare, show her a motorcycle in the store and perhaps have her touch it. Talk about the big noise it makes when it is going; read a book that includes motorcycles.

▶ Be sure she has her favorite lovey nearby to snuggle with.

▶ Sometimes having a pet for nighttime company works wonders. Even a fish can feel like company.

▶ Perhaps you may want to have siblings sleep in the same room for company. Their presence is comforting and reassuring.

▶ Joanne Cuthbertson and Susie Schevill in their book *Helping Your Child Sleep through the Night* state that nightmares are normal expressions of fears that indicate that the child is worried about something. They say, "If the child is normal and well-adjusted during the day, you don't need to worry about nightmares." As a child increases her language skills, you will be able to better understand her concerns.

▶ Avoid frightening and violent TV shows, news, and videos.

▶ If nightmares become more frequent, consult with your child's doctor.

Night Terrors

Night terrors, sleep walking, and sleep talking are different than nightmares in many ways. They all occur during the deepest sleep stages (Stages III or IV), not during REM sleep as nightmares do. If the child is awakened during a night terror, he has no recollection of any images.

In preschoolers, night terrors are not associated with physical or emotional problems, rather they are signs of an immature nervous system. Research indicates that the child may have difficulty making a smooth transition from one sleep stage to the next. The number of night terrors may increase with stresses such as separations, starting school, fatigue associated with giving up naps, and so on.

Most night terrors will disappear on their own and be outgrown by age 6. Four times more boys have night terrors than girls, and they can run in the family; the incidence is about 3 percent of children, usually preschoolers.

It is good to know what a night terror looks like so that you will not be frightened if and when one occurs. Your child may scream, sit bolt upright, and be glassy-eyed. He may seem like he is having a terrifying dream. His heart is pounding; he is breathing heavily and may be sweating. The best way to tell a night terror from a nightmare is that your child will be unresponsive to you. He will not reach out to you and be soothed by your presence, like he is with a nightmare. He appears agitated and inconsolable; within a few minutes, he relaxes and resumes peaceful sleep.

The best strategy is not to awaken him. Stay nearby until he is sleeping peacefully to keep him safe. Sometimes a child will get up, walk around, and have awkward, purposeless movements. They could harm themselves. To make yourself feel better, you can talk calmly and reassuringly to him and stroke his hand or back, but do not try to wake him up. Dr. Ferber suggests that you "keep your distance," because trying to arouse him may make the episode last longer. He will only be confused and frightened by your anxiety.

Do not question him about the incident in the morning. He will have no recollection of it, and it may make him anxious to think that he is doing something at night about which he was unaware and had no control over.

Sleep experts offer the following strategies to reduce the number of night terrors:

► Have a calm bedtime routine.

► Make sure your child gets plenty of sleep. Being overtired increases the number of night terrors.

► Your child may have more night terrors when sleeping in an unfamiliar place, such as at a friend's house or on a camping trip.

► A regular daily schedule may decrease the number of night terrors.

The sleep needs of the child *and* the parents need to be in balance to face our days with energy and enthusiasm.

11
Toilet Learning

It is very helpful to realize that learning to use the toilet is just another step in growth and development. It is a learning process, learned by the child with parental guidance and help, such as learning to zip a zipper or button a button.

Envision your arm around your child's shoulders and saying, "I am your helper in learning to use the toilet. We are a team. I will give you ideas and pointers, and you will learn when you are ready."

Learning to use the toilet must be turned over to the child to accomplish when she is ready. You describe the steps, and the child takes over the task. Breaking the task into parts helps you realize how hard a task it is to master: your child must recognize the urge (the hardest part), hold the urine or bowel movement, get to the toilet, pull his clothes down, and release the urine or bowel movement into the toilet. Waiting until the child is ready and willing to learn is very important.

Discipline has no place with toilet learning. Any pressure from the parents to perform can cause withholding of the bowel movement and lead to the constipation cycle. In the constipation cycle, the child withholds the BM, and it hurts when he finally goes. This discomfort is a further deterrent to going. With a hard movement, the anal sphincter may develop a crack or fissure and may bleed a little. The pain and discomfort is a further deterrent. The sphincter may go into a reflex spasm from the pain, and chronic constipation may follow. When a child is tense from pressure to perform, his sphincter may tighten and it will be difficult to go. Even if he is motivated to perform, his tenseness may make a bowel movement too difficult to push out.

I remember one mother sharing that her little girl wanted so much to learn to use the toilet. She would willingly sit on the potty and try and try. One day, she cried out, "Help me Mommy! Help it come out!" She wanted to be successful but she did not know how. She could not figure out how to release her sphincter. With seriousness, her mother ran the tap water and placed her fingers in her daughter's curls and said "Pssssss!"

We laugh at this but it relays an important message: Even with the motivation of wanting to learn this task, it takes children time to learn how to release their sphincters. Children have to experience trying to go in a peaceful atmosphere. Once they go by coincidence while trying, they begin to learn what it feels like right before they have to go. Words are hard to find to exactly describe what it feels like for a 2-year-old to understand. They learn by experiencing it.

Capitalize on the child's drive for autonomy between the second and third birthdays. Use the "me do it!" mentality to the child's advantage. It can provide the motivation to learn something so difficult as using the potty in an otherwise negative or "NO!" stage in personality development. There is an inner drive to be independent, and learning this developmental task gives her the pleasure of "I can do it myself!" Her little chest puffs out and her eyes sparkle with pride: "I did it!" It is her accomplishment! Her mastery of her bodily functions increases her self-esteem. This sense of mastery is more self-rewarding than a desire to please.

I have witnessed repeated successes with Dr. Brazelton's step-by-step toilet teaching method as outlined in his early book, *Doctor and Child*. Waiting until the child is ready is very important. The timing is as individual as the timing of learning to walk or talk. Trying to teach her before her body is ready can lead to months of frustration for you and your child. Toilet teaching a year too early may lead to a year of frustration.

If you wait until your child is ready, toilet learning may take only a matter of a few weeks. Dr. Brazelton states in *Doctor and Child*,◆

> In a study of 1170 children using this method, 940 trained themselves for bowel and bladder simultaneously and almost overnight. The average age for this initial success was 27.7 months. There were only 16 (1.5 percent) who were still wetting the bed after five years of age. On the average, daytime training had been completed by the age of 28 months; and in 80 percent of the cases, night training was done by the age of three. Boys took 2.5 months longer to complete training than girls.

The Signs of Readiness for Toilet Learning

▶ He shows an interest in the toilet, what it is for, and how it works.

▶ He imitates the parents' behaviors such as sweeping, shaving, or mopping up spills.

▶ He can understand the words *wet* or *dry, before* and *after,* and *go.* These concepts will help him understand your explanations.

▶ He is able to understand explanations of the process: feeling the need to go, holding it, going to a special place, getting his pants down, and putting it in the toilet.

▶ He may show a desire for his toys to be organized and may even be compulsive about things being in their proper places or in a certain order.

▶ The 17 to 20 month old flits from discovery to discovery. A sign of readiness is when the child is able to sit quietly for a time, finishing a puzzle or making a block tower. You begin to notice an increased attention span.

▶ Control of the sphincter muscles becomes voluntary by 20 months. Before

20 months, his immature nervous system is unable to voluntarily contract and relax the sphincter muscles that encircle the openings to his bowel and bladder. You may be able to catch his immature reflexes but that is not mastery.

► He is able to pull his pants up and down on his own.

► He is showing the ability of his bladder to hold urine by staying dry for 2 hours or by waking up dry in the morning or from naps. Before this increased bladder tone, urine would dribble out in small amounts. Now you go to change him, and he is dry. In the next few minutes, you find his diaper saturated. His bladder is becoming able to hold urine and then release it all at once.

► He has an increasing awareness of when he has wet, is wetting, or will wet.

The child has an awareness that he has already gone and progresses to being aware of when he is in the act of going. Infants are usually oblivious when they urinate or have a BM. Toddlers will begin to be aware of wet or soiled diapers and will show you in some way. They may pull on their diapers or bring you a diaper to change them.

With increasing awareness, they will become aware of the fact that they are in the act of going. For a BM they may squat and grunt. You get a hint that they are urinating when they look up from their play with a quizzical look, seemingly asking, "What just happened?"

The next awareness is feeling what it feels like right before they have to go. This last awareness can be learned during the toilet-learning process.

Preparatory Steps

You can help your child learn the concepts of wet and dry by discussing them as they come up in your daily activities. For example, she is wet in the tub and then you dry her off. You wash her hands, they are wet, and then you dry them.

When you change her diaper, talk about it being wet and the new diaper being dry. This will encourage her awareness. When you notice that your child is aware of the act of going, make a matter of fact comment: "I see you are having a BM," to bring it into her cognitive awareness.

Do not "whisk" a child off to the potty when she is going in her diaper; that would most surely tighten her sphincters, and she would not be able to go once she is on the potty. Whisking her in the act causes anxiety and applies pressure. Parents tell me, "But she knows she is about to do it because she hides behind the sofa or door! Why doesn't she just go over to the potty?" She is beginning to be aware but is not ready yet.

Teach the concepts of before and after by saying things like, "Before lunch, we will wash your hands," or "After your nap, we will go to the park." She will begin to understand what you mean when you describe what it feels like *before* she urinates or has a bowel movement. The concept of *go* can be learned as you use it in everyday language: "Let's go for a walk," or "Let's go get the ball." She will learn that "go" means something is about to happen.

Choose names for urine and bowel movements that have no negative connotations. Avoid names like "stinky" or "smelly" or "yucky," so he isn't shamed or embarrassed. You could choose "wee-wee" or "tinkle" or "pee-pee" for urine and "doo-doo" or "BM" for a bowel movement. Be sure to pick names that his teachers and caregivers will understand. He will begin to differentiate between urinating and having a bowel movement when telling you he has gone.

Newborns get diaper rashes on their sensitive bottoms. As time goes by, the skin gets used to having urine next to it and fewer rashes occur. With increased bladder tone, urine is held and then released all at once. The skin goes for a period without urine next to it, and then the skin is saturated. A toddler may get a diaper rash at this time. The skin becomes unused to having urine next to it all the time.

It is recommended that you purchase a little potty chair for several good reasons. Your child can sit down independently, without the need of being lifted onto the toilet. We are turning the task over to her so she can go potty without assistance. All of us can bear down more easily to have a bowel movement if our feet are flat on the floor, not dangling.

In addition, she will have pride in ownership—her very own potty. Being able to move the potty nearby is a plus, as you shall see with this step-by-step method. Choose one that looks like the real toilet (remember how much toddlers like to imitate). If it comes with a deflector for boys, remove it. Both boys and girls can painfully bump themselves on the deflector as they sit down. Teach the little boy to point his penis down, and listen for the sound as he urinates.

There are adapters that fit over the hole in the toilet to make it smaller. Some come with armrests and steps. These are not recommended for several reasons: If the child pulls his pants down and tries to mount the steps with his pants at his ankles, he may fall. He may want to take his pants off each time he goes, so he can climb the steps. Taking his pants off usually necessitates taking off the shoes, too, which will become too inconvenient and time consuming. If the child steps up the step, turns around, and then pulls his pants down, he may fall on his head as he leans over to remove his pants.

A foldable toilet adapter that makes the toilet hole smaller is helpful when you are using public toilets. It folds to about a five inch square and can be carried in your bag. Keeping a potty in the car can be helpful when the need arises at a park or while traveling longer distances.

When a child is learning, he does not get much forewarning that he will need to go. When he has to go, he usually has to go "right now." You could pull off an exit and let him use the potty. It is not a good idea to teach a little boy to urinate on a tree at the park, because he may use someone's favorite rose bush when at a friend's house!

Little boys should be taught to sit down

to urinate until they are completely bowel trained. If they learn the fun of standing up to urinate, they may not take the time to sit to have a bowel movement. Constipation may result. Daddies need to sit to urinate during this stage if the child follows them to the bathroom. He will want to copy his father.

A step stool is needed by the sink for hand washing after going to the bathroom. Build that into your child's potty routine.

If the constipation cycle occurs, ask your pediatrician for advice. He or she may recommend stool softeners. "P" fruits can help keep your child regular: prunes, peaches, plums, pears. Making sure that your child has plenty of fluids can also help. Hydrating her from within can help the BMs be more moist and easier to expel. Increasing fiber with whole grains, added bran, and green and leafy vegetables can also help prevent constipation.

Brazelton's Step-by-Step Method

(Adapted from Doctor and Child *by T. Berry Brazelton, M.D., copyright 1976 by T. Berry Brazelton. Used by permission of Dell Publishing, a division of Random House, Inc.)*

Keeping your child in diapers or pull-ups until mastery is accomplished is an important difference from past training methods. This avoids repeated "accidents" before your child understands how to control his sphincters. Repeated accidents lead to a sense of failure and worry that she is disappointing you.

Step 1.

Take the child to the toilet to sit with her clothes on once a day for a few days to help her get used to sitting with a hole under her. Encourage her to sit on her potty when you go.

Step 2.

Take her to sit without her diaper on once a day, preferably at BM time. Choose a convenient time, such as first thing in the morning or before a bath, when you are changing or dressing her. Build it into her daily routine at the same time each day.

Step 3.

With repeated success one time per day, work up to several times a day. All the while, you are keeping your child in diapers—diaper on, diaper off—to try. When your child has repeated successes two times a day, increase to three times, and so on.

Times to try could be when he gets up in the morning, before nap, after nap, after meals, after being dry for two hours, before bath, and at bedtime. The important thing is that the times to try are built into their days as a part of their daily routines.

I don't recommend the "Toilet Training in a Day" strategy because it takes the process out of their normal daily routine, gives them lots to drink so they will have more urine, and places *pressure* on the children to perform. It is so much better to have the learning be part of their everyday experiences.

Children's books can be fun and helpful in getting them to see that everyone uses the potty. They help the child see that everyone uses the potty every day and that you are not singling them out to learn this hard thing. One is *Toilet Learning* by Allison Mack. It has pictures of a fireman going potty, a policeman going potty, a doctor going potty, and so on. It also has a picture of the pipes under the street to show children where their urine and BMs go. Another book is *Everybody Poops* by Taro Gomi. This book helped one little girl get over her fear of having her BM in the potty. Perhaps it could help yours as well.

Step 4.

Only with success several times per day, proceed to the next step of playing near the potty without diapers and pants on. Your little girl could wear a dress and your little boy could wear a longer t-shirt. An explana-

tion is made to the child that this is done to turn the process over to her.

As soon as she feels the urge, all she has to do is sit down and go. The middle steps of holding it, getting to the potty, and getting her pants down are eliminated. What a sense of mastery and pride! A little urine may come out at first, and then she becomes aware and sits down quickly to put the rest in the toilet.

It is recommended that this 1- to 2-hour playing near the potty with a bare bottom be done once or twice a day on a washable floor or outside on the patio. This step usually only needs to last 1 to 2 days. You will know when she gets it, when her eyes light up and she thinks, "Aha! Now I know what it feels like right before I have to go!" You may be able to skip this step altogether if your child, during Step 3, asks to go and goes. She's got it! She now knows what it feels like right before she goes.

Step 5.

After success in the steps above, allow your child to wear panties for a short time, about 2 hours at a time. If she stays dry and uses the toilet, the time in panties can be increased gradually. For trips out of the house, place her back in the pull-up or diaper until she is able to go most of the day in panties with no accidents.

When learning, children need to keep the awareness of the bodily sensations in their cognitive awareness. This takes energy. Soon it will become second nature; but before it does, limit the wearing of panties to short "practice times." She may get involved in her play and forget to be aware of the sensations.

When you know that your child knows what to do and she has an accident, it can be very frustrating. Remember that discipline does not have a place in toilet learning. If there are frequent accidents during the panties practice times, go back a step or two. If the child stops showing an interest or refuses to cooperate, go back to pull-ups or diapers and table the potty learning for awhile.

I have seen many children become very excited to learn, and they do beautifully in learning how to use the potty for awhile— sometimes a month or more—and then stop being interested. I think that the reality sinks in and they think "This is too much trouble. I just want to play without thinking about it all the time." They are feeling society's pressure, even when the parent does not pressure them. The best tactic is to give them a rest from the expectations and place them back in pull-ups or diapers. If it is handled matter of factly, they will soon revive their interest by themselves. They will one day ask for 'big-boy pants," and they will do beautifully.

If children are cajoled into using the potty, or if discipline is used, going to the bathroom can become a lifelong vulnerable spot. Any time they are upset or sad, they become constipated, have diarrhea, or experience frequent urination. Some bed wet into the teen years. One parent shared that her niece and nephew were "trained" too early and without the signs of readiness. Now, at ages 4 and 5, they are having frequent accidents at home and school and are showing anxiety whenever they do have to go.

This method leaves the learning up to the child. If the child balks at any point, the parent can move back a step or stop altogether for awhile. Please feel confident in going forward or backward in the steps, following your child's behavioral cues.

Helpful Hints

Praise your child for trying and for going, but do not overdo the praise. If we get very excited when they actually perform in the potty, jump up and down, and call Grandma in Illinois, the child may be frightened and may refuse to try again for awhile; this over-praising feels like pressure. "Mommy is *so* happy if I go in the toilet this time, and if I can't make it come out the next time, she will be *so* sad" is what she may think. Some children may be afraid to try again after such praise. Praise quietly and say, "You must be so proud of yourself." I love the phrase "You did it!" It emphasizes that this is something they did and that they should be proud!

Dr Brazelton thinks that children view urine and bowel movements "as precious parts of themselves and sometimes do not want to give them up." He suggests to not flush the urine or BM away in front of them, rather wait until they lose interest. Many children seem excited and want to flush and flush. Later on they may express fears about it; some children are frightened by the noise. One parent told of how her child would open the door for a quick escape, get his pants back up, wash his hands, then flush and run out the door.

Asking a 2-year-old a yes-or-no question usually leads to a resounding "No." Asking "Do you have to go?" or "Do you want to try?" often gets a negative answer. A great tip is to say, "It is time to try." A timer can be a helpful objective reminder. You could set the timer for 30 minutes after a meal or a drink and explain that the timer is helping her learn to remember to try.

Use the word "try" instead of "go." That way the child feels success even if she can't "go." Sometimes the sphincters tighten when the child is trying, and after he has tried unsuccessfully, he may stand up and urinate on the floor. This can be frustrating. However, he is not being willful or disobedient; the sphincters relaxed when he stood up, and the urine was released. He will be able to control his sphincters with practice.

Do not allow your child to play with bowel movements. Divert his attention to other messy play, such as finger painting, play dough, or sand and water.

Children do not need to learn to empty the potty by themselves. This is not a skill they will have to learn for the future; it just leads to spills and frustration. Do keep an inch of water in the bottom of the potty for easier clean up.

The best incentive for toilet learning is to regularly see a friend use the potty.

Using the timer can be so helpful. It is not you saying it is time to try; it is a "third party" saying it is time to try. Some children enjoy making a game of it. If he says no, don't push it. Respect the child. Remember that it is his task to learn.

One helpful hint when having to use an adult-size toilet when you are out is to have the child sit backwards facing the tank. Some children feel more secure if they can hold on to the tank.

When you get to the point of going out of the house with panties on instead of diapers—only after they show you they can reliably use the potty at home with just panties on—take a little "emergency kit" with you. This should consist of a large Ziploc bag containing a cloth diaper or rag and clean pants. If they have an accident, you can matter of factly wipe up the puddle with the cloth, put the wet pants in the bag, and put the clean pants on.

Explain to your child that she eats food to build strong bones and muscles but that her body does not need all of it. What is not used comes out as BMs and urine.

If an "accident" occurs, say something like "That's okay. It is a part of learning. Soon you will be able to hold it and get to the potty."

If they are having to go back a step or two due to lagging interest or several accidents, and they are balking about going back in diapers or pull-ups, you could allow them to wear big-boy pants on top of the pull-up or diaper.

Sometimes children are urinating in the potty, but they refuse to put the BM in the potty. Some ask for a diaper when they need to make a BM. This can be very frustrating, because if they know when it is coming and ask for a diaper, why can't they just go to the potty? The answer is that they are not ready. It may be related to feeling that the

BM is a part of themselves. Something is making them afraid. The best strategy is to give them a diaper and after they go, change them.

One mother said that every day before her nap, her little girl asked for a diaper. She would make her BM in the diaper, call to say she was done, was changed, and then went to sleep. Remember, no pressure and no discipline can be used for learning to use the potty: The constipation cycle is sure to ensue. Reassure the child that it is perfectly okay to save the BM for his diaper.

I have found three things that have helped children feel more comfortable about putting a BM in the potty:

1. After the BM is made in the diaper, take it to the little potty and drop it in while the child is watching. Say, "This is where the BM will go when you are ready." This is a concrete association that will help them learn. Be sure you say it matter-of-factly, without a chiding or cajoling tone in your voice.

2. Another strategy that has worked several times is to place the diaper in the potty, draped open across the potty, and say nonchalantly that they can put the BM in that diaper. For some reason this feels less scary for some children. It seems irrational to us, but it works. After 1 to 2 weeks of this, the child is able to go in the potty without the draped diaper.

3. The children's book *Everybody Poops* has encouraged several children. If you do not make a big deal about the book and simply add it to your pile of books to read, the child will realize that having a BM in the toilet is something everyone does.

Some children seem to know what to do about toilet learning but need some extra incentive to get over the hump and do it. I have seen a sticker chart work well to solve this issue.

I like a relationship award chart. That means that the child gets extra one-on-one time as a reward instead of a material reward, like a toy car or a doll. You can have the child choose the stickers they like at the store and draw a "key" for the chart in the corner with pictures. For example, you could draw two stars or stickers equaling a trip to the park along with a drawing of a park swing. Three stickers could equal lunch out with Daddy or Grandma; draw one big stick figure and one small stick figure at a table. You can think of what your child likes to do with you and add that and so on. I remember one 3-year-old girl who seemed to know exactly what to do but would not put her BM in the potty. This chart helped her face her fear and do it on her own in one day.

Night Toilet Learning

It is within normal limits for children to bed wet until age 6 or 7. Some doctors are not concerned up to age 8. Luckily, there are large sizes of overnight pull-ups widely available. If you are unable to find them, call the 800 number on the box of pull-ups.

A child should never be shamed for wetting the bed. Many children sleep very soundly and are therefore unable to be aware of the bodily sensations that precede urinating. Others have small bladders that cannot hold the amount of urine that collects overnight.

Some children have an "I don't care" attitude about wetting the bed. Sometimes this means that they care too much. Keep up the attitude that you are on their team and ready to help. The children's book *All by Myself* by Anne Grossnickle Hines can offer encouragement. It is about a little girl's determination to give up her diapers at night and her mother's relaxed attitude.

Night training sometimes coincidentally happens with daytime training, or it may happen 1 to 2 years later. The best rule of thumb is to keep them in diapers at night until they have been dry for 3 to 6 months. It gives them a rest period from trying to be aware of the bodily sensations night and day.

The best tactic is to wait until they express a desire to be dry at night or to not wear diapers at night anymore. If he wets his diapers nightly, keep him in diapers; it is embarrassing to wet the whole bed. When he asks for help, you could try the following, but be sure to "talk ahead" to explain the plan:

1. Wake him when you go to bed, and see if he is willing to get himself up to go to the toilet. Carrying him will not achieve the mastery that is needed.

2. He may need help to awaken early enough in the morning to urinate.

3. Use luminous tape or paint on his potty next to his bed so he can easily find it in the dark. If it is next to his bed, he can easily slip out of bed, use it, and slip back into bed. Sometimes the length of the trip to the bathroom can seem very long and is a deterrent to getting themselves up.

4. You may want to warm the house at night for awhile, because another deterrent is the cold air outside the covers.

5. Use nightlights to light his way to the bathroom.

Helpful Hints for Wet Beds

Encouraging independence at night can be very important for self-esteem. You could offer one or more of these ideas to your bed-wetting child so she will be able to take care of it herself. Remember, if bedwetting is a nightly occurrence, it is best to leave the child in diapers or pull-ups. If it happens occasionally, you could try these helpful steps:

1. Be sure you have a plastic mattress cover on the mattress to protect it. The type that goes on like a pillowcase and zips closed is the best kind.

2. Keep extra pajamas handy.

3. Remember to protect the pillow also.

4. Make up the bed with two sets of sheets with a rubber sheet between. When the top set gets wet, the child can pull the top set off with the rub-

ber sheet and place it in a plastic laundry basket in his room. He can climb into the second set after changing his pajamas.

5. Another idea is to keep a sleeping bag handy. The child could take off his sheets, place them in the plastic laundry basket, change his pajamas, put the sleeping bag on the plastic mattress cover, and fall back to sleep.

6. Nonchalantly taking the laundry basket to wash the sheets should be done without words and without negative body language. The child should never be shamed for wetting his bed.

Let toilet learning be the child's task to master when he or she is ready.

Children's Books That Can Help Your Child with Toilet Learning

Going To the Potty by Fred Rogers. Putnam Juvenile, 1997.

Everyone Poops by Taro Gomi. Kane/Miller Book Publishers, 2001.

You Can Go to the Potty (Sears Children's Library) by William Sears, MD, Martha Sears, R.N., and Christie Watts Kelly. Little, Brown Young Readers, 2002.

Koko Bear's New Potty by Vicki Lanski. The Book Peddlers, 1997.

Toilet Learning by Alison Mack. Little, Brown Publishers, 1978.

All by Myself by Anne Grossnickle Hines. Houghton Mifflin Publishers, 1985.

12
Reading Right from the Start

The Joy of Reading

Discovering the joy and value of reading to a child is one of the pleasures of parenthood. Begin daily reading in early infancy. Reading encourages language development, encourages learning, and encourages a love of reading and books.

Holding the child on your lap and encircling her with your arms as you are reading gives reading a pleasurable association to the child. She associates books with being held lovingly. She is comforted by your gentle, melodic voice as you read.

Each new book brings new words and new experiences. Children who are encouraged to think and talk about the pictures, characters, and situations in books will become good readers. They learn how to hold a book, how to turn the pages, and that the marks on the page represent words. They learn the value of the written words and how to approach them.

The Types of Books to Share

Many kinds of books can be shared. Books with one picture on a page are wonderful. You can label the item and talk about the child's experiences with the item pictured: "That picture looks like your red wagon," or "That puppy looks like the puppy we saw

at the park." Colorful, realistic, and familiar objects engage the child's attention. Children are delighted to recognize a familiar object in a colorful illustration or photograph. Infants and toddlers particularly love books with photographs of babies' and toddlers' faces. Touch-and-feel books, and open-the-flap books engage participation. Babies and small children are delighted to touch and feel the textures or open the flaps to find things. *Pat the Bunny* by Dorothy Kunhardt (Golden Books, 2001) is an all time favorite touch-and-feel book. Lakeshore Learning (http://www.lakeshorelearning.com) has a great set of *Touch and Feel Discovery Books*. Encourage her to lift the flaps, peek behind doors, and peek into boxes. This will help your child develop small-muscle control and understand the concept of disappearance and reappearance. By repeatedly playing peek-a-boo games with the books, she will learn that objects that are temporarily out of sight still exist and can indeed reappear.

Finding objects on a page of many pictures introduces the idea of scanning the page for details, which is a prereading skill. Babies as young as 9 months can begin pointing to pictures. Ask, "Where is the cow?" At first you point to the object and your child will soon be able to point, too.

Usborne Books has a series of board books that encourage the child to find the puppy or duck on each page. Richard Scarry books have numerous pictures on the page; ask your child to find a particular person or thing and watch him develop scanning abilities. Usborne Books also has a set of books with things to spot on each page: *Things to Spot on the Farm* (Education Development Corporation, 1999), *Things to Spot in the Sea, Things to Spot in the City*, and so on. An extensive set of *I Spy* books, by Jean Marzollo and Walter Wick (Cartwheel Books), will also encourage your child to find things on the page.

Concept books are wonderful introductions to colors, numbers, size differences (big and small), or different groups of things, such as a book of kinds of animals or trucks. Choosing books that are of par-

ticular interest to the child can help get his attention. One little boy loved trains, and his mother searched for train books that he loved to "read." Books about everyday events that happen in your family, or about going places like the grocery store, the dentist or the park are interesting to children.

Books can teach children about their experiences and their feelings. Fred Rogers has a wonderful series of books to help children cope with new experiences. Mister Rogers' First Experience Books (Putnam Juvenile) include: *The New Baby, Moving, Going to the Hospital, Going on an Airplane, Going to the Potty, Going to the Doctor, Going to Day Care, Going to the Dentist, When a Pet Dies* and *Making Friends.*

Each book you read will introduce new words to your child. The larger your child's vocabulary, the easier he will learn to read. As discussed in the next chapter, Learning in the Preschool Years, the brain develops more connections as the child hears and sees familiar objects in the pictures in books; for example, she sees a picture of a cat in the book, and she recalls the cat basking on the neighbor's front porch that she saw this morning, or she thinks about the cat stuffed animal that she has in her room. Talking to her about what she sees in the book and relating it to personal experiences will reinforce her brain connections and help her learn. She is practicing her thinking skills.

I worked with the Even Start Program, a National Family Literacy Program sponsored by the Lucia Mar Unified School District and held in Oceano and Nipomo, California. The Hispanic parents were

learning English in the Adult School, and an important aspect of the program was called PACT—Parent and Child Together Time. Parents were taught the importance of reading to their children. Many of the children had never seen a book, nor were they talked to regularly. Miraculous development occurred when the parents began interacting in the learning centers with their children and reading to them every day.

I attended a National Literacy Conference and learned about the most engaging ways of reading to children: reading with enthusiasm, following the child's cues, and "picture walking." In the latter, parents are taught to talk about the pictures in the book by discussing what is happening in the pictures, what might happen next,

and what the characters might be feeling. Picture walking can be used in reading any picture book, especially when the text may be too difficult for your child. Many books are only pictures telling a story, which encourages picture walking.

Try to read with enthusiasm to engage the child's interest. Use your imagination. Change your facial expressions and use different voices for the different characters. Smile and ask, "Then what happens? How is the little bird feeling?" Do not hesitate to use your child's name in the book, substituting his name for the main character. He will love it!

Making story time a special part of every day is an important way of helping a child learn. Read at different times in the day, not just at bedtime. If your child does not want to go to bed, he may associate reading with something he does not like. Infants and toddlers like short, simple books that repeat the same words over and over, and children often like to read the same story many times. Ask them what will happen next before you turn the page.

Rhyming books are popular and fun. Rhymes encourage children to listen carefully to sounds. Read poetry to your child to nurture her love of words. Very young children respond to the music of poetry—its rhythm, meter, imagery, sound, and playfulness. Books with nonsensical words, like the Dr. Seuss series of books, also encourage children to listen to the sounds in words. It helps with their sound discrimination, which is an important prespeaking and prereading skill.

Children love sound effects—oink like a pig, quack like a duck, or neigh like a horse. Have sturdy, cardboard books that they can freely handle. Always keep books handy in the car, in the stroller, and in the diaper bag for those unexpected waits you encounter throughout your day.

Bring a basket of books home weekly from the library for variety. Keeping the library books only in one particular basket will help you easily find them when it is time to return them. Most libraries have enjoyable story times using big books and puppets. The Public Broadcasting System (http://www.pbs.org) has a wonderful computer learning center called "Between the Lions" for you and your child to explore together. (It is produced by the New York Public Library that has lion statues out front.)

Some toddlers are so eager to explore that they cannot sit still for a whole book. They want to jump off your lap and keep discovering. Try two or three short reading times for a few minutes each. Find a time when he may be more relaxed and attentive, such as bedtime or after a nap.

Another strategy for the curious, active toddler is to place an interesting picture on the wall and "picture walk" as the child passes by. Having a child touch or hold an object similar to the one in the story can help the story come alive. As he listens to *Corduroy* by Don Freeman (Viking Juvenile, 40th revision, 2008), he could hold a stuffed bear. As you read *The Very Hungry Caterpillar,* by Eric Carle (Philomel, 1994), gather real foods so that he could touch the different foods in the story. If your infant grabs at the book and tries to mouth it as you are reading, give him a toy or a vinyl book to keep his hands busy as you read.

As you have probably figured out, some fairy tales may need to be edited as you read them because they have scary parts. Substitute with gentler words or change the story line. Such books as *Bambi,* by Felix Salten may need to have whole parts skipped.

Follow Your Child's Cues

Follow your child's cues when you are reading to him. If he loses interest, stop. Never force a child to read with you; it must be a pleasurable time. To encourage the love of reading, a pleasurable association with books is important.

Develop Thinking Skills

As your child gets older, help her develop her thinking skills while reading. Ask who, what, when, why, where, and how questions to encourage her language and encourage her to use her reasoning abilities. You could ask, "How did the paint spill?" or "What is the mother doing?" You can leave off a word, and she will fill it in with enthusiasm.

Encourage her to join in repeating parts, such as the monkeys saying "Tzz Tzz Tzz" in *Caps for Sale* by Esphyr Slobodkina (Harper Festival, 2008). Ask open-ended questions about the pictures or the story, such as "What is the bunny doing in this picture?" Invite your child to notice the details in the pictures. Pick something small and ask her to find it. Notice a favorite or funny part and comment "That was funny, wasn't it?" or "What part did you like the best?" Wonder what might happen next by asking her or telling her what you might think will happen next. Help her to interact with the story.

Older children love reading chapter books with you. They eagerly anticipate what will happen in the next chapter. Do not give up reading aloud to your child after she learns to read; even teenagers can enjoy being read to. Sometimes parents and children alternate reading chapters to each other.

Literacy experts encourage you to move your fingers under the words to teach your child that the marks on the paper stand for words. The child also learns that we read from the top of the page to the bottom, and from left to right. Ask your child to tell you a story as you write his words down, and then read them back to him. Ask him to tell you about all the things he saw at the park or the farm or the zoo, and write his words down. Have him draw a picture that goes with his story, and he is on his way to writing his own stories. What a wonderful way to learn that the marks on the paper stand for words!

Be a role model for your child. Set aside a reading time to allow her to read her books and you read your books. Let her see *you* enjoying reading!

13
Learning in the Preschool Years

The Brain: A Work in Progress

There are many simple, everyday ways to influence how a child's brain develops in the first 5 years of life. Brain connections grow at an amazing rate in the first years reflecting the learning that is happening.

Newsweek Special Issue had an excellent article entitled "How to Build a Baby's Brain," by Sharon Begley; it said that at birth the brain weighs a pound; by age 1, it has doubled in size, and it reaches 90 percent of adult size—3 pounds—by age 4. The number of cells does not increase; it is the weight of the connections that add weight to the brain.

An infant is born with 100 billion brain cells called *neurons*. These 100 billion neurons form 50 trillion connections at birth. In the first few months, the number of connections will increase twentyfold, to 1000 trillion.

At one end of each cell are dendrites that look like fingers or branches on a tree limb. At birth there are only a few dendrites or branches on each cell. With experiences using the senses of touch, hearing, smelling, tasting, and seeing, more dendrites rapidly develop. With more dendrites or branches, more connections are possible between cells.

In other words, enriching experiences cause more connections between cells. Every time your child touches, sees, hears, tastes, or smells something, messages are sent to her brain, and a connection is made. At birth the only part of the brain that is fully functional is the brain stem, which regulates breathing and the heart beating. Genes determine the basic wiring that is in place. Early childhood experiences make the connections between brain cells; brain

scans show that the young child's brain consumes twice as much energy as an adult brain because of the furious pace of making connections.

Reinforcing Connections

With repeated experiences, the connections are reinforced. These connections, called *synapses* grow stronger with learning. They will disappear when not used; they are "pruned away." Just as a memory will fade if not thought about from time to time, so will the synaptic connections if not used.

In an infant/toddler brain, synapses form at a rate of thousands a second. By 8 months of life, there are 1,000 trillion connections. These gradually begin to decline after this time, which leaves 500 trillion that last most of life.

These numbers are difficult to grasp. To visualize this, think of a wheat field where one person has made a path by walking through it. If the path is never taken again, the wheat will likely recover, stand back up, and the path will be gone. If many people also walk on the path, it becomes worn and easily recognizable. This metaphor illustrates what happens in the brain.

If the child experiences something once, a wispy connection is made. If he never experiences it again, it is likely that the connection will be "pruned away" and will disappear. If he experiences the same thing again and again, a well-worn path will develop and a firm connection is made. For example, if a child sees an actual elephant, his brain makes connections for "elephant." If he never sees an elephant again, that

connection will prune away. If he sees a picture of an elephant in a book, he will connect that with his idea of the actual elephant. If he has an elephant toy, he will begin to make firm the connections associated with "elephant."

This explanation supports the early childhood educators' encouragement to read the same books from day to day and to repeat experiences. It also may explain why children often ask you to read their favorite books over and over. These early synaptic connections form the *foundations* for thinking, language, vision, attitudes, aptitudes, and other characteristics. Most of the architecture of the brain is completed in the first years of life.

All the experiences your child has will increase the connections and add to his thinking skills, or cognitive growth, and knowledge. All the time you spend with your child, interacting and offering experiences, helps build his brain. For example, if you read a story about a goat and then on another day, you take him to see a goat at a farm, a deeper or well-worn connection will be made. He will begin to be able to picture a goat when he hears the word or sees a picture. All this happens even before he has spoken a word or is able to make the sound of a goat.

Playing Builds Connections

Play develops thinking skills: recalling experiences, figuring out how to replay them, and solving problems. It develops social skills as children work together and share ideas.

Play is the work of childhood. As a child plays, she makes brain connections about what she is handling: "Does this match something I touched before? Is it smooth or bumpy? Is it soft or hard? Does it smell like anything I smelled before? Oh, this round bead looks like the shape of my ball!" With each discovery, she is categorizing, and trying to compare this new thing to past experiences. What a miracle the brain is!

Playing improves large- and small-muscle coordination, hand–eye coordination, and the ability to make choices and decisions. Play encourages language development and fosters the ability to express feelings, ideas, imagination, and creativity.

Play teaches the concepts of size, shape, color, and texture. Children do not need fancy or expensive toys: The home provides many things to touch and feel with different textures, and many smells. Perhaps

you will now have a greater understanding of the "yes" environment, as described in Chapter 8: Creating a "Yes" Environment, which allows the child to touch and feel freely without frequent "no's." You do not want to say no to the child's learning.

Touching, feeling, and handling various toys and manipulatives—puzzles, matching games, pegs, or beads—will also encourage connections to be made. Your child will practice hand and finger control, learn how to handle new materials, and practice problem solving. Offering a variety of things to play with is important. The home has a wealth of things to play with or things that can be easily made.

The Benefits of Music

New brain research shows the benefits of playing music for young children to encourage brain connections. Music affects spatial-temporal reasoning that underlies math and engineering. An example of spatial-temporal reasoning would be the ability needed to see a disassembled picture of an object, such as a kitten, and mentally piece it back together.

Classical music seems to have the most effect; the child begins to hear patterns. Learning to play a musical instrument, particularly piano, seems to make the connections that encourage better math skills and understanding later.

Singing songs together prepares your child's brain for listening and speaking. Your toddler will sway, bounce, and clap as she enjoys the music. Make up songs about what you are doing each day. As you sing familiar songs, use her name in the songs: "Little Miss Jocelyn sat on a tuffet" Find things around the house that she can make music with: pots and pans, a wooden spoon, an oatmeal box, or her xylophone. Make music together!

Memory and Learning

It is interesting to note that learning researchers have found that there is a working memory and a long-term memory. Through testing they have found that things are held in our working memory 18 seconds. Whether something goes into our long-term memory is determined by whether the brain can find some related previous experience or learning to attach it to.

Attention to and engagement in the things to be learned are necessary for learning to take place. Novelty, meaning and emotion are factors that influence whether a child is paying attention and therefore able to learn. Is the new experience meaningful? The brain is constantly attempting to make sense out of its world. It attempts to determine what is meaningful in its experiences. Every encounter with something new requires the brain to fit the new information into an existing memory category or network of neurons. If it cannot, the information will have no meaning; with meaning, it is more likely to be stored in long term memory.

As future experiences occur that are related, the long-term memory will be reinforced. It may be pruned away if it is not accessed. That is why we cannot easily recall many of the facts we learned in our high school classes. As your children are having new experiences, try to "hook it" to past experiences. Recall other encounters they may have had with this information. For example, you see a red cardinal and comment, "It is the color red just like your wagon" or "It is a bird, too, like the brown bird eating at our birdfeeder this morning."

Our brains are working all the time in our subconscious. They may be processing stressful thoughts, reactions, and emotions we are not consciously aware of. If we are trying to remember something and cannot, our brain works on it when we are not aware, and the item will pop up, and we will remember it later.

It is said that if we think of a concern or problem during the day, sometimes our brain will work on it all night and you wake up with a creative solution in mind. Positive thinkers believe it is important to think about the good things that happened to you that day before retiring, so your brain is focused on those things as you sleep.

The Emotional Hook

Think of your earliest memories. Most likely they are imbedded with emotion. When emotions are high, we remember better. Learning in an emotional context seems to stimulate connections more powerfully than information alone.

Being enthusiastic about your child's discoveries and experiences can help her learning. Smiling broadly and showing interest with enthusiasm will "hook" the child's interest and encourage learning. Playfully act out what you see, or ask the

child to picture in his head the last time you saw something. "Can you picture in your head how the other bird looked that we saw this morning?"

Teachers have found that singing a jingle will help children remember better. How many jingles do you sing to help you remember? "30 days has September, April, June—" New songs have been developed to help children learn the sounds of the letters.

The brain loves music, acting, and stories. These can be used to help a child learn, because they use more parts of the brain and connect the new information to several sets of neural pathways.

Who, What, Why, and Where

Children who discuss the most learn the most. Talk about what you saw or what you did. Ask who, what, why, and where questions. "What is the elephant eating?" "Where is the elephant's nose?" "What can he do with his nose?" "What other animal has a long nose?" Discussing will help the information become connected to other learning.

Learning Another Language

If you or someone who spends time with your child speaks another language fluently, I encourage you to speak that language with the child. Researchers have found, with the help of brain topography scans, that language is learned in the early years in the language center of the brain. After puberty, a new language is learned in the cognitive part of the brain, and learning is much more difficult.

Have you ever wondered how Europeans speak multiple languages? Most likely, they learned two languages simultaneously from birth. Neurons are available at birth for registering the sounds in other languages. They are activated when the other sounds are heard; if never used, they will be pruned away.

It works very well for one parent to speak one language and the other parent to speak another language. I have had several parents in my classes use this approach. Speech pathologists say that the words may be scrambled in early sentences. For example, a child may intersperse a Spanish word in an otherwise English sentence. They say

that by age 3, the child will be able to sort it out.

One mother told me that her 3-year-old began to translate for her. His father would speak in English, and the child would translate it into Spanish for his mother! Ideally the language will be used throughout life. Spanish, French, or Italian caregivers or grandmothers can give a lasting gift to your child. For this to be effective, the person must be fluent in the language. Many schools are teaching languages in the early grades.

The Value of Pretending

When your child begins to make believe, it is a very important step in her learning. A child who can pretend play is able to hold a picture of something in her mind. She is remembering different experiences she has had in order to take on a pretend role.

In pretending, she is beginning abstract thinking. Abstract thinking is needed for learning to read and do math. *Encourage her pretending.* If she pretends she is a puppy, ask her what her name is, if she would like a drink of water, and if she lives with you. Make pretend cookies, offer her one, and pretend to eat it. Pretend to be a doctor and ask her how her tummy is feeling or listen to her heart. Pretend to be a waiter and ask what she would like for lunch. Pretend you are driving a bus and ask her if she would like a ride. Be creative!

Art Experiences

Art experiences are another way to express ideas and feelings. Art gives rich, sensory experiences through touching and feeling various art materials. Connections are being made in the brain each time a child makes a mark on an easel with paint, finger paints, glues, or pokes and squeezes play dough. The experience with the materials is the valuable learning experience, not the end product.

The act of creating is important. Give her materials and let her create. Let her learn to explore and make decisions on her own. Restrain yourself from saying, "Oh, no. The eyes are supposed to go here." Art builds thinking skills. The paint on the brush makes a mark: she is learning cause and effect, not to mention perfecting small motor skills.

Art is a way to practice problem solving: "What shall I make?" or "What color shall I use first?" When children make marks with crayons or markers, they are learning prewriting skills and practicing using fine motor skills.

Scribbling is the first stage of writing. Nearing 3 years old, your child will begin to make more deliberate marks that begin to look like symbols: a short line, a small circle, a half-moon shape. As you show them, they will try to make letters.

In our parent participation classes, the parents are encouraged to let even the youngest child experience the art. Sometimes the child will make one mark on the easel paper or one swipe with the paint roller. Even one mark will send messages to the brain, enrich their experiences, and build connections.

Everyday Learning

With all these ways of building connections in the brain, you are helping the child build the organizing framework for later learning. Lots of prelanguage, prewriting, and

prereading skills are perfected in the first 3 years. The more connections that are made as the brain is growing, the more your child will be able to learn in the future.

The Carl Reiner Foundation's Early Childhood Initiative's phrase is "First Years Last Forever." It lets us know that if a child does not have enriching experiences in the first 5 years of life, the window of opportunity may be closed. Scientists call these "windows of opportunity" *sensitive times,* in which the connections are more easily made. In my work with Even Start, a federally funded early literacy program, I encountered 2- and 3-year-old children who had never seen a book or a puzzle and had no idea how to make marks with a crayon. The program provided experiences for the children and also worked with the parents. Parents had PACT time—parent and child together time—to model for the parents and teach them opportunities for encouraging learning in daily life.

Head Start Programs have enriched the experiences of untold numbers of preschoolers, helping their brains be ready to learn once they enter Kindergarten. The First Five Commission encourages preschool for all with its commercials on how attending preschool can impact the rest of a child's life. There are also many effective public service announcements encouraging parents to play with preschoolers. It can make a significant contribution for the rest of their lives.

Building thinking skills and learning can occur in daily activities throughout the child's day. Here are some specific examples:

► Sorting socks by size or color as you are folding clothes can be a learning opportunity.

► Comparing your shirts with their shirts can be a lesson in size comparison. Have them sort the clothes by type with all the pants in one pile, all the shirts in another, and all the socks in another.

► Count the items of clothing. It is important for your child to learn the one-to-one correspondence to numbers. Many children can count by rote but have no idea what each number represents. Point to items as you count them. As they get older, have them point to objects as they are counted.

► Gathering several pairs of shoes in a pile can be a matching game and could lead to a size comparison game. Have her match the pairs and talk about small, medium, and large shoes. Hold one shoe and ask her to give you one that is different to learn the concepts of same and different.

► Making sandwiches can be a learning opportunity: "How many pieces of bread are needed?" "What will we need to make the sandwich?" Enhance her vocabulary by using words to describe what you are doing: spreading, cutting, and so on. Talk about the sequence of making a sandwich. "What do we do first, next, and last?" Even a shape lesson evolves as you talk about the square of the bread being cut into triangles or rectangles or little squares. "How many corners do we have?" "How many pieces do we have after we cut it?"

▶ The concepts of full and empty can be learned when pouring his juice into a glass. You could ask, "What else can we put in a glass?" Put glasses in a row: one different glass and the rest the same. Ask which one is different. Ask how it is different.

▶ Cooking offers multiple opportunities to learn new concepts, such as pouring, kneading, measuring, and so on. As you measure, he is learning math skills. Give him opportunities to make choices.

▶ Gather pots with lids and mix them up. Ask the child to find the lid that fits each pot. Talk about the biggest, the smallest, and the middle-sized ones.

▶ Discussing things that go together encourages thinking skills. Gather things that go together: crayon and paper, a sock and a shoe, toothpaste and toothbrush, a comb and a brush, a quarter and a penny, a water bottle and a cup. Mix them up and have the child find the pairs. What a vocabulary lesson! Discuss how they go together.

▶ You can play a word game. I am thinking of something I use in the kitchen. Keep giving hints until the child guesses.

▶ Play Pick-a-Number and then give clues (higher or lower).

▶ Hide-and-seek can be played with objects. Hide the object in the room and give hints as to where to find it until it is found. "It is close to somewhere you sit." This has the side benefit of helping the child learn to follow directions.

▶ A walk outdoors can be enriched by noticing and commenting on the things you see. Build vocabulary by pointing out new words like *curb, fire hydrant, dandelion* and *squirrel.* Compare sizes of trees, bushes, houses, and cars. Talk about the colors you see on cars, shutters, and houses. Have him draw a picture of something you saw when you get home.

▶ Ask your child to find something that starts with the letter "A"; point to it or draw it. Ask your child to find something red or draw things that are red, blue, or yellow.

▶ Hands and feet can be traced. Compare the sizes of your hands and feet to her hands and feet. Spend a day talking about all the things that hands can do and another day talking about all the things that feet can do. Count the fingers and toes. Talk about fingernails and knuckles and name the different fingers.

▶ Label all the parts of the body including the more difficult parts, like cheeks, eyebrows, forehead, knees, ankles, and so on. Ask, "Where is your nose? Chin?" Encourage the child to point to the part. If they cannot, you point to and touch the part. Play "What is it?" by giving clues of the part you are thinking of,

such as, "I am thinking of something you use for seeing."

▶ As you ride around in the car, talk about where you are going and what you will do there. Comment on the things that you see as you drive along, such as houses, a fire station, the grocery store, or a bus. Draw attention to the sounds you hear: a fire engine, a plane, or a horn. As you return home, talk about all the things you did together.

Homemade Learning Games

Following are easy directions for making homemade learning games:

▶ Size, shape, and color matching games—Use varying colors of construction paper to make circles, squares, triangles, and rectangles in each color. Make each shape in three sizes: big, little, and medium. The possibilities are endless!

Match the shapes by color—"Place all the blue circles here."

Match the shapes by shape—"Put all the squares in a pile here."

Identify shapes by size—"Give me the biggest yellow square." "Show me the littlest one."

Mix things up—"Find the red triangles. Which triangle is the biggest? Littlest?"

At first, make one color of each shape. Progress to one shape in each of the different sizes. As she understands the concepts, increase the sets of shapes and colors in different sizes.

▶ Give her the blue square and go on a scavenger hunt with her to find all the blue things in the house. Repeat with the other colors on other days.

▶ Involve your child in painting cylinders to compare small, medium and large heights. Use paper towel or toilet paper cardboard rolls and cut them at different heights. Painting them to have a yellow set, a green set, and a red set can add a sorting dimension.

▶ The Outline Game—Collect a few objects from around the house—such as a wooden spoon, a toy zebra, a jar lid, a comb—and trace them onto a piece of construction paper. Voila! You have a puzzle. Mix the objects up, and ask your child to place each object on its outline. Keep the pieces together to play with again and again.

▶ A variation of the outline game could be to trace puzzle pieces on paper and ask the child to place each puzzle piece on its outline.

▶ String games can be fun and are great for increasing perception and improving thinking skills. Cut a 12-inch piece of yarn. On several pieces of paper, draw different lines that the yarn can be matched to. Begin simply and make the designs more intricate as the child perfects the skill of laying the yarn on the drawn line.

▶ A variation of the string game can be to cut a 3-foot length of string and lay it on the floor in a simple design.

Give your child his own 3-foot piece to copy your design; then ask him to lay his string in a design and you match it. Take turns laying out a 6-foot string in a design to walk along.

▶ A string could be used to trace around the shapes you make or to trace letters. Shapes and letters can be traced in a tray of sand also. Using the sense of touch will enhance your child's learning.

▶ What Is Missing? is a fun, lively memory game to play. Gather household objects such as a spoon, a pair of sunglasses, a small toy, a crayon, or anything you wish; have your child help you choose the objects. Spread them on a tray, ask her to remember them, then cover them with a dishtowel. While your child hides her eyes, whisk one object away. Take the cover off of the tray with enthusiasm and ask eagerly if she can tell you which object is missing. You begin with two or three items and work up to several. Naming all the objects will build her vocabulary. Vary the objects and have fun!

▶ What's in the Bag? is another game that challenges a child's thinking skills. Secretly place any object in the bag. Ask the child to name the object just by feeling it. A variation would be to hide something in the bag and give hints about the object as the child guesses what is hiding in the bag. Another variation is to place many things in the bag and tell them to pull out a certain object, such as a spoon.

▶ To teach the concept of wet and dry, have your child touch a wet sponge and a dry sponge or a wet washcloth and a dry washcloth. You could put one wet or dry item in a bag and have your child reach in and tell you whether it is wet or dry.

▶ To encourage sound discrimination, place rocks, buttons, and sand respectively in coffee cans with lids taped shut and talk about loud, medium, and soft sounds. Then have your child shake the cans and tell you which are loud, medium, and soft sounds. You could make a second set of identical sound cans and ask your child to match the sounds.

▶ To stimulate the sense of smell, you could place different items with distinctive smells each in a separate bag and ask your child to smell the contents and identify the objects. You could try bananas, lemons, oranges, pine needles, apples, and so on.

▶ Explore taste by giving an assortment of things to taste to experience sweet, sour, and other flavors.

▶ You could teach your child the concept of "sticky" by cutting a marshmallow in half or using a piece of tape, sticky side up, and having her touch it.

▶ There are many opportunities for sorting in the home. Use buttons to talk about colors, size and shape (discount stores have bags of assorted buttons in the craft section). You could use an egg carton to sort buttons that are alike. Nuts and bolts can be sorted—of course close supervision is necessary with small objects. Go on a rock hunt and collect rocks in a container. When you come home, spread the rocks out and discuss the size comparison—big, little, or medium-sized—and compare the textures using descriptive words, such as smooth, or rough. Make piles to categorize them. Use your imagination!

► For a sequencing game, use any objects: colored beads, colored blocks, even silverware. At first arrange three items and ask the child to copy your design. For example, place a green bead, a red bead, and another green bead in a row. Give your child several beads to chose from and have her arrange them to match your sequence. Gradually increase the number of objects to place in a sequence. There are several commercially made sequencing games from catalogs: try Lakeshore Learning (http://www.lakeshorelearning.com) or Discount School Supply (http://www.discountschoolsupply.com). Learning to sequence is an important prereading skill. Older 2- and 3-year-olds will be able to begin sequencing.

Your role as your child's first teacher is to create opportunities for your child. Each time you play and interact with your child, you are impacting her future. You are using the windows of opportunity to structure her brain's framework. How important all those hours of playing over those first five years can be for your child's future ability to learn and succeed!

14
Your Child's Safety

A safe environment allows children to touch, feel, experiment, and discover freely without harming themselves. To safeguard a child's safety first and foremost, you and anyone who takes care of your child should take an Infant and Child CPR class and a First-Aid class (available through the American Red Cross). With this knowledge, you can take better care of your child when he or she is hurt, chokes, or stops breathing. This chapter supplements that knowledge, to make you aware of safety hazards for children. *Accidents are the leading cause of death in children. More children die from accidents than from the next five leading causes of death.*

Conditions Leading to Accidents

Boston Children's Hospital did a study concerning when accidents are most likely to occur, published in the *Accident Handbook: A New Approach to Children's Safety.*♦ They had parents complete a questionnaire when their children were brought to the emergency room for an injury. The study found that most accidents are triggered by a chain of events, not by a single event. The conditions the study found that most often precipitate accidents involving children are:

- ▶ The child is hungry or tired.

- ▶ A safe place to play is not available.

- ▶ The mother is sick, about to have her period, or pregnant.

- ▶ Hazards are accessible to the child, such as medications, sharp scissors, knives, or a busy street.

- ▶ There is tension between parents.

- ▶ Parents think the child is hyperactive.

- ▶ A child's surroundings have changed, such as during vacations or moving.

- ▶ Other family members are sick, taking attention away from the child.

- ▶ The family is rushed, especially on Saturdays.

- ▶ The child is in the care of an unfamiliar person or someone too young to recognize dangers.

- ▶ Parents are not foreseeing what to expect next in the child's development.

Two or three of these conditions occurring together greatly increases the chances of an accident occurring. Slow down and be more watchful when you feel stressed or anyone in the family is sick. Anticipate your child's next step in growth and development

151

and childproof accordingly. No matter how much you think your child will not run in the street because you have repeatedly told him about the dangers, he may unwittingly run in the street after a favorite ball or a kitten. You cannot assume that your child has learned all the safety rules and will abide by them.

Infant Safety

Infant safety guidelines include always putting your infant to sleep on his or her back. Studies show that this practice greatly reduces the rate of Sudden Infant Death Syndrome (SIDS). It is also recommended to avoid having anything soft in the child's crib, such as pillows and stuffed animals, for fear that they may block the child's breathing. Do not take your hand off the child on a changing table. Do not place the infant seat on counters, tables, or any high places: a sudden movement will cause the baby to fall. Reflexive movements, such as the Morro reflex—when an infant throws both arms wide as if startled—can cause a child to fall off high surfaces even when she cannot turn over yet.

Formula or breast milk should not be heated in the microwave, because it could have hot spots and scald the baby's mouth and throat (microwaving also alters the nutrients). Baby food warmed in the microwave needs to be stirred and temperature tested before serving.

Safety Tips for the Mobile Child

When your child becomes mobile, many other safety precautions need to be taken. Gates must be placed at the top and bottom

of the stairs. The top gate must be the type that fastens with hardware in case the child falls against the gate. A pressure gate can be used at the bottom of the stairs. Be aware of the following safety guidelines to keep your child safe in every room. This list is by no means all inclusive.

► Keep medications locked up, even iron tablets and vitamins. A climbing child can reach the medicine cabinet. Do not store medications there unless you install a lock.

► Look for toxic substances—nail polish remover, after-shave lotions, colognes, mouthwashes, and perfumes—and place out of reach. Keep alcoholic beverages out of reach. Sunscreen lotions can be toxic and food extracts and kitty litter are potentially poisonous.

▶ Keep aerosol cans containing deodor-ants, hair spray, insecticide, and so on, out of reach.

▶ Cleaning fluids and disinfectants must be kept out of reach, even scouring pow-ders. The plastic cabinet latches cannot be trusted for toxic substances, because you do not know when your child will be able to figure them out. Place toxic substances in a high, unreachable—preferably locked—cabinet.

▶ Drano and other drain cleaners are so caustic that they can burn through the esophagus, the tube between the mouth and the stomach. If you must use such a product, use it immediately after buying it and discard any leftover. Do not keep them stored anywhere. I remember one toddler at Children's Hospital of Los Angeles who had gotten into Drano crystals, resulting in third-degree burn "dots" all over his body.

▶ Be aware that dishwasher detergents can cause severe mouth burns. The dispens-ers in the dishwasher door are at the perfect height for little fingers. When filling the dispenser, be sure your child is across the room and close the dish-washer right away.

▶ Use back burners and turn pot handles in toward the back of the stove so that a child cannot pull the handle and dump the hot contents on himself.

▶ Be aware that children hide in ovens; the child could have turned the knob to "on" before he got in. One mother pan-icked when she could not find her child for 5 minutes. He was hiding inside the oven! Velcro oven locks are available. Front loading washer and dryers pose the same risk.

▶ Most stove handles can be removed and placed in a high cabinet. They can easily be replaced to turn on the burner and immediately removed again. Several of the safety catalogs have knob covers and Lucite barriers that protect the stovetop from little fingers reaching up.

▶ Do not place hot liquids, such as soup or coffee, within reach on a table. One little boy received a third-degree burn on his entire arm when he pulled hot soup down off the table. It is best not to use tablecloths that children can pull on. *And do not drink hot liquids while holding your child.* He may reach up and grab the cup or accidentally knock the cup and spill the hot liquid on himself.

▶ Never leave a bucket of liquid unat-tended, even for a minute. Children have drowned in buckets.

▶ Keep foods that can be choked on out of reach. Such foods include nuts, corn, peas, dried beans, grapes, blueberries, or hot dogs. Grapes need to be cut and blueberries and peas need to be pierced with a fork before serving.

▶ Plug all electrical outlets to prevent chil-dren from sticking things in the holes and electrocuting themselves. Many children figure out how to take the caps off the outlets. There are safety devices that cover the entire outlet if plugs need to be plugged in and also outlet covers that are easy to install that require a two-step process to plug something in (either a sliding motion or a twisting motion).

▶ Keep knives, pointed scissors, needles, pins, tacks, and matches out of the reach of children. Older children's toys with small pieces must be kept out of reach.

▶ Floor lamps, especially the ones with attached tables, can easily be pulled over on top of a child who is using them to pull up to stand. Loan them to a friend until your child is older.

▶ Another item to loan to a friend is a glass coffee table or a coffee table with sharp corners and edges. Coffee tables are at the perfect height for children to fall against or bang toys on. The glass could break and cause a severe injury.

▶ The corners and edges on tables can cause lacerations. You can buy corner guards and edge guards.

▶ Beware that recliner chairs can pinch fingers or even trap bodies.

▶ There are hearth guards as well. Place them, or a heavy quilt, over the edge of the hearth. Fireplace screens need to be secured. Hearth gates are also available.

▶ Use a harness in the high chair and in shopping carts. They have ones that look like a vest and zip up the back. There are side hooks that attach to the sides of the cart or high chair. Harnesses keep your child from wriggling out of a lap belt, standing up, and subsequently falling on her head. Severe head injuries have occurred when children have fallen out of shopping carts or high chairs. The same harness can be used if your child tries to wriggle out of his stroller.

▶ Precautions for avoiding scalding burns from hot tap water include always testing the bath water with your wrist or elbow before placing your child in the tub, and turning the hot water heater temperature down to 120 to 130 degrees. Never leave a child alone in the tub or even in the bathroom, because he could turn on the hot water faucet and burn himself. Place a soft guard on the tub faucet to avoid bumped heads and burned fingers. Reduce falls on a slippery tub bottom by adding nonskid grips or safety strips. Use a nonskid bath mat outside the tub.

▶ Even when turned off, hair dryers, electric shavers, and curling irons can cause a severe electric shock if dropped in water. Keep them unplugged and out of reach.

▶ The bathroom poses a drowning hazard. Never leave your child alone in the bathtub for even a *second*. If you have to answer the phone or door, wrap her in a towel and take her with you. Children have drowned in toilets. They lean over to reach in or retrieve a toy, and their heavy heads tip them into the toilet head first. A safety clip to secure the toilet lid is a good idea. Lock the bathroom door to keep it off bounds; you could use a doorknob cover or a hook-and-eye lock placed high out of reach.

► Use unbreakable glasses, even for yourself. Your child often will ask for a sip or drink from a glass left around.

► The safest homes have no guns. If guns must be stored, store them unloaded, locked up, safety on, with ammo locked up separately.

► Watch for any dangling cords from small appliances or dangling plants that could be pulled over.

► VCR and DVD guards are also available to safely block the openings.

► Watch for frayed parts of an electrical cord. It will attract a toddler's attention. Keep all cords out of reach. Place cords behind heavy furniture or use a device that will allow you to coil the cord around it (cord shorteners).

► Cords hanging from blinds can be very dangerous. Use devices that secure the long cord in an encasement high up out of reach. Newer blinds have short cords or the cords are attached to the wall with hardware.

► If possible, open windows from the top down. Even screens in good condition are not made to prevent falls from windows. Perhaps you could use a locking device that allows the window to open only a few inches.

► Keep your handbag and those of visitors out of reach. They could contain medications, nail files, make-up, matches, and other dangers.

► Keep plastic bags out of reach, including dry cleaner plastic bags. Beware of plastic bags in garbage cans that are in reach. When discarding plastic bags, tie them in knots.

► The railings on balconies, decks, and banisters can also be hazardous. Slats should be no more than 4 inches apart to prevent a child from falling through or getting his head stuck. Lucite railing covers and attachable netting are available to cover the openings.

► Walkers are not recommended, even the newer ones with gripping mechanisms. The babies are often stronger than the mechanisms, and falls in walkers can be serious.

► Door-jam hanging jumping seats are not recommended. Babies can get themselves jumping very fast and hard. They can bang the sides of the doorway, and the impact may not be healthy for their developing spines. It has been hypothesized that the brain may also bang against the skull as the baby jumps, which could cause brain bruises. Tossing a baby up in the air could also cause similar damage.

► Dressers and bookcases need to be secured to the wall so they cannot fall on top of a child using them to climb on. One child's thigh bone was broken when he climbed up his dresser and the dresser fell on him.

▶ Think garage safety also. Insecticides, paints, paint thinners, weed killers, gasoline, kerosene, and fertilizers need to be locked up or not stored (used and the remainder discarded). Power tools need to be out of reach. Insecticide spraying equipment could have a lethal dose on the equipment after use. Do not think that your child will never be in the garage; toddlers have been known to slip out of the house and curiously explore garages, yards, and neighborhoods.

▶ The garage refrigerator or freezer needs to have safety locks so children are not able to hide inside and suffocate. Discarded refrigerators or freezers need to have the doors removed before they are left out for garbage pick-up.

▶ Glass doors need to have decals on them to keep children from running into them.

▶ Make sure doors to the outside are safely locked in a way that your child cannot open. This may mean that you have to install a sliding bolt or hook-and-eye up out of the reach of your child.

Buckled Up

Never take your child out of his car seat when the car is in motion, not even for a second. On a long car trip, it is tempting to nurse the baby as you drive along, but don't do it. If an accident were to happen, you would never forgive yourself.

A child not in a car seat is a projectile in a collision. If you are holding her, the weight of your body will further propel her forward in a collision. One mother shared that they were at a party and her child was asleep in the back room. As she carried her out, she thought about just holding her on the way home. She decided against it and strapped her securely in her car seat. That night they were hit head on by a drunk driver on a mountain road. Her husband had nowhere to go to avoid the drunk driver driving down the centerline. Her husband and child were both killed. She asked me to tell the parents in my classes her story. She said she could not have lived with herself if she had not put her child in her car seat. She would have always believed that her child's death could have been avoided—and that it was her fault.

Fire Safety

Keep matches and lighters out of reach. Do not smoke in bed and be sure to dispose of butts, matches, and ashes carefully. Having your children wear flame retardant sleepwear is important. Check that the garment has been treated to comply with the United States Product Safety Commission's Flammability Standard.

It is important to make sure you have a working fire extinguisher and that you know how to use it. Smoke alarms outside bedrooms are imperative. Be sure to check the batteries twice a year; when we change to and from daylight savings time is a good way to remember. Carbon monoxide alarms are also good to have.

Every family should have an emergency escape plan. Teach children where to meet you if you are separated. Teach them not to hide in case the firemen need to come and find them. Teach them and yourself to crawl in case of a fire, because heat and smoke rises. Remember that smoke and hot gases are as dangerous as flames. Most deaths occur from suffocation due to hot fumes and smoke, not from direct burning.

Never open a door that is hot to the touch. Roll something in front of the crack under the door, and use your alternate escape route. Make sure each room has another way out, whether it is a garage roof or a chain ladder that hooks over the windowsill. Never leave small children in the house alone even for a minute. Conduct home fire drills. In the event of a fire, get everyone out of the house immediately; call the fire department from a neighbor's house.

Poison Prevention

Toddlers have the highest rate of poisonings each year—in the hundreds of thousands. They explore, touch, and put most things in their mouths. It is up to you to keep poisonous substances out of reach and locked up. Fortunately, the incidence of poisonings among children has reduced dramatically with the advent of the childproof caps on medications and cleaners. Do not rely on childproof caps, however, because many clever children have figured out how to open them. They are a deterrent but not a solution. Always buy products with childproof caps to add the deterrent, but realize you still have to lock up toxic substances.

Place the number for Poison Control next to all your phones. If your child ingests any substance, grab the container and call Poison Control. They will ask you to read the ingredients and estimate how much was ingested. They will give you clear directions as to how to proceed.

Ask your pediatrician beforehand what items to have on hand. It is a good idea to have your pediatrician's choice of Activated Charcoal or Syrup of Ipecac—both may be found in the first aid section of the pharmacy—on hand in case Poison Control directs you to give it. There will not be time to run to the pharmacy to buy it.

Never administer any remedy without Poison Control directing you to give it, because it may worsen the condition. The American Academy of Pediatrics states that Syrup of Ipecac can complicate the doctor's efforts to rid your child's body of the poisonous substance.

I recommend that you have a first-aid kit in the car for those trips to the park and visits to the homes of others. Keep the Poison Control number and the remedy suggested by your pediatrician in it. Many poisonings occur in someone else's house, one that is not childproofed.

To further poison-proof your home:

► Never call medicine "candy" to encourage your child to take it.

► Realize that many medications look like candy, such as M&Ms. Some capsules, like Contac, have colored beads inside that look like candy sprinkles.

► Some laxatives and rat poisons look like chocolate.

► Keep products in their original containers. Do not put poisonous substances in food containers. For example, do not put turpentine in a cut-off milk carton to clean paintbrushes. The paint from the brush will turn the turpentine the color of milk or a smoothie! One father put turpentine in a Coke bottle for a clean-up job, and his teenage son came behind him and took a gulp; it looked like Coke.

► Another reason to keep things in their original containers is that the ingredients are usually listed on the bottle. Poison Control will need to know the ingredients in order to give you directions if your child ingests the product.

► Do not take medications in front of your child; children love to imitate.

► Read the medication label two times before administering, and never give or take medication in the dark.

► Discard unused or outdated medications by flushing them down the toilet and rinsing the container before throwing it away.

► Be aware that many common plants are poisonous including oleander, lily of the valley, wisteria, laurels, rhododendrons, and azaleas. Acorns from oak trees, buttercup, mistletoe, and poinsettias are poisonous, as are many other plants. The United States Department of Agriculture Regional Extension has a list of the poisonous plants in your area.

► Install carbon monoxide detectors in your home and have your furnace serviced and checked at least annually.

Babysitter Safety

Entrusting your child to the care of a babysitter can be difficult. The best babysitters have had the First Aid and Infant and Child CPR classes. The YMCA and the Red Cross have Babysitter Safety classes and give certificates of completion. You will need to review the extensive list of safety precautions listed above with any babysitter you use.

The U.S. Consumer Product Safety Commission (800-638-CPSC [2772]) has a *Super Sitter* book that is excellent.

Be sure to leave a complete listing of phone numbers near the phone for the babysitter. Be sure to list the number where you will be in case your cell phone is out of range or out of power. Keep a permanent list by the phone that includes numbers for all of the following:

► Reminder Fire/Police/Ambulance 911

► Poison Control

► Your child's doctor with phone number and address

► Relative's phone numbers

► Work numbers

► Neighbors' phone numbers with their positions on the street (next door blue house, yellow house across the street, and so on)

▶ Write out the following for the sitter to read in an emergency:

"This is an emergency. I am at___ _____Street, between_____ and _____ streets, in _____ (town). I need help because_____. Please tell me what to do until help comes."

This is an excellent idea, because in an emergency, you or the sitter may temporarily forget the cross streets—and even the address.

Toy Safety

Selecting the right toy for the child's stage of development is very important. You must use discretion and not always go by the age listed on the box. For example, when a toy states that it is for children over 3 years old, it means it has small parts that could break off. If mouthed, the small parts could choke a child, so that toy would not be appropriate for a 3-year-old who still puts things in his mouth. Balloons have caused numerous suffocating deaths, because as a balloon pops and startles the child, the child will usually breathe in with an audible "Huh," sucking the balloon in to occlude the trachea (breathing tube).

Other toy safety precautions include:

▶ No sharp edges

▶ Beware of small parts

▶ No loud noises

▶ No long cords or strings

▶ No sharp points

▶ No propelled objects

Additional considerations: glass or button eyes on dolls or stuffed animals pose a choking hazard. Clumps of Raggedy Ann or Andy Doll's hair can be grabbed and choked on. Check any squeak toy for a separate squeaker inside that could be dislodged and choked on. A separate squeaker can be cut out with scissors, and the toy could still be valuable as a chew toy that does not squeak. Inexpensive rattles—like those used to decorate packages—can splinter easily when banged on a hard surface.

Open plastic bins are the safest way to store toys. If you use toy boxes or chests, they need to have ventilation holes for fresh air in case a child gets trapped inside. They also need lids that will stay open in any position to which it is raised, so it will not fall on a child. Check all toys periodically for breakage and potential hazards.

A curious child's world is one of innocence. They see objects not as hazards but as fun. We need to protect them as they explore their worlds.

Safety Resources

A Sigh of Relief, the First-aid Handbook for Childhood Emergencies, produced by Martin I. Green, Bantam Books, Inc., 1997.

Safer-Baby, The One-Stop Baby Proofing Shop; 800-356-0654

One Step Ahead Catalog at http://www. onestepahead.com; 800-274-8440

The Right Start Catalog at http://www.right-start.com; 800-548-8531

U.S. Consumer Product Safety Commission at http://www.cpsc.gov; 800-638-2772

The American Academy of Pediatrics, Division of Publications, 141 Northwest Point Blvd, P.O. Box 927, Elk Grove Village, IL 60009-0927; http://www.aap.org

National Safety Council, Child Safety Program, 444 N. Michigan Ave., Chicago, IL 60611; http://www.nsc.org

Toys to Grow On has a "No-Choke Testing Tube" at http://www.toystogrowon.com; 800-987-4454 (2695 E. Dominguez St., Carson, CA 90895).

15
Easing Separations: Hello and Goodbye

I hope this chapter will reassure you about the developmental nature of separation anxiety and give you new ideas, skills, and solutions to help ease separations. With understanding, you will be able to be more calm and in control when a separation occurs. Your child will look to you for your reaction and will be comforted if you are calm, smiling, and reassuring. If you are anxious and frowning, the child will pick up on your anxiety and her fear will be increased.

Your child's bereft crying, as if her heart is breaking, hurts you; yet it is important that you understand that it is her way of coping. Protest is her way of enduring separation. She is expressing her feelings, saying, "I will miss you!" She trusts you enough to show her feelings, and she is using a skill that has worked before.

Crying is her way of trying to get you to stay. It shows how strongly attached to you she is. One of the key pieces to helping her is to make sure she knows and trusts the person you are leaving her with. As her cognitive thinking skills grow, she will exhibit changing reactions to separation.

Separation Theory

For better understanding, I want to give you some theory about attachment and separation. Psychoanalyst Margaret S. Mahler, in her book *The Psychological Birth of the Human Infant*, laid down the "map of self-organization" that is used by psychologists today. It begins with three assumptions:

1. The child is *born as selfless*, with no sense of identity. The process of individuation, or gaining a sense of being an individual, occurs by 3 years of age. The child is "psychologically born into selfhood" by age 3.

2. Establishing a self is *done in the context of a relationship*.

3. *The interaction is reciprocal* with active participation on the part of the infant and the adult.

    Dr. Brazelton refers to this reciprocal interaction as the *rhythm of interaction*, a dance between parent and child. Parent and child are taking turns responding and initiating.

    Mahler says that the child has an inborn capacity to attach. Through evolution, the child innately knows that he has to attach to someone in order to survive; he "hooks" someone to fall in love with, and Mother and Father are poised for attachment.

With caring and sensitive responses from you, your child begins to engage you with a social smile and eye contact. With head control, your infant actively searches for you and learns turn-taking in interactions. A "rhythm of interaction" ensues with intimate looking, touching, hearing, speaking, and seeing. Mahler believes that the infant feels what she terms an "oceanic self" or feeling "one with mother." Your baby will mold herself next to you and feel like part of you. Mahler calls this "molding and melting" with mother. This is why infants like to be held and cuddled.

Your baby shares in your feelings of contentedness and oneness. Your baby feels the love, and she gets strength from it. This early attachment is the basis for later human relatedness, the ability to be friends and lovers later in life.

Mahler believed that between 3 and 6 months the child begins to associate mother with pleasure and stress reduction. The child develops a preferential smile and she begins to differentiate mother from others. Recent studies show that even a 4-day-old infant can differentiate her mother from others.

These reciprocal interactions lay the foundation of trust. Mahler defines trust as "the confident expectation that there will be an available caregiver to me," one who answers my needs with steady, dependable, loving care. The attachment message is that your child needs your emotional availability and responsiveness in order to thrive emotionally. Responsiveness is defined as being there for your child, sensitively attuned, consistently available, and seeking out opportunities to be close to her.

"Hatching" is the word Mahler uses to describe when the infant discovers that mother is a separate object—"the baby hatches out of the common membrane." He says to himself, "Aha! We are not in the same skin!" Hopefully, the infant will leave this feeling of oneness well-stocked with love, confidence, and trust. He realizes he is separate and needs you to take care of him.

Separation anxiety begins at this point, and your child will cry loudly if you go out of sight. He is not convinced yet that you still exist if you are out of sight. With increased experience and improved thinking skills, he will realize one day that you exist even when out of sight (this understanding is called "object permanence"). With increased cognitive growth and physical maturation, he begins to not want to be held so closely and prefers to face out toward the world.

Stranger anxiety appears now also, a sign of the strength of attachment. The child is so attached to the parents, a stranger causes anxiety.

Between 10 and 15 months, babies have a love affair with the world. Mahler calls this the *practicing stage*. Your child is upright, robust, and curious. She freely wanders off to see new and thrilling sights. She goes to the edge of her world to discover, practices coming and going, goes out to explore and comes back to sit on your lap for emotional refueling. Separateness is a physical reality, and she realizes she is vulnerable and needs care and protection. She may just look back to make sure you are there and continue exploring. She is checking in with her trust base. This checking in gives her a feeling of safety and keeps her connected. Language provides another way to stay connected over a distance.

A key to understanding separation is to understand what Mahler meant by "rapprochement." With increasing cognitive ability, a child of 16 months has a rude awakening. He suddenly realizes: "I am separate! I am out here, and now I realize that I cannot take care of myself. I want to go explore, but I am afraid. I need to hold on to Mommy. I am confused, angry, and sad. I want my autonomy, but I need Mommy too." Being less independent than the 10 to 15 month old, the child regresses to clinging to Mommy.

The mother or caregiver needs to be available and permit regression. Your child needs a period of reassurance, a refueling time, and a time to regroup. It is not unusual for a 16 to 24 month old to exhibit prolonged crying, intense rage, and uncontrollable sobbing upon separation. It is recommended not to begin child care or go on a vacation without them at this age if possible; separation or even suspected separation can be especially difficult. He may become inconsolable. With increasing cognitive skills, your child has a profound understanding of your very special importance to him and how much he relies on you. This knowledge increases his terror and panic when you leave.

Nancy Balaban, in her excellent book *Learning to Say Goodbye*, describes what a child might think upon separation: "I really know that you are my parent. I know that I need you to take care of me in all situations. I am afraid that if you leave me, I won't be able to take care of myself. It makes me angry that you want to go away like that, and I feel sad and hurt. So in order to not feel that way, I'm going to do what I know best to keep you here. I can cry. I can hold onto you. I can follow you. I can call you. These things ought to work, because they have worked before."

Mahler suggests being quietly available to the child experiencing rapprochement. Do not push him away and say, "You were able to play independently before, why can't you now?" Rather, be emotionally available and be empathetic. "I see that you want to hold me right now. I am here when you are ready to go and play with the other children." Be an anchor. Reassure him that you will not abandon him.

Two-year-olds want to be big and want to be babies; often these feelings clash in the same moment. They have been likened to mini-teenagers, with the similar task of autonomy, wanting to assert their independence with statements like "Me do it" or "No!" to everything you ask of them. The frequent "no's" are showing you how much they are trying to separate, to establish themselves as separate beings with thoughts, feelings, and wishes of their own. Chapter 3: Living with Your Toddler—Tips for Daily Life explores ways to handle this striving for independence.

Individuation

By 3 years of age, your child will feel like an individual able to take some care of himself. He is more cooperative and more interested in his peers and outside interests. He has the ability to reliably picture the person he is missing and is able to comfort himself. He is finished with his tumultuous twos and has completed the personality task of individuation; individuation means that your child sees himself as a separate self with positive feelings about himself and an inner reserve to cope. He has an enduring inner conviction of "being me and nobody else."

Gradually Encouraging Independence

You want to create a secure world for your child through the many hellos and goodbyes throughout his day. Playing peek-a-boo and hiding a toy are ways children learn that an object still exists even when they cannot see it. As mentioned, Jean Piaget calls this learning "object permanence." At first, a child thinks you have gone forever if you go out of sight. With repeated comings and goings, he begins to learn that you return.

Make an effort to tell him you are going before you leave his sight, and say you will be back. When you come back say, "I'm back!" Practice this coming and going when you go get a drink of water, when you run to the store, or when you head upstairs. These mini-separations will prepare him for the bigger ones; he sees that you come back each time, so he begins to relax when you are out of sight. With each goodbye, your child is becoming more competent in learning to

say goodbye. Going to sleep is an everyday goodbye. What are some others?

- ▶ Weaning from breast, bottle, or pacifier
- ▶ Outgrowing clothes
- ▶ When her crib is replaced by a "big-girl bed"
- ▶ When Daddy or Mommy goes off to work
- ▶ When a lovey is lost
- ▶ When the high chair is replaced by a booster seat
- ▶ When Grandma or cousins come to visit and then leave
- ▶ When a ball rolls under the couch
- ▶ When a squirrel scampers up a tree and out of sight
- ▶ When a parent goes on a business trip
- ▶ Going to school or child care
- ▶ Going to birthday parties and then leaving them
- ▶ Going to play at a friend's house then leaving to go home

Fears of Separation

Separation for all of us is a sadness at being away from the people you most love. Your child needs to begin to understand that he is okay if left for a few minutes. If he is never left with Daddy or someone else, he fears that he cannot exist without Mommy's presence. Children under 3 need support from adults when separations occur. The young child has not yet developed coping skills, such as language, or an understanding of time. The child worries that no one will take care of him, that he will not know how to get home, that he will not find his parents, or that his parents will not be able to find him—even if they dropped him off there.

Ways to Support Your Child During Separations

Remember that your child's crying is saying, "I will miss you!" Tell her that you will miss her, too. Ask the caregiver to reassure her that Mommy will be back. When you come back, say "I am back now. I missed you." Spend a few minutes to reconnect and for your child to refuel emotionally.

Your child needs to transfer trust to the new person who is with him, whether it be a babysitter or a nursery school teacher. He has trust in you—trust that you will take care of him. We need to help the child gain trust in the new person and to know in his heart that this new person will take good care of him.

A very effective way to facilitate this transfer of trust is to phase him in gently to the new place and to the new person. That means staying with him in the new setting for a time and conveying to him that you think this new person is very nice and dependable. You talking to and smiling at the new person confers your "stamp of safety." It says, "This person is someone you can trust. See how I trust her to take good care of you?" Allow the new person to talk and play with your child with you nearby. Let your child see that this new person can take care of him. This time also helps *you* develop trust in the new person.

One study found that if the new caregiver waited at a distance from the child without moving in too quickly, the child responded better than if the adult rushed in and picked up the child. It also found that the caregiver's use of a toy to make indirect contact with the child was better than touching or making direct eye contact. The child forms a relationship with the teacher first, then to the activities, and then to the other children.

Children are never too young to need this phasing-in. I remember one little 4-month-old named Heidi who cried for an entire 8-hour day, did not eat or have eye-contact with anyone on her first day in child care. She had no phase-in. She was frightened and did not trust these new people to take care of her.

We instituted a phase-in program to avoid what I called "The Heidi Syndrome." In our registration materials, the phase-in program was described: "In order to facilitate our philosophy of partnership between parent and caregiver in nurturing your child, we have developed a phase-in program which is part of our curriculum. The program as been developed to support your child in his/her transition to this new environment in order to foster trusting relationships between caregiver and child as well as caregiver and parent." The proposed schedule was as follows:

Day 1: Two hours in the classroom together

Day 2: One hour together and leave your child for one hour

Day 3: One hour together and leave your child for two hours

Day 4: Leave your child for two hours

Day 5: Regular day

Have you ever had the feeling, when embarking alone on a new adventure, that you would rather have had the company of a familiar person? Is it more comfortable for you to walk into a room full of strangers with another known person than by yourself? Your child feels the same way. Having your child learn to trust the caregiver is very important in easing the transition to a new environment.

Spending time with the new people in the new place with someone he trusts near him will help him begin to trust the new people and to feel safe. The same thing could be used for a new babysitter for you to go out in the evening. Have her come over a few days ahead of time and spend time together for your child to transfer trust. If the babysitter is familiar but has not sat for you for awhile, have her come over a half hour before you leave and spend time together.

Always be sure your child sees the babysitter before he goes to bed. It would frighten him to see an unexpected face if he were to wake up. Some parents tell me that their child never wakes up during the night once asleep, but that night could be an exception.

In addition to helping your child trust the new people and feel comfortable in the new place, here are several other ways to ease separations:

▶ It is important for the caregivers to talk about the parents during the separation for reassurance.

▶ Your child needs to pick up on your positive feelings about the goodness and safety of the new person and place.

▶ Your child needs to pick-up feelings of respect and friendliness between you and the caregiver/teacher.

▶ The caregiver needs to respect the child's feelings and be encouraged to say something like, "I know you miss your Mommy," or "You were sad yesterday and Mommy came back. She will be coming to get you after your nap."

▶ The child could bring in a special book from home to have read to them to encourage the home-school link.

▶ To further encourage the home-school link, your child could bring other home items to school. Most schools will allow a lovey, such as a blanket or a special teddy, but it needs to be kept in the cubby. Your child could go to the cubby and touch the blanket for comfort occasionally. Perhaps your child could decide together with the teacher when it will be blanket time (perhaps at naptime). Remember that the lovey has associations with you imbedded in it and can be a real source of comfort. However, carrying it around is not a good idea, because his hands need to be free to play and explore.

▶ You could read books to your child about going to child care as a teaching tool and also as a forum for talking about his feelings about going to child care. See the list at the end of this chapter.

▶ Make sure you say goodbye to maintain your child's trust. Never sneak away. Your child will be very upset that you disappeared and will worry that you will disappear the next time you are together. This may result in clingy behavior. Your child might think, "I better hold on to her so she won't sneak away again" or "I can't trust her not to disappear again."

▶ Have family pictures readily accessible for your child to look at. You can make up a little album to keep in her cubby. We put up large sheets of Plexiglas and placed family pictures behind them for easy access at the Princeton Family Resource Center's Child Care Centers. The children could go over and touch the pictures.

Sometimes seeing the pictures caused tears to flow. This is a good thing to have the feelings brought to the surface and have the child comforted and reassured that Mommy will be back. It is not healthy for the children to keep their feelings inside. Sometimes children keep their feelings inside and become what has been referred to as a "subdued child." This child looks forlorn and does not engage in the world around him. His face does not exhibit varied emotions but appears flat, without expression. If and when this happens, the parents need to spend more time in the center to help their child trust the new people.

The length of the day can be long for your child to be away from you. If your child is having difficulty, perhaps a lunch time visit would help. I remember one little girl who protested strongly when her parents left and remained sad and uninvolved. She was becoming a subdued child. I asked the parents to come at lunch. At first they protested, because she would cry heartbreakingly when they again left her at lunch. Yet after 3 weeks of lunchtime visits, she began to cope and became enthusiastic about the center's activities—and the lunch visits were no longer needed. During the lunch time visits, she was allowed to refuel emotionally and it helped her get through what seemed to her to be an interminable afternoon. In crying a second time at the parting after lunch, she was expressing her strong feelings instead of keeping them inside. With repeatedly seeing her parents, she knew they knew where she was and they conveyed their trust in the teachers, and therefore she began to trust them also.

Another preschool places a picture of the child and Mommy or Daddy taped to the inside of the cubby. It has two purposes: to identify the cubby and to keep the image of Mommy and Daddy alive. Studies have shown that young children, especially if they are stressed, have a difficult time conjuring up a picture of Mommy or Daddy in their minds. Having a picture readily available keeps the images present and the child reassured. Think about how you feel comforted by pictures of loved ones you are separated from. You look at the features and expressions and feel closer.

Toy telephones could be placed by the family pictures to encourage "conversations" with parents. You could tape a picture inside your child's lunchbox or put a picture in one of those Lucite key chains and hook it to a strap or belt loop so your picture is with her.

▶ Try to attend any special events that the school holds for parents, like a special lunch or music program. Seeing you at school helps your child feel that Mommy and Daddy are a part of the school, too.

▶ Ask the child's caregiver to invite your child to draw a picture and dictate an "I Miss You" letter to you.

▶ Establish a separation ritual. Just as a bedtime ritual eases a child into bed, a separation ritual when you leave him eases him into the time apart. Do the same separation ritual activities each day, so your child knows what to expect. For example, you could give two hugs, two kisses, and kisses in the palms for each pocket. The kisses for the pockets become a tangible connection to you in the child's mind.

One child was having a difficult time with separation when dropped off at nursery school. We talked about the importance of a ritual. The little girl did very well with the kiss for her pocket. Yet one day, her friend was sad and she gave away her mommy's kiss to comfort her. She then became inconsolable, and Mommy had to come back to replenish her supply of kisses! From then on I always recommend a kiss for each pocket in case one is given away.

Your child could also give you kisses for *your* pockets, and you could talk about using them during the day. Sometimes part of the ritual could be the teacher holding your child's hand for support or standing nearby for support. After a kiss and a hug, my grandson waves out the same window each time my daughter drops him off. She turns at the gate and waves again.

▶ Have your child visit your workplace so she can visualize where you are. When she visits, let her be the leaver and leave you there. Give her a picture of you at your workplace.

▶ Your child will be comforted if you leave an article of yours with her, such as a sweater, an old purse, or a set of old keys. Remember that one of her fears is that you will not know where to find her. For some inexplicable reason, she thinks you will return for your purse or keys and find her there, too.

▶ In addition to daily practicing of telling him you will be back and then upon returning, saying "I'm back," you could role-play the same scenario with a teddy bear or a doll. Encourage your child to say "Bye, Teddy. I will be back" and when he returns, encourage him to say "I'm back." Taking it a step further, the teddy bear could be placed in the car seat after you have taken your child out. Say "Goodbye Teddy. We will be back." Then say, "We are back!" when you return. This role-playing will encourage him to learn the concept of coming back.

▶ Play is your child's work. She can work through her feelings, and feel some control of the comings and goings, by playing in the housekeeping center, pretending to be Mommy and Daddy saying hello and goodbye. You could role-play at home and play through saying goodbye, or switch roles and let her tell you goodbye. Role-play scenarios of separation with puppets, too.

▶ Encourage special friendships by finding out the names of a couple of children that are going to be in your child's class and inviting them over to play ahead of time. He will already know someone when he gets there and will feel more comfortable. He may look forward to seeing his new friend at school.

▶ One very helpful strategy is to make a time line of the day: "A Day in the Life of Katie." You could use a poster or a strip of Velcro and put Velcro dots on the backs of photos that depict her day. Take pictures of getting ready for school, eating breakfast together, driving to school, saying goodbye at school, her playing at school, you at your workplace or doing a chore at home, her taking a nap (if that is done at school), and then your reunion at school, you driving her home, and all of you at dinner together. "Read" her the story each morning so she knows what to expect. The biggest value is that she will see you all together at the end of the day in the picture and be reassured. Alternately, you could use a little photograph album with one picture on a page to tell the story. The ease of the Velcro buttons or the little album allows you to change the pictures as the daily routine changes.

▶ A home visit by the teacher can be a very helpful strategy if the teacher is willing. To see his teacher in the child's familiar setting can be very reassuring. Then when he goes to school, he feels that he knows her. She also knows his room, his pets, his siblings, and his favorite toys to talk to him about. He feels closer to her after she visits him.

Suggestions for Easing Longer Separations

If you are going on vacation or a business trip without her, let her see you packing your suitcase, talk about the trip ahead of time, reassure her that Grandma or her caregiver will take good care of her, leave pictures of you for her to see and touch, and talk to her about you missing her. Tell her that you will call. Videotape or audiotape you reading a story to her with her voice also on the tape. Ask Grandma to play it every day to keep you close. When you call, talk about what you will do together when you get home.

Realize that she may be angry with you when you get home and may turn her head and refuse eye contact for a little while. Stay nearby and she will warm up and you can reconnect. A lot of ideas listed above apply like role-playing, giving your child something of yours to hold and using a photo story to show that you will all be together soon.

Children's Books about Separation

For Toddlers and Twos

Hello! Goodbye! by Aliki. Harper Collins, 1996.

The Runaway Bunny by Margaret Wise Brown. Harper Collins, 2005.

The Blanket by J. Burningham. Candlewick, 1996.

You Go Away by Dorothy Corey. Albert Whitman and Company, 1976, rev. 2008.

Are You My Mother? by P. D. Eastman. Random House Books for Young Readers., 1960.

Mama, Do You Love Me? by Barbara Joosse. Chronicle Books, 1991.

Swimmy by Leo Lionni. Dragonfly Books, 1973.

Will You Come Back for Me? by Ann Tompert. Albert Whitman and Company, 1992.

Owl Babies by Martin Waddell and Patrick Benson. Candlewick, 1996. Book and CD combination, Walker Books Ltd., 2007.

For Preschoolers

I Don't Want to Go to School by Nancy Pando. New Horizon Press, 2005.

Shawn Goes to School by Petronella Breinburg. Thomas Y. Crowell, 1974.

You're My Nikki by Phyllis Rose Eisenberg. Puffin, 1995.

Young Mouse and Elephant by Pamela Farris. Houghton Mifflin, 1996.

My First Day of School by P.K. Hallinan. Ideals Publications, 1987.

Come With Me to Nursery School by Edith Thacher Hurd. Coward, McCann and Geoghegan Publishers, 1970.

What Will Mommy Do When I'm at School? by Dolores Johnson. Atheneum, 1990.

Froggy Goes to School by Jonathan London. Puffin, 1998.

Guess How Much I Love You by Sam McBratney. Candlewick, 2008.

Dinofours: It's Time for School by Steve Metzger. Cartwheel Books, 1997.

The Kissing Hand by Audrey Penn. Tanglewood Press, 2006

My Nursery School by Harlow Rockwell. Mulberry Books, 1990.

Going to Day Care by Fred Rogers. Putnam Juvenile, 1985.

Off to School by Ann Schweninger. Puffin, 1989.

Maybe Tomorrow I'll Have a Good Time by Mary Soderstrom and Charlotte Epstein Wein. Human Sciences Publishers, 1981.

Have You Seen My Duckling? by Nancy Tafuri. Harper Collins, 1991.

16
Preparing Your Child for the New Baby

Many things can be done to help your older child adjust more smoothly to the coming of a new baby. It can take a lot of energy for your child to make the adjustment so other milestones—such as toilet learning—should be left for another time. My rule of thumb is to defer other milestones 3 months before and 3 months after the new baby's arrival.

There are three main themes when considering preparing your child for the new baby:

▶ Use every opportunity to encourage your child to *feel special and loved.*

▶ Use *concrete terms* in discussing and describing the arrival of a new sibling. That means that whatever the child can touch and feel and actually see regarding this change will be most easily understood.

▶ Encourage your child to feel that he or she is part of the team in welcoming the new baby. *Create a sense of family.* Convey that you are in this together and show your child that he or she is an integral part of the family. Too many families, in the effort of trying to protect their child from overwhelming feelings,

exclude the child from preparations. Your child needs to feel included.

Sharing Mom and Dad

When do children learn how to share? The answer is particular to your child's temperament and environmental concerns. However, most children are not good at sharing until well into the third or fourth year.

We are asking a child to share her most precious things—Mom and Dad—when she is not good at sharing yet. This is at the crux of sibling issues. They may ask themselves, "Aren't I good enough? Why do they want another child?" You are the center of the world for them. It is painful to have to share your love, time, and attention.

Many people have likened a new sibling in the family to having your spouse say, "I want to welcome a new husband (or wife) into the family, because I like the one I have so much, I want another." We chuckle about this and dismiss it as never happening. Try to envision this analogy to have a better understanding of how your child might feel—as if he is being replaced or displaced. The new wife (or husband) is very cute, and your husband smiles at her fondly, and hugs and kisses her. He wants to buy her things and even wants the new wife to use your things. Maybe he asks you to give up some of your things that are too small or old toys you have outgrown but still treasure.

It is not the new baby herself that the child becomes upset with, it is less time and attention from you. This less time and attention can represent, in their hearts, that you love them less. Offer daily reassurance that you still love her just as much as before.

Many children view love as finite, like a pie full of love. With the new baby's arrival, they see the pie as cut in half. We need the older child to know that another "pie" was created. Your heart has more love.

Jealousy

Your affection and attention are very hard to share. Jealousy may occur, and it takes many forms. It may be expressed indirectly by too much concern and affection for the baby, refusal to go to school, not eating, not sleeping, or open attacks on the baby. It may manifest as regression and behaviors such as whining, wetting pants, wanting a bottle, wanting to breastfeed, acting silly, needing more attention, whiney baby talk, crying more, clinging to you, demanding, stuttering, and more frequent temper tantrums.

These strong reactions point out how constantly our little ones need parental support and affection; once he feels secure, the regression will stop. Regression may even begin before the arrival of the new baby. Many things can be done to allay the jealousy. With preparation, the child may actually be able to work through some of her feelings ahead of time, before the arrival.

Acting Like a Baby

Sometimes regression takes the form of acting like a baby. Your child might think, "The baby is getting attention. Maybe if I act like a baby, I will get more attention too." Two things might help:

1. Allow your child to *pretend* to be a baby. Hold him like a baby; feed him like a baby, and he will quickly realize that it isn't as much fun as big-boy things like coloring or riding his bike.

2. Encourage him to copy the baby's actions. Lie them both down on a quilt and have him mimic the baby's movements. Again, he will realize: "This is boring!"

Reassurance of your love, and that you still have time for him, is the best remedy.

When Do I Tell My Child?

Parents often ask, "When should I tell my child that we are having a new baby?" I feel strongly that it is a good idea to tell her when you begin to tell others. She understands so much of what you say, and if she overhears you telling someone, she may wonder why you are keeping it a secret from her. She may become anxious or afraid of some impending change she cannot understand.

When You Were a Baby

Telling him the story of his own babyhood can be very helpful. Talk to him about the way he was cared for, how he was fed, how he was rocked to sleep, and how you gave him many hugs and kisses. Parents tell me that the best idea of all is the suggestion to make a "Big Brother" or "Big Sister" Book. You can also tell his babyhood story with the use of his baby book or other albums. Let him see pictures of you holding him, bathing him, caring for him, and loving him. Making a special book is a wonderful idea because he can handle it as much as he wants. He feels special that you took the time to make him a book telling his story.

Pages you might want to include:

1. Drawings of how the baby grows and grows inside his mother (perhaps a page out of one of your books describing intrauterine growth). Remember that the more concrete you make the explanation, the more he will understand. Pictures make it more concrete.

2. A picture of you pregnant with him. "You can see how much you were growing because my tummy got bigger and bigger."

3. A picture of the hospital where he was born.

4. "Here is what you looked like when you were born. The doctors and nurses helped Mommy and Daddy have you." Include a picture of him in the hospital as a newborn.

5. "Mommy and Daddy loved to hold you." Use pictures of you both holding him.

6. "Look at all the things you learned to do!" Include pictures of him sitting up, crawling, feeding himself, learning how to walk, and riding a tricycle. "Our new baby will learn how to do these things too. You can help her. How lucky she will be to have you for a big brother!"

7. Have a space on the last page to add a picture of the new baby. You can make a special fuss over placing the baby's picture in your child's Big Sister or Big Brother Book.

Be as creative as you want. Over the years, parents have shared their books with me, and I have been amazed. You can use a little photo album to create the book easily. The key piece is to make copies of the precious photos so your child can handle the book as much as she likes. (The easy way is to lay the original pictures side by side in a color copy machine and just cut them out.) Have fun with it! This is a great way to help your child feel special and loved.

Teach Your Child about Newborns

Talk to your child about the newborn baby. Show him pictures of newborns. Help him realize that a newborn does not smile and cannot play yet. Describe how they sleep a lot and cry to convey their needs.

Capitalize on the infant's grasp reflex. Have your child place his finger in the baby's grasp and tell him that the baby loves him so much. Use the Big Brother Book and other books about babies to show that the baby will soon learn to smile, sit, roll a ball, crawl, and walk. Your older child may be disappointed that the baby cannot play as soon as he arrives.

Give a realistic impression of what it is like to have a new baby in the house.

1. Give your child his own doll to care for. With the doll, show him the care that the baby will need: diapering, feeding, and burping the doll. After the new baby arrives, he can care for "his baby" while you care for the newborn. Try to get a doll that can be immersed in water, so he can bathe his doll while you bathe the baby. A towel on the floor with a basin of water for bathing his doll is a lot easier than having a toddler on top of you as you bathe your newborn.

2. Arrange to babysit for an infant so your child can get used to you holding and caring for a baby. Show him the feeding, diapering, and comforting. When the baby cries, discuss that this is the way the baby communicates.

3. If you are going to nurse, show him a baby nursing and talk about it with him. Foresee that he may want to nurse again once he sees the baby nursing. Think about what your response will be ahead of time, so you can respond calmly. Will you allow him to try? He won't recall how to suck. He will try to suck as he sucks through a straw, and it won't work. Perhaps you will decide to express some breast milk into a cup. He probably will not like the taste or the bluish color! Or you can say that he had breast milk as an infant and now he drinks milk from the refrigerator, and give him some.

Arrangements for Care of Your Older Child

Talk to your child about the arrangements made for her care when you go to the hospital. It is best that this discussion occur about 4 to 6 weeks before your due date, in case you go early and to give time for her to grasp the idea. As you know, the timing of labor is unpredictable. It would be best to have a Plan B in case the Plan A person cannot come right away due to illness or if you cannot reach her.

It is best for the child to be cared for in her own home with someone she knows and trusts. The reason is that more things will be familiar in a situation that is changing; such as her own bed, her own toys, her own kitchen, and so on. If that is not possible, the second best way is to be cared for in a home she knows with someone she knows and trusts. It is helpful to have a dry run, to practice the care when there isn't the anxiety of labor and the imminent birth. Let her get used to the new place and the new person ahead of time.

With your child, make up a chart entitled "A Day in the Life of (*her name*)." List her daily schedule, showing mealtimes, naptimes, and activities for the person taking care of her. This way, she will be reassured by familiar schedules and activities. Keeping things as familiar as possible is helpful when everything around her is changing.

It is helpful to use play to describe the arrangements. It makes it more concrete or real for her. Gather a family of dolls; use figures you have or purchase a doll family (Fisher Price has a family of figures that works well). Use a box or building that represents home and another that represents the hospital. Use the figures to tell the story of Mommy saying, "It is time to have the baby now, and Daddy and I need to go to the hospital. Grandma is here to stay with you." Actually take a car, put the figures in it, and drive to the hospital waving goodbye to the child and Grandma figures.

Using play helps her visualize what will happen. An added benefit is that then you can ask her to show you with the dolls what will happen to check her understanding. Let her play with the dolls in the setting and replay the scenario over and over.

Playing Through the Visit to the Hospital

Playing through scenarios helps a child understand what will happen, allows her to feel a sense of control over a situation over which she has no control, and enables her to express her feelings with the dolls. One situation that play helps the child cope with is the visit to the hospital.

Playing through the visit to the hospital can be invaluable. Use the figures and buildings described above and play through the visit ahead of time. Have the car bring Daddy from the hospital to the home to pick her up; the two of them drive to the hospital and go in to visit. Have dialogue saying something like, "Hi Mommy. "Hi Sweetheart. I missed you! Here is our new baby." Then play through the fact that Mommy and baby stay at the hospital and Daddy and child leave and drive home.

Play through this part several times. Have her replay the events using the dolls so you can be sure she understands. Again, leave everything out for her to play with, over and over. I remember overhearing my son acting out the story many times by himself.

Even if there are tears, it is best to have the child visit. Tears can be soothed; his feelings are being expressed instead of held inside. I had parents refuse to have their child visit, even with an extended stay due to complications, because they thought she would be upset to have to leave Mommy in the hospital at the end of the visit. She sat at Grandma's worrying and holding in her feelings. When Mommy did come home with the baby, the child literally clung to her for weeks. It is most important that the child is reassured that Mommy is okay by seeing for herself. Your child's greatest fear is that something has happened to you.

Your child may cry or act angry when he sees you. He may look away and not have eye contact. You left him! It will take a few minutes for him to warm up and be reassured.

Keeping the Closeness

There are several ways for your child to feel close to you while you are separated by the hospitalization:

1. Make sure your child is familiar with the sound of your phone voice. Place your hospital number next to the phone so he knows how someone can call you for him. Point out the telephones by the beds when you tour the hospital, so he can visualize how he can reach you.

2. Hide little presents around the house before you leave. When you call, you can tell him where you hid a surprise. This shows him how much you are thinking of him.

3. Before you leave, make an audio or video recording of you reading a story to her. Let her voice be on the recording too. She will feel closer to you to hear your voice and remember when you read the story. (You can also use these recorded stories at future bedtimes when you are home. Your older child can fall asleep listening to your voice.)

4. If possible, take your child on a tour of the hospital so he can visualize where you are when you are gone.

5. Make some meals together and freeze them. When he eats them he will remember when you prepared them together.

6. With a cell phone or a digital camera, send a picture home of Mommy, without the baby, to reassure the child that Mommy is okay.

    One of your child's greatest fears is that you will be hurt and unable to come home.

7. Take the child's picture to the hospital in a frame to reassure her that you will be thinking of her while you are away. Tell her you are going to show the picture to all the doctors and

nurses and tell them this is the big sister! She will see it when she visits, feel included and be reassured.

Do Touch Our Baby

Show your child how to touch the baby instead of telling her not to. Do not allow others to keep her away from the baby. Show her how she can touch, such as rubbing the baby's back or patting the baby's leg. The hammock-like baby seats are ideal to have the child sit with her legs underneath, get close, and have a "conversation." Allow her to hold him with supervision. An easy way is to have her sit crossed legged with a bed pillow on her lap. Place the baby's head in the crook of her arm and the rest of the baby's body is supported by the pillow. Allowing this closeness helps her realize that this is her baby, too. It encourages the beginning of a relationship and fosters the sibling bond.

Hurtful Actions

Sometimes the actions of your older child can be harmful to the baby. As discussed in Chapter 9: Discipline Styles, small children do not have self-control over their actions until they are consistently taught that hitting, pushing, throwing things at other people, and so on are not acceptable. Yet even when you are confident that your child has learned not to hurt others, his feelings may well up and he may hurt the baby. Remember, it is not the baby he is upset with but rather the decreased time and attention with you that the baby represents.

Many hurtful actions appear to be accidents. Your child may be playing quietly with blocks across the room and then a block flies toward the baby. I have seen a toddler run across the room and step on his little sister as he runs past. A 6-year-old, with good intentions, was found carrying her newborn brother down the stairs to her mother because he was crying and she wanted to help.

Newly crawling babies and newly walking babies are sometimes pushed down. You need to be aware of the older child's whereabouts at all times, especially in those early weeks. Bring the baby near you when you are out of the room. Some parents feel more secure with a gate at the baby's door, or they may even put up a screen door on the baby's room to keep the older child out while the baby is sleeping (air can circulate and it has the side benefit of keeping cats out of the baby's bed). Older children may hoist heavy toys into the baby's bed for the baby "to play with" or may climb in the crib to play with the baby without Mommy being aware.

Be sure to acknowledge the older child's feelings. If he does hurt the baby, he will often be devastated over his lapse in self-control. Prevention is the best solution. Actually catch his hand in a hit or push and say, "I can't let you hurt the baby, but you can show me how you feel with the doll." Allow him to knead and poke and cut play dough to let out his angry feelings, or draw you a picture of how he feels.

It is important to allow expression of his feelings, not just to tell him to not hit the baby. Feelings held in will burst out and cause hurtful actions later. Please review Chapter 9: Discipline Styles on how to set limits on hurtful actions. Remember all feelings are allowed; hurtful actions have to be stopped.

Special Alone Time

Try to have some special time alone each day with your older child, even if it is just for a few minutes. No matter how much time you have, the child will wish for more.

Acknowledge his feelings saying, "I wish we had more time with just you and me." You could set a date for a Saturday for an hour or two of alone time with the child. During the rest of the week, talk about how much you are looking forward to your time together. Your child will feel valued that you want to spend time with him.

You can squeeze out an hour or two while someone else stays with the baby. The "alone time" doesn't have to be without the baby. Sometimes the baby is content in the sling or a seat, and you can direct your full attention to the older child. He just needs to know he is still important to you and that you have time for him, too.

Setting up Outings

Seeing Mommy with the baby day in and day out can be overwhelming. It has been likened to the adult feeling sleep-deprived (at your wits end and unable to go on). Plan for some outings or play dates for her. Your friend or Grandma could take the child out and away from the sight of you holding and feeding the baby.

Maintaining Rituals

Maintaining old rituals offers the child security. "Not everything in my world has changed." If you do not have a bedtime ritual, begin one before the baby is born and continue it afterward. Before the baby is born, parents should switch roles occasionally to have the child get used to the other parent caring for him. If Mommy always puts him to bed, switch off to let him get comfortable with Daddy doing it, too.

It can be very helpful for Daddy to spend some quality time with the older child soon after he gets home. The child gets her "love bank" refilled and is more able to cope with the rest of the evening. It has the side benefit of giving Mom a breather before the evening routine.

Gifts, Gifts, and More Gifts

Here are some ways to help your child feel special and loved:

► Your child will have fun buying the baby a welcome gift to give the baby when she sees him for the first time (of course, buy it together well before the arrival date).

► You may want the child and infant to exchange gifts.

► Consider the gifts of others. Most people are considerate and give a gift for the older child, too, but some do not. You have a few choices on how to handle this scenario:

  1. Purchase small gifts for the older child in case visitors don't think of it. Think about the mailed gifts also. People are more likely to forget the older child when mailing a gift.

  2. Having your child open the gift can be fun the first few times, but after the fifth baby outfit, it isn't fun anymore. Use your gift stash for him.

  3. Another option is to point out all the gifts she got after her birth—the lamp from Aunt Sue and the Teddy from Uncle Bill. Now it is the baby's turn to get gifts.

  4. Another choice is to explain that these are the baby's birthday gifts and that she will get gifts on her birthday too.

► You may want to buy some small, special treats to give your child at times when a distraction is needed. I think

of that Calgon commercial where the baby is crying, the doorbell is ringing, the dog is barking, and your older child is hanging on your leg. It might be time to pull out a gift from your stash, such as a book, a paintbrush to paint with water on the sidewalk, play dough, a little car, or new crayons and paper. It may give you precious moments to regroup.

The Visit to the Hospital

Planning the visit to the hospital takes some forethought. Envision a hospital room and your older child. What will you and your child do? Plan some things to do together:

► I encourage you to have your older child hold the baby, even for a few minutes. Sit with him on the bed, place a bed pillow in his lap, and lay the baby's head in the crook of his arm. The rest of the baby's body is supported by the pillow. We talk a lot about mother and father infant bonding: I think there is sibling bonding also. With any luck, the baby will cooperate.

► This is the baby's birthday! Consider bringing in a store-bought cake with a candle and some hats and sing the baby "Happy Birthday." Many parents have told me that this worked out splendidly.

► Tuck a book and a pack of crayons and paper in your suitcase so that the two of you could share a story or color together. It will be a more pleasant visit if you have ideas of how to spend the time.

More Ways to Help Your Older Child Feel Special

Another way to help your older child feel special is to throw a big brother or big sister party. Invite a few other children and family members, have cake and ice cream (no presents needed), and let the older child be the center of attention and celebrate being the Big Brother or Sister. There are many t-shirts available stating, "I am the Big Sister (or Brother)" that would be perfect for the occasion.

Compare photographs of your older child to pictures of the new baby at the same age. Talk about how they are alike and different. It could be fun to cut a piece of string the length of the baby and one the length of the older child to show how much bigger she is.

Encourage your child to talk into a tape recorder to express how she feels about having a new baby, what she likes to do with the baby, and what she looks forward to doing together. Also record some of the baby's sounds. It will be fun to listen to together over and over as the children get older. Trace your older child's hand and trace the infant's hand inside to show the difference in size—it makes a nice keepsake.

Part of the Family Team

Here is a list of ways to help your child feel like a valued, important member of the family team. She will feel involved and helpful.

1. Help pick out the baby's coming home clothes and place them in the suitcase.

2. Accompany you to the doctor when possible and listen to the baby's heartbeat.

3. Feel the baby kicking in Mommy's tummy.

4. Help Mommy pack her suitcase.

5. Help choose a name.

6. Choose some of her toys to share with the baby.

7. Put lotion on the baby's back.

8. Help dress, feed, and burp the baby.

9. Smile and talk to the baby, especially when the baby is fussing. This genuinely can be helpful.

10. "Read" to the baby by showing pictures in books.

11. "Teach" the baby the sounds of the various animals, shapes and colors, and so on.

12. Assist in making the birth announcement. An older child could draw a picture to be reproduced on the announcement. My daughter liked drawing houses, so she drew a house and we entitled it "We have a new baby at our house." Another child drew a family on the announcement. Imagine how proud and included she feels if her artwork is sent to all your family and friends.

13. Be included in the birth announcement by saying something like, "Johnny announces the birth of his

sister, Ann Marie." Or listing his name along with yours on the announcement: Proud Parents Jean and Tom Sands and Big Brother Johnny. I have a large stack of examples that I have been sent over the years. My favorite has a black and white picture of the big brother and new sister with the words, "Nathan is proud to announce the birth of his sister, Erika."

14. Have a basket of some of your older child's toys in the baby's room so he feels welcomed when you are caring for the baby there.

15. Have your older child show visitors "our baby" so he can be center stage as everyone admires the baby. There is an image on a commercial that shows a crowd of adults around the bassinet in the background, and the little boy in the foreground all alone is looking in the mirror saying, "But I had blue eyes first!"

Take your cue from your child. If she wants to help, encourage her. Be sure to show enthusiasm and praise for her efforts.

When You Leave for the Hospital

If you have to leave for the hospital in the middle of the night, it is recommended that you awaken your child to say goodbye and show him who is with him. My children only murmured "Bye, Mommy" groggily. If you disappear in the night without saying goodbye, it can violate the child's trust.

After you come home, bedtime can be difficult, because he thinks you might disappear in the night again. I have heard of children sitting at the top of the stairs with blanket and teddy waiting for Mommy to return all night. Your child may literally hold onto you, for fear that you might disappear again. The main deterrent in saying goodbye is the fear of tears. It is far better to have the child cry and be comforted by whomever is taking care of him, reassuring him that Mommy will be back, than to be afraid when he wakes up without Mommy.

The Nursing Couple

It is hard for your older child to see the nursing couple, cozy in the closeness. Try to include your child in the circle when she is around. One idea is to nurse on a sofa so that the older child can sit cuddled close and you can talk or read a story. When you have to change breasts, make a game of the child changing sides, too, by sitting on your other side.

Another suggestion is to prepare your older child a snack before you sit down and have her eat near you. When she sees the baby sucking, it often prompts a request for a drink or food. Settling her ahead of time works wonders. One of my favorite suggestions is to make up a "Nursing Box" filled with small toys, puzzles, or books that can be played with at your feet only while you are nursing.

Try to consider your older child's well being as you settle yourself down for a nursing. Parents express the concern that the baby is not receiving undivided attention during the nursing. Be reassured that your baby is getting the closeness he needs and he loves hearing your voice. He will have you all to himself at evening and night feedings.

Acknowledging Feelings

I remember a pediatrician in one of my classes who was dismayed when her child emphatically stated about her baby brother, "Send him back to the hospital!" It can be so upsetting when your older child says, "Throw him away in the garbage" or "Send him to live with Grandma." Our inclination is to say, "You can't say that! You love your baby!" However, such comments deny his very strong feelings.

A better strategy is to acknowledge his feelings by saying such things as, "It is hard to have a baby brother who takes so much of my time. Tell some more." Or you could say, "I didn't know you felt so strongly. Take all the time you need to tell me how you feel." Focus on the underlying feeling behind the words instead of the actual words. "It can be upsetting when each time we sit down to read, the baby wakes up crying for a feeding."

If you deny feelings, your child may hide her feelings. Her feelings may come out in nightmares, pulling her own hair, asthma attacks, hurtful actions, or nail-biting.

Having a child draw you a picture of how he feels can be very therapeutic. One child drew a picture of his mother and little sister in a pool holding hands, and he drew himself very tiny, up in the corner of the picture. It clearly conveyed how left out he felt. Children can express their feelings in drawings. Another way to encourage feeling expression is with play dough or with a teddy bear. Say, "Show me with the teddy bear (or the play dough) how you feel." All feelings are accepted; limits are set on hurtful actions.

Changing Sleeping Arrangements

It is recommended that the changes in your child's routine—including changing beds, getting a new babysitter, or going to nursery school—be made at least a month before the baby's birth, as soon in the pregnancy as possible is best. If things change too close to the baby's birth, your older child might feel displaced or exiled.

If your child is close to 3 years old, she is probably ready for a "big-girl bed" with a bedrail. It is recommended to take the crib down, store it, and take it out right before the birth. If your child is younger than 3 years old, try to keep her in the crib so that she is contained at night. You do not want a toddler wandering at night while you are in a deep sleep. A well-meaning toddler may get the idea that the baby wants to play with a big truck and push it up over the side of the crib. Use a bassinet, cradle, or portable crib for the baby for awhile so your toddler can have the crib for awhile longer.

Thoughts on the Homecoming

Perhaps your child can come with Daddy to pick you up. Show her how she can help by carrying a blanket or some flowers; it can help her feel that she is a valued member of the family. It is imperative, however, that she be accompanied by another adult besides Daddy. If there are delays or Daddy has to carry a lot of things, or the child begins to misbehave, another adult can step in to help.

Another downside to your child coming to take Mommy and baby home is that the infant may react to being outside or in the car seat and howl all the way home. It can be quite disconcerting to the older child not to mention everyone else in the car.

Because of these unforeseen circumstances, I think it is a good idea to leave your older child home with whomever is caring for her. When you arrive home, have someone else bring the baby in and have your arms free. Sit down—you shouldn't be picking your older child up yet—and gather her up in your arms and cuddle, expressing how much you missed her. Give lots of hugs and let it be her day as much as possible. Keep calm; she may act clingy or tearful or be cold or angry toward you. It will take her awhile to be reassured that she is still important to you and loved.

Children need daily reassurance of their own secure, special place in the family. When she is sure there is room for her in the family, she will make room for the new baby.

Handling sibling rivalry can be very challenging for most parents. My favorite book on siblings is *Siblings Without Rivalry* by Elaine Mazlish and Adele Faber. They give life-changing suggestions for encouraging sibling loyalty.

Children's Books about a New Baby in the Family

Children's books can be very helpful in teaching your child about having a new baby in the family. They also act as a sounding board for feelings to be expressed. A child describing how a character in the book is feeling is often really expressing how she feels.

Here are my favorites:

The New Baby by Fred Rogers. Putnam Juvenile, 1996.

A New Baby at Koko Bear's House by Vicki Lansky. Bantam Books, 1987.

Getting Along Together: Baby and I Can Play by Karen Hendrickson. Parenting Press, 1985.

Noisy Nora by Rosemary Wells. The Dial Press, 1973

Hi New Baby by Andrew C. Andry and Suzanne C. Kratka. Simon & Schuster, 1970.

A Tiny Baby for You by Nancy Langstaff and Suzanne Szasz. Harcourt Publishing, 1955.

A Baby Sister for Francis by Russell Hoban. Harper Publishing, 1964.

A New Baby is Coming to My House by Chihiro Iwasaki. McGraw Hill, 1970.

Nobody Asked Me if I Wanted a Baby Sister by Martha Alexander. Dial Press, 1971.

On Mother's Lap by Ann Herbert Scott. McGraw Hill, 1972.

Peggy's New Brother by Eleanor Schick. Macmillan, 1970.

Peter's Chair by Ezra Jack Keats. Harper Publishing, 1967.

We Are Having a Baby by Vicki Holland. Scribner Publishing, 1972.

Whose Mouse Are You? by Robert Kraus. Macmillan, 1970.

Sometimes I'm Jealous by Jane Werner Watson and Robert E. Switzer, M.D. Western Publishing Co., 1972.

That New Baby by Sara Bonnett Stein. Walker and Co., 1974.

Baby on the Way by Martha Sears. Little, Brown Young Readers, 2001.

How You Were Born by Joanna Cole. Harper Trophy, 1994.

I'm a Big Brother by Joanna Cole. Harper Collins, 1997.

I'm a Big Sister by Joanna Cole. Harper Collins, 1997.

The New Baby at Your House by Joanna Cole. Harper Trophy, 1999.

Waiting for Baby by Annie Kubler. (The New Baby Series) Harper Collins, 1997.

My New Baby by Annie Kubler. (The New Baby Series) Harper Collins, 1997.

Before You Were Born by Jennifer Davis. Workman Publishing Co., 1999.

The New Baby by Mercer Mayer. Random House, 2001.

Hello Baby by Lizzy Rockwell. Dragonfly Books, 2000.

I'm Going to be a Big Brother by Brenda Bercun. Nurturing Your Children Press, 2006.

What to Expect When Mommy's Having a Baby by Heidi Murkoff. Harper Festival, 2000.

What to Expect When the New Baby Comes by Heidi Murkoff. Harper Festival, 2000.

What Baby Needs by William Sears, M.D., Martha Sears and Christie Watts Kelly. Little, Brown Young Readers, 2001.

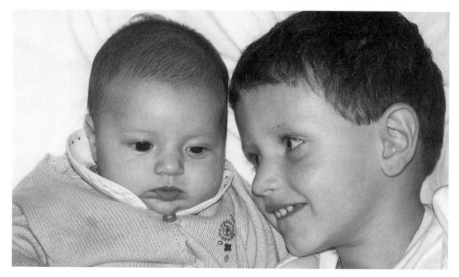

Select Bibliography

Ainsworth, Mary D. Salter and John Bowlby. *Child Care and the Growth of Love.* London: Penguin Books, 1965.

Balaban, Nancy, Ed.D. *Learning to Say Goodbye: Starting School and Other Early Childhood Separations.* New York: Signet, New American Library, a Division of Penguin Books USA, 1987.

Begley, Sharon. "How to Build Your Baby's Brain," *Newsweek Special Edition: Your Child from Birth to Three,* April 23, 1997.

Bowdoin, Ruth. *How to Teach Your Child at Home.* Brentwood, TN: Websters International, 2001.

Brazelton, T. Berry, M.D. *Doctor and Child.* New York: Delacorte Press, 1976.

Brazelton, T. Berry, M.D. *Families, Crisis, and Caring.* New York: Ballantine Books, 1989.

Brazelton, T. Berry, M.D. *Infants and Mothers: Differences in Development.* New York: Delacorte Press, 1969.

Brazelton, T. Berry, M.D. *On Becoming a Family: The Growth of Attachment Before and After Birth.* New York: Delacorte Press, 1992.

Brazelton, T. Berry, M.D. *Toddlers and Parents: Declaration of Independence.* New York: Delacorte Press, 1974.

Brazelton, T. Berry, M.D. *To Listen to a Child: Understanding the Normal Problems of Growing Up.* Reading, Massachusetts: Addison-Wesley, 1984.

Brazelton, T. Berry, M.D. *Touchpoints: Your Child's Emotional and Behavioral Development.* New York: Perseus Books, 1992.

Brazelton, T. Berry, M.D. *Working and Caring.* Cambridge, MA: Da Capo, 1992.

Brazelton, T. Berry, M.D. and Stanley I. Greenspan, M. D. *The Irreducible Needs of Children.* New York: Perseus Publishing, 2001.

Brazelton, T. Berry, M.D. and Joshua D. Sparrow, M.D. *Discipline the Brazelton Way.* New York: Perseus Books, 2003.

Briggs, Dorothy Corkille. *Your Child's Self-Esteem: The Key to Life.* New York: Doubleday, 1975.

Chess, Stella and Alexander Thomas. *Temperament: Theory and Practice.* New York: Taylor and Francis, 1996.

Cuthburtson, Joanne and Susana Schevill. *Helping Your Child Sleep Through the Night: A Guide for Parents of Children from Infancy to Age Five.* Main Street Books, 1985.

Department of Health Education, Boston Children's Hospital Medical Center. *Accident Handbook: A New Approach to Children's Safety.* New York: Dell Publishing Co., 1966.

Dodge, Diane Trister and Cate Heroman. *Building Your Baby's Brain: A Parent's Guide to the First Five Years.* Washington, D.C.: Teaching Strategies, 2002.

Faber, Adele and Elaine Mazlish. *How to Talk So Kids Will Listen and Listen So Kids Will Talk.* New York: Harper Collins, revised 1999, reissued 2004.

Ferber, Richard, M.D. *Solve Your Child's Sleep Problems.* New York: Simon and Schuster, revised edition 2006.

Green, Martin I. *A Sigh of Relief: The First-aid Handbook for Childhood Emergencies.* New York: Bantam Books, 1997.

Greenspan, Stanley I., M.D. *The Challenging Child: Understanding, Raising, and Enjoying the Five "Difficult" Types of Children.* Cambridge, MA: Da Capo Press, 1996.

Kaplan, Louise J. (Foreward by Margaret S. Mahler). *Oneness and Separateness: From Infant to Individuation.* New York: Simon and Schuster, 1978.

Karp, Harvey, M.D. *The Happiest Baby on the Block.* New York: Bantam Dell, 2002.

Karp, Harvey, M.D. *The Happiest Baby on the Block DVD.* New York: The Happiest Baby, 2002.

Karp, Harvey, M.D. *The Happiest Toddler on the Block.* New York: Bantam Dell, 2004.

Karp, Harvey, M.D. *The Happiest Toddler on the Block DVD.* New York: The Happiest Baby, 2004.

Kenda, Margaret E. and Phyllis Williams. *Natural Baby Food Cookbook.* New York: Avon Books, 1988.

Kotalak, Ronald. *Inside the Brain: Revolutionary Discoveries of How the Mind Works.* New York: Andrews McMeel Publishing, 1997.

Kurcinka, Mary Sheedy. *Raising Your Spirited Child: A Guide for Parents Whose Child is More Intense, Sensitive, Perceptive, Persistent and Energetic.* New York: Harper Paperbacks, Revised edition, 2006.

La Leche League. *The Womanly Art of Breastfeeding:* Seventh Revised Edition (La Leche League International Book), Plume, 2004.

Leach, Penelope and Jenny Matthews. *Your Baby and Child: From Birth to Age Five.* New York: Knopf, 1997.

Ludington-Hoe, Susan, PhD. and Susan K. Golant. *How to Have a Smarter Baby: Infant Stimulation Program for Enhancing Your Baby's Natural Development.* New York: Bantam Books, 1987.

Lupine, Missy Chase. *The Sneaky Chef: Simple Strategies for Hiding Healthy Foods in Kids' Favorite Meals.* Philadelphia, PA: Running Press, 2007.

Mahler, Margaret S., Fred Pine and Anni Bergman. *The Psychological Birth of the Human Infant.* New York: Basic Books, 1975.

Melville, Greg. "Build your Baby's Brain," *Parents,* October 2003, pp. 160–64.

Olson, Cathe. *Simply Natural Baby Food: Easy Recipes for Delicious Meals Your Infant and*

Toddler Will Love. Arroyo Grande, CA: Goco Publishing, 2003.

Pantley, Elizabeth. *The No-Cry Sleep Solution: Gentle Ways to Help Your Baby Sleep Through the Night.* New York: McGraw Hill, 2002.

Pryor, Karen and Gale Pryor. *Nursing Your Baby.* New York: Harper Collins, 1973, revised 1991, revised 2005.

Rothman, Phyllis, M.S.W. and Irene van der Zande. *Parent/Toddler Group: A Model for Effective Intervention to Facilitate Normal Growth and Development.* Los Angeles: Published by Phyllis Rothman and Irene van der Zande, 1990.

Satter, Ellyn. *Child of Mine: Feeding with Love and Good Sense.* Boulder, CO: Bull Publishing Co., 2000.

Sears, William, M.D. and Martha Sears, R.N. *The Attachment Parenting Book: A Commonsense Guide to Understanding and Nurturing Your Baby.* New York: Little, Brown and Company, 2001.

Sears, William, M.D. and Martha Sears, R.N. *The Discipline Book.* New York: Little, Brown and Company, 1995.

Sears, William, M.D. and Martha Sears, R.N. *Nighttime Parenting: How to Get Your Baby and Child to Sleep.* New York: Plume Publishing, 1985, revised 1999.

Seinfeld, Jessica. *Deceptively Delicious: Simple Secrets to Get Your Kids Eating Good Food.* New York: Collins Living, 2007.

Turecki, Stanley and Leslie Tonner. *The Difficult Child*: Expanded and Revised Edition. New York: Bantam Books, 2000.

White, Burton L., PhD. *The First Three Years of Life, the Revised Edition.* New York: Prentice Hall Press, 1985.

Wingert, Pat, and Martha Brant. "Reading Your Baby's Mind," *Newsweek*, August 15, 2005, pp. 32–39.

Wolfson, Randy Myers and Virginia DeLuca. *Couples with Children: Helping Couples Survive the Strains of Parenthood,* New York: Warner Books, 1981.

Van der Zande, Irene. *1, 2, 3…The Toddler Years: A Practical Guide for Parents and Caregivers.* Santa Cruz, CA: Published by the Santa Cruz Toddler Center, 1995.

Index

About the Author

Joan Rice, R.N., B.S.N., Parent Educator and Pediatric Nurse, is a graduate of Duke University and holds a California Adult Education Teaching Credential in Parent Education. She has worked as a Pediatric Nurse at Duke University Medical Center, Children's Hospital of Los Angeles and on a Child Psychiatric Unit at the Medical University of South Carolina. She taught Pediatric Nursing and Psychiatric Nursing at the Memorial Hospital School of Nursing in South Bend, Indiana.

For the past thirty years Joan has taught parenting classes. As the Director of Parent Education and Staff Development of the Princeton Family Resource Center for fourteen years, she was responsible for a parent education and support center serving approximately 250 families a week. She was the Infant/Toddler Program Director for the Warner Bros. Children's Center for its opening year. She is now teaching parenting classes in California at the Burbank Preschool Education Program, the Parent Participation Programs of Arroyo Grande and San Luis Obispo, Allan Hancock College, the Foster Parent Program at Cuesta College and at Warner Bros. Studios.

While teaching parenting classes for 30 years, she has developed a deep understanding of what concerns parents. Each chapter of *Parenting Solutions* will be like attending a thought-provoking, behavior-changing parenting workshop.